What

"*The Golden Promise* is truly food for my soul. Archangel Michael's messages have touched me deeply and his loving energy continues to resonate throughout my being as I let these new truths settle within. Thank you with all my heart." D.S.

"The thoughts of each and every page of *The Golden Promise* ring with truth. The messages are so very clear and give such wonderful guidance and hope for the future." C.R.

"I feel the beauty, love and incredible energy that pours forth from the words as I read them. It touched me deeply and validated some things for me that I have felt for so long, but couldn't believe were true. Love and Light," E.K.

"My soul has been thirsting for this elixir—I have been waiting a long time for these wisdom teachings." L.L.

"It seems Archangel Michael says just the right thing to help me see my problems or life situations in a different light so that I can deal with them in a more 'Light-hearted' way." M.K.

"The meditations and affirmations are so helpful and the information on the rays and chakras is wonderful. Lord Michael's loving guidance helps us, step by step, to build a vision for the new millennium." J.D.

"What a treasure of love and vital information. Archangel Michael's loving messages help us to remember our magnificence and to reflect the Light to others so that they may see their own inherent goodness and beauty." D.L.

"The messages get more and more profound and give us such a clear picture of our origins, why we are here and what our future holds. Whereas, in the past, I was so uncertain and fearful of the future, I now live in joy and expectation." P.B.

Book Review by Russ Michael

Once again, Ronna Herman, who is an incredibly pure channel for the powerful Archangel Michael, has transmitted another colossal book of awesome new spiritual information.

This book is cram-packed with needed information, meditations, and great "spiritual tools" which when read, understood and utilized, can definitely lead anyone who chooses faster toward spiritual enlightenment and self-mastery!!

Several chapters are devoted to explaining our seven solar rays and the five cosmic rays, their colors, their aspects or attributes, and what gems or stones that can be worn, held or viewed to accentuate or magnify any one of these divine ray qualities within our own divine beings.

Other chapters give insights into the seven major "chakras" or etheric centers of the body and how to activate or enhance them with the physical use of the colors related to each one, wearing that color daily for a month, writing with that color ink, meditating on that color, etc., etc.

This grand book also contains an outstanding "New Age Creed" that all of us would be wise to embrace in our daily lives—as well as a selection of superb and powerful "Mantra Petitions" to Masters, Archangels, or divine beings.

The overall tone and feeling of this book is greatly uplifting and tremendously inspiring. If you are planning to read only two or three books this month, *The Golden Promise* should definitely be one of them.

NOTE: Russ Michael is author of 26 books selling in 11 languages, including his long-time best seller, *Finding Your Soulmate,* and his new book, *Your Soulmate Is Calling.*

The Golden Promise

MESSENGES OF HOPE
AND INSPIRATION

FROM ARCHANGEL MICHAEL

CHANNELLED THROUGH RONNA HERMAN
A COSMIC TELEPATH

MT. SHASTA LIGHT PUBLISHING

The Golden Promise

Published by:

Mt. Shasta Light Publishing
P. O. Box 1509
Mt. Shasta, CA 96067-1509 USA

Phone: 530.926.4599

Fax: 530.926.4159

Email: aurelia@mslpublishing.com

Website: www.mslpublishing.com

Ronna Herman may be contacted at:

StarQuest
6005 Clear Creek Drive
Reno, NV 89502 USA

Phone/Fax: 775.856.3654

Email: ronnastar@earthlink.net

Web site: www.ronnastar.com

CONTENTS

CREDITS:

The Golden Promise was lovingly edited by an angel friend: Jodi Hopkins of Los Angeles, California.

Final proofreading was carefully completed by Barbara Herbert of Reno, Nevada.

Book design and formatting was done by Aaron of Mt. Shasta Light Publishing.

Front cover photo of Archangel Michael by Peggy Black: "Sacred Sound Salutarist" guided by angelic realms, the essence of Kuan Yin, and the energy and presence of the Hathors. A world traveler, lecturer, she conducts workshops and retreats for women. She is passionate about sharing the incredible wonders of the "Sacred Sounds" as a healing modality. She is a creative artist with a line of angel greeting cards and a series of "Angel Montages" photographs. Phone: 831.335.3145, Address: 661 Felton Empire Road, Felton, CA 95018, Website: www.healingmusic.org/PeggyBlack.htm, Email: peggyblack@aol.com

1. MESSAGE FROM RONNA

To all my beloved Soul/Star Sisters and Brothers:

Much has transpired since Archangel Michael's first book of messages, ON WINGS OF LIGHT, was published. People tell me their lives have changed dramatically, mostly for the better; I know mine certainly has. My husband and I moved from San Diego, California to the high desert in Reno, Nevada, to be near our children and grandchildren. ON WINGS OF LIGHT has been translated into four languages: Dutch, German, French and Portuguese. Archangel Michael's monthly messages have been translated into most major languages and read by thousands, possibly millions, around the world. I have traveled extensively throughout the United States and Europe holding seminars and workshops—meeting so many wonderful people whom I consider to be my extended soul family.

The favorable response I have received from the messages and my work is almost overwhelming. I am eternally grateful for having been chosen as messenger for Archangel Michael's loving wisdom and inspiring messages to the world during these swiftly changing times.

I write this letter of love to you on the eve of the new millennium and I, like so many of you, feel the excitement building for the wonderful things we know will be happening in these next critical years. It has not always been easy, but I cherish the experiences, both the lessons and the many gifts I've received, for they have made me who I am today. I can truly tell people, "I know how you feel," for I have had to experience all the things that I teach so I can "walk my talk" and "fly my vision."

Everything Archangel Michael has told me has come true—

not always as I expected or in the time frame I'd hoped for, but in looking back I can see it was all for the best and the highest good of all. What more can we ask?

Again, I invite you to take a journey with me, a journey into the unseen realms where angels dwell. Put your analytical minds aside, if you will, and feel with your heart and inner knowing. Allow the words to resonate and see if they do not touch a cord deep within, a memory of times long past when we communed and walked with the angels.

Archangel Michael's messages have become increasingly more profound as he has gently led us into a greater awareness of our cosmic lineage and the universal laws by which we must live—as he explains what is happening in our world and to us. I present his messages to you in the form they were given to me, with little editing or grammatical corrections. He has updated a few of the messages, but they are timeless—as relevant today as they were when he first gave them to me. The messages have a flavor, a style; Lord Michael uses words in a way that may not be acceptable in literary circles, but they resonate with his essence of love and compassion and therefore, I bring them to you in the same way.

Our physical, emotional, mental and spiritual realities are expanding by leaps and bounds, as we begin to access a higher truth and greater wisdom. Humanity is coming of age—we are no longer children, stumbling in the dark, or following others without question. A consciousness level is emerging that will incorporate not just our families, neighborhood and cities, but races, cultures, countries and planets, and even our solar system, galaxy and universe.

As we begin to resonate with the higher frequencies of love, compassion and non-judgment, there will be no fear, limitation or disease, and we will move into a sense of unity instead of a feeling of isolation and aloneness. We are in the process of healing and releasing all energies and frequencies which no longer serve us and which cannot exist in the Light body we are building. As we release all the dark crystals (as Lord Michael calls them), we can fill those vacancies with pure crystalline Light Substance. These old imbalanced energies hold the memories of pain, suffering and limitation from our ancient past.

It is time for us to release the misconception or sense of separation: good and bad, light and dark—duality or polarity consciousness. We are here on Earth in a physical body, on the material plane, to experience duality and polarity. It is balance and harmony we seek, not the elimination of duality or polarity.

It is time for us to return to a sense of Oneness or wholeness. All creation is an aspect of the Divine Creator, our Father/Mother God. It is also time for you to remember that you are a master. You came to Earth as a master of cocreation: to build, experience and enjoy the paradise world called Earth. Are you ready to move from being a master of lack, limitation, fear and suffering? It is time to reclaim your heritage as a master of love, beauty, bounty, abundance and joy.

Never since our arrival on planet Earth, so many aeons ago, have we had so much assistance from the higher realms: archangels, angelic helpers, masters, teachers, guides and wondrous Beings from far distant galaxies. But you must ask and then follow your inner guidance until you find your way back onto that wondrous path of higher awareness, illumination and mastery.

We are all in this together, on this wondrous journey back

home. Every victory, every gain you make, smoothes the way for those following behind you. My hope is to help make your journey a little easier and the experience more joyful.

Love, Light, joy and blessings beyond measure, Ronna

2. RELEASE YOUR PAST BY GOING
BACK TO THE FUTURE

*M*y beloved ones, this is a most critical time in your transmutation/ascension process, a time when you are most vulnerable to outside influences and concepts. New information, methods and theories are brought forth daily for you to contemplate, investigate and integrate. But what is true and what is not? How do you discern? Have we not told you that you are to sort and glean through the multitude of concepts that are being brought forth and discern what is your truth? You, and you alone, can decide what is right for you and what path of awareness you are to follow, for you are a unique and vital creation of the Divine Mind.

There are many smaller dramas being played out in the greater drama of transformation and evolution, and you cannot totally comprehend or envision what is occurring in this beautiful dance of ascension back into the realms of en-LIGHT-ened reality. It is just one more step on the path back to your home among the stars. What may seem to many of you as negative or punishment is in reality a necessary step toward jolting you out of your complacency or out of your old patterns of thinking.

Many beautiful and brave servants of the Light have accepted the task of being the catalysts for mind- and heart-shaking events so that they will be shocked into their higher awareness, and will begin to think for themselves. At a Divine level, they accepted the opportunity to do the Creator's work, no matter what the cost or condemnation. We honor these magnificent and wondrous Beings, for their task is not an easy one.

Because you are in a very critical phase of your

illumination process, a time when you are most vulnerable and your trials and tests are not as dramatic as in the past, quite often you are confused and do not know what the next step is or what the next truth is that you are to incorporate into your ever-changing reality.

Many of you are falling back into the old patterns of allowing others to do your thinking, to lead the way without question, without validating what is your truth by going inward and connecting to that infallible source, your own Divine Presence. You are still seeking outside yourself, turning to those you think are more powerful or more knowledgeable than you, hoping they will lead the way so you will not have to step to the fore, into the line of fire or into untested territory. We tell you, beloved ones, this will not work. You, as a Light Warrior, must lighten your own path, draw on your own precious wisdom, which has been paid for and won through many long ages of experience, trials and suffering.

A great variety of loving, dedicated messengers and teachers has been thrust out into the arena of public service in order to give you access to the multitude of new information that is pouring forth since the "Ring-Pass-Not" or the quarantine was lifted from the Earth. But with the plethora of information, much of which is in harmony with the concepts and teachings of the hierarchy and Beings of Light, there is still information that is brought forth in thought forms that are filtered through the belief systems and reality of the messenger; information that is conflicting and confusing— some partially true, much shaded truth and even some distorted fallacies picked up from the myths of mass-consciousness.

This is a testing ground, you see. You are learning to use

gifts and abilities that have lain dormant for centuries beyond centuries. You are not judged by your score or level of authenticity as you move into the realms of illumined truth, only by your intent. Each person who channels or brings forth information will find a following for that level of knowledge, those who will learn from it, much of which has not been available to you before—insights, tools and methods you will need to traverse the spiral of ascension. Sometimes they will bring forth the innocence of Spirit, a gentle loving nature that resonates with unconditional love to be a shining example of a true master. And others may be teaching the lessons of discernment, quite possibly through painful experience, so that you will come to realize you can no longer give your truth or power away to another.

You must take the information offered and validate it in your own heart center, thereby attuning more and more with your own Divine Intuition. You may not have all the knowledge, and it is not necessary, for that is the role of these messengers of the higher realms—to give you a wide variety of viewpoints, a panorama of information gleaned from the Universal Mind or from their own memory banks of ancient experience, so that you can choose what resonates most closely to your lineage, your heritage and your destiny. But you must find your own spiritual truth via conscious awareness, mental discernment and intuitive attunement with your Higher Self.

You have within your Divine Blueprint a memory of where you came from—your cosmic origins. You have indelibly stamped there how it was in the beginning, this Garden of E-Don, Planet Earth—this most wondrous place of beauty and perfection. But as aeons passed, those perfect memories have faded, been covered over, replaced or distorted by all

16

the effluvia, negativity, limitation and isolation you came to accept as your reality.

We ask you to release your past so that you can recapture that memory of perfection, that perfect you that descended, a fully empowered representative of the Creator, in order to assist in bringing forth all the great varieties of expression and creation to the precious planet Earth. Each level of higher vibration you attain sets up a resonance within your physical vessel that sends waves of this new frequency down into the very core of your Being. It then begins to vibrate loose those core memories or energies that are not compatible with these more refined frequencies. Many of these residual energies come from your ancient past, memories of your first experiences of failure, betrayal and separation in the physical. They have been with you so long that you have accepted them as who you are, and they have had an impact on you, in some way, in every lifetime you have lived since you became disconnected from Spirit and sank down into the quagmire of limitation and the swirling negative energies spewed out by humanity.

In order to release those ancient memories that are still holding you in bondage, you must go back to that time of perfection when you were in a beautiful etheric/physical body, when you were a cocreator of this pristine planet, living in paradise, and when we interacted, communed and labored together in perfect harmony, building a new world from a blueprint sent forth from the God Mind. This was a wondrous, new experiment, a unique concept in a never-ending spiral of creation, a time when you were innocent and pure in your delight of expressing, creating, experiencing and sharing. But in order to get there you must break through the layers upon layers of thought forms that are no longer yours—they are not who you are. Let them go—you have learned your lessons, you have integrated the knowledge and wisdom this physical experience had to offer. IT IS TIME TO LET THEM GO.

Run the words through your mind that create pictures or activate memories—if they create feelings of love, peace, harmony and unity, then they are memories and energies that you brought with you from your Divine Self, but if they bring fear, depression or anxiety, then they are concepts of limited thinking that you have incorporated into your reality since assuming your cloak of flesh.

Failure, unworthiness, abandonment, scarcity, rejection, betrayal, bondage, slavery, manipulation, imprints, encodings, devils, demons, Satan, hell and darkness are all words that set off frequencies and memories of fear in you. More crippling in some than others, depending on how much of these impacted energies have been released and set free back into the Light of illumined truth. Words cannot hurt you, but these memories and impacted energies can keep you tied to the wheel of Karma and enslaved in the illusion of the third dimension.

You no longer walk through the shadows alone, you no longer tread through the dark night of the soul alone, for the angels and your Divine I AM Presence are with you. Even though you may veer from the straight and narrow path now and again, you are quickly nudged back by Spirit, for these are most wondrous and exceptional times. Never before has humanity had such a precious gift offered to them—that of mastership and illumination in one lifetime. But there are pitfalls, tests and trials along the way. We will assist you and walk beside you, but we will not hold your hand and lead you. We will guide you, but we cannot remove or help you evade your lessons. That responsibility lies solely with you, for you are in training to, once again, be a master of cocreation of paradise worlds.

Leave the fear behind, precious warriors; leave the memories of failure behind as well, for this time you WILL NOT FAIL. It is imperative that, once and for all, you decide how you will create your future, your new reality. Will it be from someone else's blueprint, their point-of-view, or your own? Will it be by someone else's methods, or your own? Will you live someone else's dream, or your own? You must decide NOW!

The wonderful servants who so faithfully devote their energy, time, effort and creative endeavors are to be honored and commended, and theirs is a momentous task, but they are gifted with their abilities and insight to give you guidelines, to give you a variety of viewpoints and concepts to choose from, so that you may gain a broader spectrum of the higher truth, so you may glean from all the information and concepts that which will increase your knowledge and awareness. Then, you must sort out the knowledge which resonates with your inner truth and incorporate it so that it becomes your wisdom and a part of your personal expression, an expression of wisdom and truth that will resonate in perfect harmony with your Divine Self so that, more and more, you will eliminate the distorted truths and energies that keep you from merging with that powerful, most wondrous part of yourself—the real you.

You are breaking through the final levels of illusion. Most of you have moved out of the third dimension of pain and suffering, and now are swirling through the emotional levels of the astral planes of half-truths, glamour, mystery and myth of the fourth dimension. There are many enticing thought forms and realities which can draw your attention away from the higher goal of illumination and ascension into unity and harmony with your Divine Self. Do not tarry along the way, my faithful ones. Your true destiny is in sight. Hold on— hold on, we are almost there. My profound love and gratitude to you all, my faithful servants of Light. I AM Archangel Michael.

3. You Will Become the Myths of Future Generations

*B*eloved masters, allow me to infuse and anchor in each of you the Aurora Borealis of cosmic energy of Creation that is presently pouring down upon your Earth. There has been a warp or an opening in the fabric that separates the dimensions, thereby allowing a great infusion of fifth-dimensional energy to permeate your Earth and all humanity. This has never happened before in the history of your Earth. It has been activated by your intent, your outpouring of pure, unselfish love and devotion for the Creator. And so, allow me to give you some assistance so that you may derive the greatest benefit from these ever-increasing and accelerated infusions of Christ Light. Make no mistake, every person on Earth, at some level, is being affected by this miracle.

Imagine, if you are willing, a perfect diamond-crystal pyramid, point facing downward, descending from your Divine I AM Presence and penetrating your crown chakra. Within this pyramid, in just the right proportion for each of you, is the essence of the five higher Rays you are now incorporating into your Being. Allow your conscious mind to be flooded with the love, joy, sense of peace and recognition that this energy infuses throughout all your brain cells. Picture or sense your conscious mind moving to the side, possibly perching on your shoulder, as an observer, a silent watcher of the process. We want your conscious mind to become accustomed to the sensation and not feel threatened as more and more of your Spirit, your Christ Mind, takes dominion of your brain functions. This is necessary so that there is no conflict as you bring in new truths, as you begin to use and access more of your brain's capacity.

In the past all knowledge or expanded truth had to move through the resistance of your linear, analytical mind, most often meeting opposition, or being distorted by old rigid concepts and thought forms. The new modality of authentication will be in your heart/soul center. Accept as your truth that which feels expansive, loving and enlightening. Set aside anything that stirs doubt or feels uncomfortable: if it is your truth it will be validated in some way by your Higher Self. In this way you will always stay in your own integrity and empowerment.

Now allow this precious, rare gift to move downward into your subconscious mind. See this as a long, dark corridor with many closed doors and compartments. Behind these doors are all your fears, phobias and obsessions; all the subjective thought forms you have accepted as your reality down through the ages that have kept you constantly at war with yourself. See these doors and compartments opening as all the shadows and energies lurking there are infused with the transforming energies of the five higher Rays you are accessing. See all that is not your highest truth, all that is keeping you in limitation and illusion, dissolving and transmuting into pure Divine Light Substance. The gift we offer you is unity and harmony between your subconscious mind, your conscious mind and your superconscious mind, or Christ Mind, so that you will no longer have to experience the battle and conflict between your multi-mind structure. Once again, you will take control and dominion of your consciousness from the vantage point of a master, no longer sabotaging your efforts, but functioning in perfect harmony with your Divine Self and your Divine Blueprint.

We know that you are experiencing much confusion. Many

of you are having difficulty speaking or expressing: words come out wrong or garbled, you hear words spoken by others and you do not understand. You are having a difficult time focusing and concentrating, and at times you feel totally disoriented. We tell you this too will pass, beloved friends. You are healing your past and the past of your Earthly experience. Picture the third-dimensional Earth slowly disengaging from the fourth-dimensional reality you are presently experiencing. Gradually, all the negativity and imbalances, illusions of that reality, will disappear from your world as you resonate with higher and higher frequencies. All you will take with you is the remembrance of the beauty, the successes and accomplishments—the wonder of your past experience on planet Earth. You will forget the pain, suffering and anguish. As your Spirit quickens, it will wipe out the illusion of separation and sense of failure—it knows only perfection.

You will become the myths of the future generations. They will look back and speak with great respect and awe of the brave and beautiful souls who had saved planet Earth from sure destruction, who had lifted and transformed it to its original beauty and perfection. Make no mistake, you are planting the seeds and laying the groundwork for the emergence of a new Heaven on Earth.

It is time for you to step forth, precious friends—either in the physical or etheric body. It is time to be counted and made accountable. What have you done with the gifts given you? Are you willing, dedicated and brave enough to move forward, to reach out and accept the new level of empowerment being offered to you? Are you willing to face your greatest fears and walk through them, watch as they dissolve into smoke, never to return—an illusion after all? Are you willing to follow the nudging of Spirit as you step out into uncharted territory, as you allow yourself to be vulnerable, to be bold enough to reach out and grasp your dreams and bring them to fruition with your thought and love power? The path of a master is not for the weak of heart and Spirit.

We have said that many special dispensations are being given to those who bravely step to the fore and claim their heritage. As the masses awaken and cry out for assistance, solutions, information and encouragement, you are needed more than ever, my precious warriors. We are waiting to empower you, to gift you with wisdom, abilities and knowledge beyond your wildest imaginings. You see, your brain has always functioned at 100% capacity—does this surprise you? But you could only access that limited portion that resonated to the frequencies of the third dimension. As you balance and integrate the higher frequencies, you will begin to access more and more of your brain power that resonates to the fourth, fifth and sixth dimensions. You cannot access those portions of your brain until you attune to those frequencies.

That is why it is important that you begin to access your brain, conscious and subconscious mind in a new way so you do not go into "overload." Too much conflicting information or accelerated information throws your mind and body into fear, making it feel as if it is being invaded. This creates all the symptoms you have been experiencing in your body. Resistance and fear bring about dis-comfort and dis-ease.

In the days ahead, as it is appropriate, we will give you many different ways to access and use the energies of these higher Rays that are now available to you. But we also feel it is appropriate to give you an admonishment. As you become more sensitive to the higher vibrational energies, it is more important than ever that you monitor your thoughts, your speech and that which you allow to filter into your consciousness. Your subconscious mind receives direction and is imprinted by repetition, rhythm and emotional responses. As you clear your subconscious of all the old debris, do not allow any thought forms to penetrate your consciousness that are not self-empowering, loving and enlightening—that are not attuned to your new expanded reality. Be aware and vigilant of the music you allow to play in the background, the words that constantly spew forth from your radio and television, what you read and allow to bombard your senses. Many of these are insidious energies of addiction, victimhood, enslavement or limitation.

More and more beautiful, young souls of your world are being indoctrinated and controlled through the power of the media, as you helplessly stand by and watch them fall into traps from which you are powerless to extricate them. Be vigilant, precious ones, take control of your senses and your destiny.

Your reality will constantly shift and your perception will broaden as your expanded awareness takes dominion of your brain and physical senses. Therefore, it is more important than ever that you attune to your beautiful body and see it as an extension of Spirit instead of a separate entity. Make it a habit in your quiet times to focus on the different parts of your body: interact and attune to the many precious parts that comprise your physical vessel. Place your consciousness in your feet: acknowledge them for their under-standing and support, for grounding you and giving you a sense of connectedness to your Mother Earth. Focus on your knees and hips: honor them for the wonderful flexibility they supply, the mobility and forward motion they give your body. Your sexual and reproductive organs deserve love and recognition for the gift of creation they afford you, as well as the ability to merge and unite with another. There is no greater earthly gift you can give yourself or another when this interaction comes with honor of self and your partner through the purity of love and unity of body, mind and Spirit. Move your consciousness through your body until you begin to feel the flow of blood and life force through your veins, and the beating of your heart as you attune to the rhythm of your Mother Earth and the Cosmic Heart. You are becoming attuned to the pulsations of creation through the energies of your Great Central Sun as you become more sensitive to this refined stimuli. Continue the process as you acknowledge and attune to the wonder of your physical vessel so that you will become aware of how truly multifaceted you are. You will form a new relationship with your body, realizing new strength, vitality and mastery.

The excitement on Earth is building, dear ones: a vision is emerging that is beyond your wildest dreams. Reach out and grasp that dream. We are there, waiting for you—within and without—to surround you in our love and protection. We are with you always. I AM Archangel Michael.

4. THE GOLDEN PROMISE

*B*eloved masters, many facets of your belief structure, as well as much of the illusion on which you have built your world, are crumbling and shifting at a faster pace each day. Indeed, it is a time of mass awakening, a time when every sentient being, no matter what level of consciousness, is beginning to question and feel an inner discontent.

As the Earth Mother becomes fully conscious, she too is beginning to bring forth from her subconscious memory the devastation, pain and suffering she has experienced since she agreed to be your host mother for this grand experiment. She also yearns to reclaim and don her garments of Light and now that she realizes this is possible, nothing will stop her from moving forward to her destiny as a star of Light. I have spoken before of the honeycomb of Light, the consciousness grids that are being reestablished around the Earth. These are now firmly in place, and through the efforts of you, the faithful Light warriors around the world, they are slowly being filled with Divine Light Substance—the resonance or frequencies necessary to lift the Earth and humanity to the next level of consciousness.

Envision these grids as the bloodstream of the Earth and when the higher frequencies hit pockets of negative, impacted energy, or blockages, it creates stress and chaos. As a result, you might liken it to the Earth experiencing the effects of high blood pressure. Just as you are being bombarded with this refined cosmic energy from without and within, so it is with your Earth. As the stargates, or cosmic freeways are opened, the influx of energy from the Great Central Sun is allowed to flow freely through this quadrant of the galaxy and into your solar system. The deepest shadows within the

Earth's subconscious mind, as well as humanity's, are being infused with refined frequencies of Light.

All the ancient memories of your past experiences in the physical are surfacing, as are the memories within the Earth's consciousness. Many of you agreed to incarnate in this lifetime in areas where the worst destruction and negativity were experienced. You were there, my brave ones, and experienced all the pain and suffering along with many others. You hold within you the memories which are waiting to be healed and balanced, and together you will bring about that miracle for humanity and the Earth as well. As I explained before, you agreed to assist in the healing and balancing of all that has occurred in the past, for this energy must be requalified and harmonized before you can move forward. The past is made up of energy and potential that has already been used. It is engraved within the memory of mass-consciousness and woven into the cosmic tapestry. But the past is fluid and flexible just like the future, and it can be requalified and rewoven, thereby eliminating the errors and imperfections.

The future is filled with unlimited promise, primal cosmic substance just waiting to be molded and used by you, the cocreators of the brave new world of tomorrow. But you must relearn and remember how to grasp and use this great gift, and it is the same with your Mother Earth. The Devic and Elemental Kingdoms, under the supreme direction of the Seven Elohim and the builders of form, were commissioned to manifest and oversee the Divine Plan/Blueprint for planet Earth. These magnificent Beings, from the greatest to the smallest, served unselfishly for aeons of time, until they could no longer stand the negativity and destructive forces by which they were constantly bombarded. They gradually began to withdraw their energy. Just as your soul-self gradually withdrew from your physical body, leaving only a thin silver cord to connect you with your Divine I AM Presence, so it was with the life force of the Earth, which is supplied through your Solar Logos to the Devic and Elemental Kingdoms. Barely enough primal life substance flowed into the Earth to keep her alive, and from self-destructing, and she too went into slumber.

That time is coming to a close. The beautiful servants of the Creator, the Devic and Elemental Kingdoms, have been given a new directive, instructions to begin to infuse the Earth in full force with their elements of life: Cosmic fire, the life force of creation; the breath of God, the air element; the cleansing and life-sustaining element of water; and the foundation of your existence on the material plane, the element of Earth. You may see the changing and erratic weather patterns and shifting earth as destructive forces of nature, but we see it as a necessary process to bring your Earth back to health and balance. The elements are not your enemies, they are Divine Gifts from the Creator, but you have misused and abused the Earth and yourselves long enough. Just as with a wayward child, it is time for humanity to be taught accountability and responsibility for its actions.

It is quickly becoming evident which areas of the planet are most in need of cleansing and balancing. We are endeavoring to keep the level of pain and suffering at a minimum, and as you have been told, the mass destruction of your planet is no longer a possibility. However, as is the case when you allow your physical body to deteriorate to the point that your life force is threatened, so it is with the Earth—drastic measures must be taken.

That is why we tell you that these times in which you

are now living are so critical. Every opportunity must be taken to assist the Earth to birth and reclaim her Light body. That is why we have asked you to come together at the time of each full moon in meditation with the intent of allowing the influx of cosmic life force to flow through you and into the Earth. You must take advantage of each opportunity offered you within the grand design of Creation. We ask you to become aware of the wondrous opportunity to be a part of the transformation of the Earth and humanity.

Join together at the Spring Equinox and at the time of the Wesak celebration during the full moon of Taurus. The Summer Solstice is a time when the creative life force available for the year reaches its peak, a time when you have the maximum potential to direct and mold your dreams and aspirations and bring them to fruition. As you come together in common purpose with unselfish intent to assist in the transformation and restructuring of the Earth, you will have all the fuel and fire of Creation at your beck and call.

It is powerful and wondrous to come together with others in the physical at such times, but if this is not possible, beloveds, know that your participation is still needed and important to the whole. At these sacred times, no matter where you are, alone, with only one other or amongst thousands, you will create a heartlink around the world and your blazing heart flame and sacred breath will capture, ignite and radiate the exquisite precious gift being offered from the Most High around and through the Earth.

Your contribution, no matter how small you may believe it to be, is of vital importance. Together you can move mountains, calm the seas and soothe stormy elements of fire and wind. Call on the blessed Devas and precious Elementals.

Solicit their cooperation and assistance as you recreate a bond and a working relationship, one with another. Just as you have reestablished a relationship with your body elemental and your Higher Self, it is once again time to begin to work in harmony with the elemental forces of Creation. You will be the winners, I assure you.

I ask you to set your analytical mind aside for a short time. See or sense your conscious mind shift to the side, as if it were perched on your shoulder. Give it a form or shape—make it real. This is advisable when you are in a meditative state or endeavoring to tap into your higher or causal mind in order to access the wisdom of Spirit. You cannot live or function within just your emotional body, nor can you function within the mental body alone (the mind). Spirit is meant to inhabit the whole body, not just the heart (emotions) or the head (intellect). It is time you become aware of the science of Spirit and not just the emotions of Spirit. Most of your current religions are based on the emotions of Spirit, resulting in fear-based reactions of guilt, shame, feelings of low self-esteem, a sense of powerlessness or not being in control of your destiny.

Now with your inner vision, give your subconscious mind a form as well. It might take the shape of a person with a body or just a fluid shape or color, but we want you to know without a doubt that these elemental parts of yourself are real and have great influence over you. There is no right or wrong way to do this; it is your personal experience and valid for you alone.

See your subconscious mind in a big room with many locked files and doors. Within these dark compartments are all the subjective, subconscious memories that have

been stored there down through the ages: fear, and the sense of failure, unworthiness and being unloved. Here are the energies of rejection, abandonment, shame and guilt— the addictions and phobias that have kept you in bonds of pain and suffering for the many ages of your earthly experience.

Call upon your Divine I AM Presence to radiate a shaft of white, crystalline Light and the Violet Flame down through your crown chakra. See this purifying, transmuting energy filling this great room. As you fling open the doors and compartments, see this wondrous Light permeating every corner, as it begins the process of illuminating and balancing all the misqualified energy stored there. Any thought forms or energies that are for your highest good remain intact and are enhanced, but those energies and thought forms which no longer serve you gradually dissolve, making way for new empowering thoughts, urges and impulses.

As you place yourself in this receptive mode so that your Superconscious mind can begin to bring forth new, vital information, your conscious mind will not go into overload, shut down or reject the input because of linear, conditioned thinking.

The last component to this process is to monitor or filter any new information through your heart/thymus area, or your truth barometer. If it feels right or expansive and is empowering, you may claim it as your truth. If it feels restrictive, if there is a sense of dread, or if it is in any way controlling or fear-based, set it aside and do not claim it. However, if there is a feeling of neutrality and you are not sure, it could be that it is a new truth waiting to be

incorporated into your belief system and it will take time for it to be validated. If you ask, it will be validated through a dream, a book, an event or a person—give it time and you will know without a doubt.

Now that I have given you the ground rules, I will give you an example of expanded truth that is waiting to be incorporated into your belief system in order that you may take the maximum advantage of what is being offered. Since the time the Earth spiraled down into the frequencies of the third dimension, in between incarnations you have always been under the guidance of your Divine Self, along with your guides and teachers. Together, you all determined what the theme of your next life would be, or what would be the best circumstances for your spiritual growth. This you already know. But in addition, you were also given an assignment, an opportunity to serve and grow in consciousness. In many lifetimes it was a very simple assignment, but at times you were given a mission of greater importance which would take wisdom, commitment and courage. See yourself going before your Great I AM Presence and being infused with cosmic Light Substance of, say, a 100-watt light bulb for an easy or nonchallenging lifetime. But when you were asked or given the opportunity to make great strides in your spiritual growth, or to assist in the Divine Plan, you were allowed to draw, hypothetically, 1,000-watts of energy, or possibly even more. So goes the saying, "When much is given, much is required in return."

You have had lifetimes when you were given great gifts, like those you may see and envy in others. Each of you has had an opportunity to forge ahead of the masses and make an impact on the future of humanity and the Earth. When you used those gifts for the good of all, more was added or made available in your bank of cosmic life substance, but you did not always bring it all into the physical experience with you. That is why we say, do not judge anyone by appearances. The homeless man on the street may have chosen to experience that facet of being, while he has great gifts and riches stored in the keeping of his Divine Self. Now this is a simplistic explanation of what actually occurs when you are between lives and before you take on another assignment on the physical plane. However, it will give you a general idea and an opportunity to expand your consciousness into a higher awareness of how Spirit moves and works within you and through you.

What I wish to instill within your consciousness is the **GOLDEN PROMISE** we made to you before you came into the physical in this lifetime. We of the higher realms, and you as well, knew that this was a "make it or break it" time in the evolution of the Earth and humanity. **The promise was made that you would have an opportunity in this one lifetime to access and tap into the full force and measure of Cosmic Life Substance stored and waiting for you within the heart of your Divine I AM Presence.** That is why so many of you are moving forward in leaps and bounds: accessing, integrating, radiating ever-increasing wisdom, love and Light.

That is why it is so important that you diligently seek to balance and harmonize your four bodily systems and allow the radiance of Spirit to pour forth to and through you. As you honor and balance the body through pure, loving thoughts and by practicing deep, vitalizing breathing and energizing motion and activity, you create a perfect environment for your Divine Essence, the spark of the Creator, to take full dominion and residency within your physical vessel.

The **GOLDEN PROMISE** will then be fulfilled. Oh, what wonders are being wrought amongst you and on your blessed planet! See beyond the discomfort of the moment and cast your gaze upon the perfection of the future, my brave warriors. Victory is in sight. Do not falter now, faithful ones. We are only a heartbeat away, surrounding, protecting and loving you beyond measure. I AM Archangel Michael.

5. Thoughts to Ponder on the Way to Mastery

1. *A true teacher will point you in the direction of your own empowerment. They actually live what they preach. A teacher is only qualified to share the truths they can demonstrate in their own everyday living.*

2. *Attitudes of emotional and mental control are the most important factors in bringing your body to a higher frequency. You must strive to prepare your lower (physical) body for alignment with the new energy vibrations now entering the earth's atmosphere.*

3. *Personal control at all times over negative emotions and feelings is necessary to create a balanced, empowered auric field around you. As you become more balanced, you will become more sensitive to higher vibrational energies, and you will be able to use these energies to manifest what you desire in your life.*

4. *The being within you that is called the soul does not think as the mind does, but perceives energies ... it senses the vibrations of your emotions via feelings. The soul does not see or hear, yet it perceives sight and sound. It is that intrinsic part of you that always "is." The mind must be trained to be the servant of the soul. An attitude of love, wonderment and gratitude places your soul in command.*

5. *As long as we are battling the polarity of the cross of matter, we are constantly out of balance in one way or another. To be free, to exercise the neutralizing power of the heart, one needs only to relax and walk discretely with wonder on the middle path—to feel, but not be a slave to feeling; to exercise control over the mind and not be enslaved by passion or excessive desire.*

6. Following the spiritual path is made easier by following an experienced traveler.

7. Negative force is nothing more than positive force in a lower vibration—the world of matter, feeling, thought.

8. The higher you rise on the spiritual scale, the more subtle life becomes and the less you are under the control of the negative forces. You will operate from a new awareness with more sensitivity and discernment.

9. You are the past life of someone in the future.

10. The soul's purpose is to learn to give and receive love without possession—learning how to love without ownership. Compassionate love is a detached feeling and not vulnerable to the mind or to the passions of emotion. Compassionate love energy is the Mother aspect. Detachment and compassion equals unconditional love.

11. If you begin to see or think of yourself as being a spark of the God force, you will have no cause or desire to feel guilt or fear, or to punish your reality by punishing yourself in any way. Remember, you are playing a role ... interacting in the game of life ... and living a dream. Change your role, change the game, and you can transform the dream into your greatest desires.

12. Use your logical mind to compare new information with past experiences. Allow new concepts time to prove their own validity.

13. Messiah complex: on the beginning path of enlightenment, but still grounded in 3D reality. Thoughts such as "Only I have the real truth and you must learn it from me." The fifth-dimensional reality is "Come, let us grow

together. I will share my enlightenment—spirit—wisdom with you and you can share yours with me, and then through our mutual resources and support, together, we will progress more quickly."

14. Be wary of anyone who wishes to take away your power or assume authority over your spiritual growth.

15. To the degree you love yourself, you will accept love from those around you.

16. The secret of change is to focus all your energies, not on fighting the old, but building the new.

17. Karma is action and reaction or cause and effect. Wisdom erases Karma.

18. Concerning anything that you feel is keeping you stuck in 3D reality, ask yourself these questions:

    A. What is the real fear behind this issue?
    B. What needs do I have or feel that are not being met?
    C. What am I doing (or thinking) that creates disharmony in my life?
    D. How can I change my behavior (or thoughts) to create more harmony in my life?

19. A change in behavior quickly leads to a change in attitude.

20. Ascension is taking place one day at a time, one thought at a time.

21. We are all doomed to perfection ... so let's relax and enjoy the ride!!

In love and light, Ronna

6. THE FUTURE IS NOW

*B*eloved masters, please do not allow the dramatically changing weather patterns or the accelerating cataclysmic events which are occurring around the world to spiral you into fear—know that out of chaos, new creation emerges. We sense the anxiety and distress you are experiencing as your old belief structures crumble and as things that you have always believed or relied upon fall away, leaving you feeling vulnerable and uncertain.

A new Earth is being birthed, just as you are emerging from the cocoon in which you have been imprisoned for so long. You are flexing your spiritual muscles and spreading your "Ray-diant" wings as you stretch and grow into your multidimensional bodies of Light. There is a plethora of probable futures which many of you are tapping into, as you merge your minds with the cosmic stream of potential realities. You must decide which of these many possible realities you wish to manifest—that is why we have asked you to take time to think about your vision for the new millennium—to refine it, and then do everything within your power to bring forth your unique vision into the world of form. Remember the popular saying, "The universe rearranges itself to fit your picture of reality." So if you hear someone predict that your city or hometown or country is in the pattern of destruction for the near future, or that there must be greater and greater cataclysms in order for the New Age to be birthed, please do not take these predictions as your truth.

You are much more powerful than you realize—especially when you join together in a unified effort to create the highest good for all. You are a creation of the God Mind and you are encoded and designed with a deep-seated desire to create.

During these most important times of evolution and transformation, each of you has been drawn (or will be drawn) to
the place in which you can be of the most service. Either by
serving those around you—sharing your unique talents and
gifts—or because you have specific energies encoded within
your Divine Blueprint that are critical to the evolution of
that area. Or, you may have Light packets or frequencies
within your brain structure that will help to activate the crystalline energies that have lain dormant within the Earth for
many thousands of years. These great structures are waiting
for you and for those who are in harmony with you, so that,
once again, they may project their radiant Light out into the
solar system and also receive the refined frequencies now
being beamed down upon the Earth. These frequencies will
also circle the globe as the golden web of Light is reestablished—a critical factor in the reunification process. Much
has been accomplished, but there is still much to be done
and each of you is a key player.

As you join together and allow yourselves to be the transformers for this energy, you will draw it through your physical vessels so that it can pick up your unique frequency
patterns before the combined frequencies are transmitted deep
within the Earth's crystalline core. Know that within your
physical vessels and with your loving intent, you hold the
keys which will help to bring these magnificent Light Structures to life once more. And in this way, you will render great
service to humanity and the Earth, for this important process will help to ease the stress and strain of releasing the
constraints and imperfections as you move through the
fourth dimension toward the freedom and harmony of the
fifth dimension.

Many of you are healing the ancient wounds and

memories of Atlantis and Lemuria—while many others are activating the wondrous memories and energies of some of the great Light centers of the past. Then you will all use these energies to help create the perfection of the future. You are being called to take brave and bold action as you go forward on your assigned missions. Remember, beloveds, you agreed.

The drama and great transformation that are taking place on Earth have never been experienced before in all creation. You will be seen as Divine Architects who have braved the unknown in the farthest outpost in your universe—assuming a cloak of flesh and submerging yourselves in the quagmire of third-dimensional illusion. Now it is time to shrug off the shackles that bind you. Now is the time for you to re-claim your Divine Birthright and your heritage. Oh, beloveds, if only you knew how you are cherished and how we honor you. If only you could remember yourselves as you were and are in the higher dimensions, you would not be anxious or sad—you would know that you have all the power, wisdom and the tools to recreate paradise on Earth, and when the task is finished, how easily you will return to your home among the stars. We wish to give you assurance that we are waiting to welcome you with open arms and that there will be a grand celebration.

As all the deep-core, negative patterns emerge from deep within your memory and DNA to be cleared and dissolved once and for all, we sense your frustration, your confusion and your fears of being punished, or of having done some-thing wrong. Let me assure you, precious ones, this is hap-pening because you are doing something RIGHT, not wrong. We will not minimize your pain or your discomfort; how-ever, we will give you encouragement and direction. A puri-fication process is underway on Earth and within every sentient Being. As you allow the cleansing energies of Light to infiltrate throughout your body, you will release and refine everything of a lesser vibration. Can you accept the fleeting discomfort as an opportunity to release that which does not serve your highest good? Then please use all the means at hand to relieve the symptoms or condition, knowing that at its completion you will be ready to accept even greater infusions of Light.

We have tried to assist you in understanding the Universal Laws of Creation and the seven Rays of Beingness, or the virtues and attributes of the Creator for your solar system. The prisms of the Seven Cosmic Rays are growing stronger as they are projected via magnified Solar Light into your bodies in order to empower you and bring you into wholeness. You are coming of age as you take on your spiritual responsibility and gain the wisdom of a master, but there is still much to be done and discernment is more important than ever. You are moving out of the harmonics of seven into the galactic harmonics of 12—this is why it is so important that you bring your physical chakra system into balance as you access the ever-increasing strength and power of the higher Rays' vibrations. Anchor your feet firmly on Earth, beloveds, as you reach for the stars—if you do not, your physical vessel will not be able to withstand the magnified influx of cosmic energy, and you will not be able to serve yourself or anyone else. You depend on the Earth to support and sustain you; now it is time for you to assist your mother planet— you are inexorably joined together until you and the Earth spiral into the next level of illumination.

As with every great change, the pendulum of popular belief or mass-consciousness swings widely before it settles down to a sensible norm. There are many teachings and claims being circulated—many to empower and assist you, and many to frighten you and take away your power. Also, there are many products being touted to speed up your enlightenment and "do the work for you." There are many legitimate tools and products which will help you on your path, but remember, beloveds, you must do the inner work—you must tread the path to en-LIGHT-enment—no one else can do that for you.

You are in the midst of the transition into the new millennium—it is a time of celebration, not of fear or uncertainty. Your fears are unfounded, for they are based on old third-dimensional illusions. If you have taken to heart the truths that we have given you, you have nothing to fear.

It is a time of harvesting and thanksgiving for many, while others in the world are suffering from deprivation. We ask those of you who live in the lands of plenty to take an inventory as to what you must have to live comfortably. It is time to decide what is truly important in your lives. Must you have more, bigger and better gadgets and material goods to be happy and live in comfort? We think not. Your world is changing rapidly, and yes, we will tell you that as these next few years of your time pass, your priorities will change dramatically. We are not asking you to give up your possessions, but we are asking you to become aware that happiness, joy and satisfaction begin internally. As you allow your soul/Spirit to take dominion within, you will no longer look outside yourselves for validation or happiness.

Will you also make this a time of forgiving? It is time to return to harmony—harmony among races, religions, cultures, as well is within the family, with friends and in the work place. Will you make a pledge to begin to see through eyes filtered with love, to hear with ears tempered by compassion and to radiate the love of Spirit through your heart? Oh, what a difference this would make, beloveds. Unity and harmony are the words to focus on during these swiftly changing times. If everyone would take the words in this paragraph to heart and practice them, how quickly your world would transform for the better. It is you who suffers when you hold anger or judgment in your heart, for you are restricting the flow of Christ Light to yourself. Love and appreciate the people around you for their uniqueness and diverse natures. If you see them as unlikable or unlovable, radiate love and compassion toward the Spark of the Divine within them. Even if they are in fear and denial, know that they are seeking love and happiness in their own way, and in their own time they will step onto the path of Divine Love and Harmony. If you teach by example, combined with your loving thoughts and deeds, you will assist in the transformation of many dear earthbound souls.

There is another issue which has been addressed before, but it needs to be refreshed in your mind. Know that you can be of great assistance to the many dear souls who are going through the physical death process. Include them in your daily prayers and add your loving energy to the column of white love/Light which extends up from the Earth into the higher dimensions. Then see all these dear souls moving upward into this column and being bathed in the blessed, purifying radiance of the Violet Flame. See the angels of mercy surrounding them and helping them in their release from the magnetic pull of the physical realm. The three lower astral planes are gradually being cleared and refined and so these beloved ones move quickly through the third and fourth dimensions into the rarified Light. We know that you mourn your loved ones and those who are taken from you, and we are here to comfort you in your time of bereavement. But we wish you to know that they are rejoicing—they will be prepared to return to Earth with a greater awareness to assist in the evolutionary process, or they will assume duties in the realms of Light and serve from the inner dimensions. The veils between the dimensions are thinning and your telepathic skills are awakening—they will be waiting to interact with you when the time is right.

Know that wherever you live, you can help in the activation of the crystalline energies within the Earth. Join together whenever and as often as possible. We have given this meditation before, but now it is more important than ever that you participate in the awakening of the Earth and humanity:

Ask our Father/Mother God and all the great Beings of Light to join you. Breathe deeply as you see your pranic tube of Light being illuminated by a shaft of Golden White Light from the Creator Source and penetrating deep within the heart core of the Earth. Breathe deeply and rhythmically of the Prana of Life and feel a vortex of energy build within your body. Sense a force begin to build, a whirlwind of Divine Power. Center your consciousness in your heart and feel the love for all Creation begin to permeate your Being down to the center of the Earth as you build this vortex of cosmic energy within. See this whirlwind filled with the magic Violet Flame and a blazing shaft of magenta, centered with electric blue and a luminous white center—you are now a pillar of Light radiating the pure Essence of the cosmic life force. Move your consciousness to your third eye and then, as we have taught you, move your focus to the center of your brain—you will ignite the keys and codes you carry within which are your gift and

contribution to the master plan. Radiate a shaft of Light from your solar plexus and your third eye, seeing them with your inner vision forming a V until they come together before you, approximately three feet above the Earth. Watch with your mind's eye as these energies ignite and spread around the globe, connecting with those of your spiritual brothers and sisters. See this column of Light expanding as it surrounds and enfolds the area you are in and then radiates out further and further each time you focus on it. Hold the vision and focus until you hear within your heart center: "It is done. It is done."

My brave warriors, do not become discouraged—it is always the darkest before the dawn. You are making dramatic progress. The shadows and dark corners of the Earth and in the minds of humanity will not be able to resist the radiance of Christ Light much longer. Hold steadfastly to your vision. Have courage and encourage others as you march boldly into the Light of the future world. We stand beside you and enfold you in an aura of God's love. I AM Archangel Michael.

7. SEEK YOUR CORE ESSENCE— WHO YOU REALLY ARE

*B*eloved masters, it is time for us to take you a step further in your awareness, your knowledge, and your transformational process. We wish to speak to you this day about core issues—the innermost core of your being, your Essence. You have been peeling off the layers of negativity, distorted concepts and old belief systems like removing the skin of an onion—layer by layer. For a number of years now, you have been delving deep within your subconscious mind, routing out and examining your shadow side—all the sub-jective beliefs, fears, limitations, half-truths and falsehoods that have taken up residence there down through the ages. Many of you have worked long and diligently to eliminate those beliefs, habits and traits that no longer serve you— those things that have kept you imprisoned in fetters of fear, limitation, guilt, and feelings of hopelessness and inferiority.

We know this has been a long, painful and frustrating pro-cess, but we wish to bring you good news and glad tidings. Those of you who have so bravely trod the barren desert of your subconscious mind, opened the locked doors of your inner world and confronted your lower ego self, your instinc-tive, emotional self and your rigid, controlling mental self have had a formidable task and worthy adversaries. After all, they were in control for many thousands of years now and were not willing to submit to a higher authority without a struggle. But you have persevered and you have won, or are winning, the battle.

Those areas of your inner being that have finally submit-ted to the glory and wonder of the Christ Light are being bathed in its healing powers and are returning to a natural state of love—a process of conformity, cooperation and re-union with the rest of your wondrous Being. They are real-izing that they will not lose their authority or their purpose in your life, but will come into even more power as they merge and blend, harmonizing with the totality of the Es-sence and magnificence of whom you are. This is the path of the master; the steps, trials and tests that must be con-fronted and conquered.

And so, we now come to the next part of the process. Just as you are beginning to get a glimpse at what a marvelous, powerful being you are, we are going to tell you that you do not have an inkling as yet.

Now it is time to acknowledge and claim ownership of your CORE ESSENCE, your true identity. You are not just a male or female human being residing on the planet Earth. You are not just a soul within a physical body, that has a Higher Self that is part of a greater being known as your Di-vine I AM Presence. You have important connections, my friends, and as some like to state, you have a royal heritage, ancestors of great renown.

You are the Starseed, the Wayshowers, and you know who you are for we have spoken much of this in the past. We do not want you to get the idea that you are "better or more than" the rest of humanity, but that it is just your time—you are at the stage of your evolution whereby the assign-ment that you have earned throughout many lifetimes and many ages has placed you in the circumstances and situa-tions in which you now find yourself.

We have told you about the unique experiment for which the planet Earth was designed, and how many of you came from far-off civilizations and even other universes to be a representative of your world or star system—to bring the expertise of your race, or to learn and gain knowledge and experience so that you could take new information back to your own civilization. All of you answered the call and accepted the duty of being a part of the "Grand Experiment"—planet Earth. Each of you was given an assignment which began at the universal level with the great councils and creator gods.

Some of you have memories (buried deep within your brain cells) of assisting in the creation of the complex, intricate design for this galaxy, solar system and the planet Earth. Many of you remember coming as guardians of Earth, watching over the development and solidification of this jewel of the universe. Some of you assisted in instilling and infusing the Earth with its magnetic grid system and ley lines—wielding great, powerful streams of electromagnetic energy and establishing the etheric web or field that surrounds the Earth.

Some brought from their worlds the DNA encodings of the minerals, precious stones, the elements: fire, air, earth and sparkling waters, while others brought the blueprints and vibrational frequencies necessary to develop the beautiful flora and fauna, the many species of animals, birds and creatures that would eventually inhabit the Earth. Some of you, under the direction and guidance of the angelic realms, helped to infuse all of these wonders with an etheric web or body, and then assisted the Elementals and the Devic Kingdom to assume guardianship over these most precious creations.

Others of you had the great responsibility of taking human form and actually seeding humanity from all the various civilizations—establishing the five major root races and many sub-races (there are two major root races yet to come). Others brought great scientific data, mental power and agility, while many came as bearers of the Goddess energy and anchored on Earth the great streams of Light that poured down from the Creator Source.

Some of you were given the assignment (when it was time for you to be fragmented into an individual soul), to carry out the part of the experiment whereby you would remember the connection you had to your Divine Complement when you separated into either the female or male body—into the polarities of physical form. It has been your task down through the ages to seek that perfect counterpart of yourself and it has been a long, painful journey. But now many of you are coming to realize that it is not without yourself that you will find this unity, this sense of wholeness, but within. And then paradoxically, you will be ready to meet a true soul-mate while in the physical or reconnect with your Divine Complement on the inner planes, if they are not presently incarnate, so that never again will you have to feel alone. And make no mistake, beloved ones, an inner-dimensional relationship with your twin flame can be even more wonderful and fulfilling than a physical relationship.

Many of you may doubt this, and you will have to trust us on this one, but once you make that connection on the inner planes with your own soul flame and your true soul family, you will never feel separated or alone.

Many of you felt betrayed and abandoned when you were eventually caught or stuck in the physical body and could no longer withdraw at will. It was your assignment to focus on and integrate Spirit in the physical body and become an extension of your Divine Presence in manifesting, developing and perfecting life in the physical expression—via the mental, emotional, astral/desire body through the gift of free

will. This is where the experiment went awry, and a love/
hate relationship began that has continued and magnified
down through the ages. Look around you at humanity at
large. How far you have fallen from the perfect, magnificent
vessels in which you came to Earth—the beautiful design,
the awesome, intricate structure you originally inhabited.

Yes, we have told you that you are not just a body, but we
have also told you that you must bring all parts of yourself
back to their original perfection. Much of humanity is still
obsessed with how much and what great variety of food they
can stuff into their bodies, or how much sensation they can
experience via sexual interaction or momentary thrills. And
yes, even these desires go back to, or have their origins in,
your original assignment which has gotten so distorted or
off track that you have no idea of the true cocreative/desire/
mental/emotional nature that was programmed or encoded
within you.

There were those of you who came as leaders, wielders of
power and authority, great planners and strategists. You can
see what has been wrought as a result of the misuse of these
gifts. When are those in power, those natural leaders that
always seem to come to the fore and affect and influence
humanity, going to awaken and realize that these gifts will
be taken from them and eventually turned against them if
they do not take the responsibility for the great honor that
was bestowed upon them and begin to use their abilities properly for the benefit of all?

There were those who came as healers and caretakers, a
most honorable duty and gift, and it is also very apparent
how this has evolved. Many are using these gifts as they were
meant to be used, but many more have taken advantage of

the masses and misused their knowledge and abilities to control humanity and to amass great fortunes. And there is a misconception that being a server or care giver of humanity is not a worthy task or endeavor and many are looked down upon or taken advantage of as being "lesser than" or not as important as other duties or vocations. Make no mistake, these beloved unselfish souls are integral to the well-being of humankind and are also Divine Emissaries of the Creator.

Those of you who came with overwhelming love for the Creator and the wonderful Earth have felt a great responsibility for the planet. You have always known (even before it was a popular belief or an acceptable concept) that the Earth is a living, breathing entity. You feel a great affinity for nature and all the grandeur and wondrous variety the Earth Mother offers as a gift to humankind. And you feel a deep personal pain, almost an assault on your own being at the misuse, neglect and selfish destruction humanity has wrought on this once perfect, pristine paradise. You are the ones who feel most at peace in the mountains, in the wilderness or sitting on the shore watching the wonder of the waves as they crest, pulse and flow, trying to soothe your ailing planet.

Send your loving energy, dear ones—feel the power surge through your being as you bring in the highest frequencies possible and then transmit this healing energy down into the Earth and see it also flowing through, clearing and healing the Earth's etheric web. This is your mission, your part of the Divine Plan. You know who you are ... you will know this is your mission by the joy, serenity and sense of peace you feel as you allow yourself to be an instrument of healing for the Mother Earth.

Ah, and those of you who came to teach, guide and keep the knowledge flowing, to transmit knowledge that will evolve into wisdom, thereby creating change and allowing new philosophies to be implanted in the fertile minds of children and those who are awakening and ready for higher truths—yours is a formidable task—for you must teach by example, as well as the spoken word as you transmit the validity of love, joy, peace, honor, integrity, unity and abundance, rather than fear, hate, guilt, isolation and limitation.

Many of you came with so much love for the Creator that it was hard to adjust to the material world and the physical body. You are the ones that have denied all things in the realm of physicality, rejecting material comfort, wealth, and desire, as well as the bodily form, in the belief that you could not enjoy or accept the sensations of the physical world and still be spiritual. But that is why you came, dear ones. We know you are capable of being pure Spirit—following the will of the Creator in the higher realms. Your assignment was to cocreate a heavenly Earth and to experience all the beauty and wonder of Spirit in solid, physical form. You have scourged your bodies, starved them unto death, abused them with harmful brain and soul-numbing substances, taken them into battle in the name of God and died with the misconception that it was the will of God. It is our Father/Mother God's will that you live in cocreative splendor, perfection, beauty and harmony with all the other Divine Emissaries inhabiting the Earth with you.

Others came to balance the masculine and feminine attributes and abilities in the physical form. We have spoken of this often and given much insight as to how far you have deviated from the balanced and harmonious energies you came with originally. Give up the battle, dear ones. First, stop warring within yourself: accept your power as well as your gentleness, accept your authority and compassion, accept your creativity, intuitive nature and dynamic, far-visioned reasoning abilities. Allow yourselves to be gentle, but strong—to love and be loved, but also to keep your integrity and your self-identity—to give unselfishly, but to receive with joy and a sense of worthiness. These are the lessons you are to learn and the balance you are seeking, my beloved warriors.

Where do you fall in this Divine Plan, dear ones? What is your role? What is the message stamped on your soul? "Go forth and accomplish ..." What is the echo in your heart telling you? You will know if you tap into your intuition or soul-self as you read this message. That is why it is being given to you at this time, so that you can focus on your particular mission ... so that you can begin to hone in and perfect your part of the great tapestry of history that is in the making. It will take each of you to bring it to perfection, to a glorious, successful conclusion, precious ones.

Claim your Divine Mission now—that golden spark which has lain dormant for so long—assume your true identity, which is waiting to be recognized and is ready to burst forth. The CORE OF YOU is calling ... please answer. I AM Archangel Michael and I bring you these truths.

8. You Have Angelic Connections

*B*eloved masters, I ask you to close your eyes for a moment before we begin our time together this day. I wish for you to sense my presence—not just read the message I offer you. We have a Divine Connection, you and I, and yes, I mean each and every one of you. You are here on this planet because we sent out a clarion call and you answered. You had to meet certain rigid criteria, and undergo what might be called an intense training process in order to qualify for this grand experiment on planet Earth.

Draw forth that memory from deep within the core of your heart/soul, allow yourself to sense a feeling of expansion, a richness, a joy, as we merge our energies, one with another. I send you a Ray of love from the center of my Being, a gift that is yours alone. We of the angelic realms are as anxious as you to reclaim our connection. We miss your presence, dear ones, we have been separated too long.

If you are willing, I will assign to each of you four beautiful angelic beings, but you must ask for this gift. These are more powerful than any other of the myriad of angelic helpers you have assigned to you, as these beloved angelic warriors will come to you at my request. There will be two with feminine energies and two with masculine energies to serve you. I assure you, THEY ARE REAL—as real as anything you can touch in the physical realm. Give them assignments, ask their names and allow a sense of their personalities to emerge—attune to them with your inner senses. Direct them to assist you in every endeavor, whether it be abundance, health, organization, protection, creativity—there is no limit to what they can do.

The more you interact with them, the more real they will

become and the more you will see how helpful they can be. It is time for you to receive some of the rewards for all your patient endeavors, all your trials and tests. Gradually, we are resuming our proper relationship with you, with all humanity. We were not meant to be separated or divided. It was intended that you would be able to interact with us telepathically, even lift your Spirit into the realms where we reside and spend time with us and receive succor.

Even when your Spirit incorporated fully in the physical vessel, it was planned that we would always be available to guide, encourage and support you, and it has been so, but in a much more limited way. We could only reach you in your dreams and through the yearnings of your heart, and the gentle nudgings of your soul. We became unreal to you—myths, fantasy, or a hope of the faithful.

More recently we have begun to rebuild our connection with you, as you cleared the static between us by refining your auric field so that you could once more access the higher dimensions. Also we have been able to accelerate the process because we were given permission to intercede in order to activate your awakening. You agreed before you were allowed to incarnate in this lifetime, that when the proper time came you would allow us to set aside your free will and direct you toward your destiny—onto the path of awakening. Many of you may recall exactly the time, place and circumstances in which this took place. We nudged you onto the path and nothing in your world has been the same since.

When the Earth was jolted off its etheric axis and sank into the third dimension, one of the greatest tragedies was that we could barely penetrate through the density of the lower astral planes to connect with you. You forgot we were all a part of the plan—in this together—this experiment on a planet you now call Earth. We are all brothers and sisters, my beloved ones, no matter what our lineage, heritage or level of awareness. You have forgotten you are Divine Beings, that you are only visitors here. Your home is out among the stars—in a vast and wondrous place that has no boundaries, no limitations—in the realm of all possibilities.

Some of you have been receiving disconnected and disturbing thoughts, and are dreaming vividly and in great detail. We tell you that you are beginning to access some of your parallel lives, other dimensions and even reclaiming parts of yourself. Some are also integrating fragments of their Higher Self, and so there is much confusing or conflicting information—distorted information and thought forms that do not seem to belong to you. Just as with the emotions and thoughts which well up from within your own being that are based on fear or negativity of any sort, see the thought forms that are not love-based or joyful instantly transmuted into pure, Divine Light Substance.

There is much taking place on the Earth, within the Earth, as well as in the dimensions beyond your Earth that you are only sensing, but cannot even begin to comprehend. I have spoken of the great crystals that are being activated, and how these are resonating at higher and higher frequencies out of and around the Earth. The Earth, your solar system, and the galaxy are being affected by these energies. As your Earth stirs and awakens (just as you are), she is, once again, sending out frequencies of love, hope, inspiration and joy. Ah, she is a brave one, your beautiful planet Earth. It will take much more than your nuclear bombs, the pollution of her vast oceans and destruction of her great forests to destroy her or break her will to survive.

She has somewhat, temporarily, quieted her rumblings in many areas around the world. She is eager, ready and willing to participate, to work with you in any endeavor, in every way possible—to heal her wounds, clean her atmosphere, stop the decay. Gradually, just as you are doing, she is healing herself from her golden etheric web inward, and from her heart core outward. Her heartbeat is accelerating, the mists are clearing. She, too, is remembering that she is Sacred—that she is a Queen of the Heavens, Gaia, a paradise, The Garden of E-Don (which means, obedience to Divine Wisdom).

Is it not apparent to you that the masses are stirring? You would have to be isolated on an island with no communication with the outside world whatsoever not to see that there is an accelerated shift in the mass-consciousness in progress. Programming about angels and psychic phenomena are becoming commonplace; allopathic and alternative healing modalities are working hand-in-hand more frequently. The scientific community is gradually testing the waters of expanded awareness, technologies where the scientific and paranormal or unusual modalities are being validated and integrated (much more often than is being conveyed to the general public).

Many of you are experiencing miraculous events in your lives, and we ask you to be bold enough to share these wonders with your friends. Do not fear ridicule or criticism; you will find approval more often than disapproval and interest more often than disdain. The religious community, partially out of fear of losing their following, are beginning to incorporate some of the more moderate New Age teachings, and while it matters not how or why, it is all for the benefit of humanity and will assist in speeding up the transformation process of Earth and its inhabitants.

There are some disturbing events occurring in your world economy and in your political arena. I ask you to be diligent and aware of the lessons that are being presented to you. It has been predicted that your financial establishments must be realigned and focused on the interests of all the people and not just the few. Your government must be held responsible, and you must demand honesty and integrity—that which will benefit the greatest numbers the most equitably and not just a few special interest groups. You must take an active part by first envisioning a healthy, just and bountiful economy, an ethical government and worldwide unity for all the populace. Then you must be responsible for your part of the plan by always operating from a point of impeccable honesty.

Examine your feelings of abundance and scarcity, beloved ones. If even one-quarter of the population of the world would believe, envision, invoke and then work towards prosperity and abundance for all, you would see a dramatic turn of events as those who hoard the wealth of the world and those who prey on the meek and poor began to lose their stranglehold on the world's economy. Are you fearfully holding on tightly to and hoarding your riches? Beware, dear ones, that your hoard does not melt into thin air. It is only a form of energy, you know. Energy is meant to be circulated, recycled— used, reformed, expanded and refined. That which you hold onto too tightly will dissolve before your eyes.

A part of the initiation process is to surrender all that you hold dear, all that you possess to your Divine Self, to the highest good of all. This does not mean that you will lose what you surrender, it just means you are willing to allow the Divine Plan to work through you, which is always for your highest good, even though it may not seem so at the time.

We watch as many of you have altered your beliefs and viewpoints as to what you must have in order to "be happy." It is wise that you are coming to the realization that abundance comes in many forms and is of great variety—not just "material things."

We are also sensing rumblings and rumors, once again, that are creating fear and a sense of helplessness in many of you—and rippling out into the mass-consciousness: dire predictions of cataclysmic events. Have we not told you that predictions are just that—a probable future, but that you have free will and can change or alleviate any prediction? Are cataclysm and destruction part of your reality? Remember you are not tossed around by the whims of fate. YOU ARE IN CONTROL, ALWAYS!

You take your cataclysms with you if that is part of your reality. You are SAFE, no matter where you go, if that is your reality. Many of you are where you are because you promised to help balance and anchor the energies within the Earth so that these great destructive forces can be quieted. Soothe your families' and neighbors' anxieties—maintain a sense of serenity and safety—be the example, the pillar of Light that casts out fear. Know that you will only experience that which you allow to become a part of your reality. As you change your beliefs, you change the picture of your reality, and the universe cooperates.

You are the leaders, you are the examples. You will represent the vision and carry the standard of what the future holds. We are ready to assist you, my brave warriors. Allow us to support you, bolster your courage, sharpen your insight and give you direction. Together, we will overcome any adversity. We will prevail. But then, I never had a doubt. I AM Archangel Michael.

9. USING THE UNIVERSAL LAWS OF MANIFESTATION

*B*eloved masters of Light, today I would like to discuss with you the law of manifestation from a more mental and scientific point of view. For the moment, we will set aside manifestation and cocreation in harmony with Spirit as a part of your Divine Right and your spiritual heritage.

Many light workers are wondering why they cannot tap into the Divine Stream of Wealth and Abundance so they can accomplish their mission and fulfill their dreams. Many are still struggling to survive and meet their everyday obligations while those who operate from a standpoint of greed and power, very obviously in the third dimension, grow richer.

There are universal laws in force, neutral laws, that all must abide by—saints and sinners alike. There were great streams of energy sent forth, aeons ago beyond remembering, by the Elohim, archangels and cocreators of your universe, at the direction of the Prime Creator. Any and all beings who carry within their soul a Divine Spark of the Creator have the ability to access and create with that electromagnetic or cosmic energy. But you must know the rules and how to tap into that source to make it work for you.

First, you must have the right mindset: you do not have to be spiritual, or good, or have lofty ideals; you can operate from a totally selfish point of view, even a desire to gain power or control of others—the laws of manifestation will still work. If you would study or take a closer look at those who have amassed great wealth and power, you will see they have a vision, a belief in themselves and their ability to accomplish anything they desire. They begin by gaining the skills and knowledge necessary to make them experts in their field of endeavor. They spend as much energy and time as it takes to make their dreams a reality. They do not listen to any negative input from others, nor do they doubt, even for a moment, their ability to accomplish what they desire and reach their goals. They draw toward them those who have like interests and similar aspirations. They have their vision firmly planted in their mind and, day-by-day, moment-by-moment, they do whatever is necessary to bring their vision to fruition.

So what is the secret? Why do they succeed when many spiritual Light workers have such difficulty creating enough abundance to live simply and gracefully so they can concentrate on fulfilling their spiritual mission and assisting others?

You are an electromagnetic force field, my beloved friends. You send out a frequency or vibrations, and those vibrations go forth and connect with like energy waves drawing to you more of the same. And so, if you have been saying affirmations and mantras day and night asking for wealth, if you talk continuously about what you want to accomplish when you have the funds, and yearn with all your heart and soul for abundance and it still is not forthcoming, why? Because you still have those old tapes lurking around in your subconscious mind that say, "To be spiritual, I must deny everything in the material world. I must sacrifice my happiness and well-being in order to serve others (the old martyr complex). If I concentrate on my spiritual growth, God will provide" ... on and on.

One moment you are excited and feel you can conquer the world and manifest anything you desire and the next, you begin to doubt yourself again. You say your affirmations for abundance and then allow your busy ego-mind to worry and fret day and night about paying your bills, or getting a new car or a higher paying job. You begrudge paying taxes, insurance, the dentist, etc., instead of giving thanks and blessing the money that flows through your hands as you meet your obligations or exchange your earnings for the services of others.

Very few of you have the mindset to handle great wealth, even if it did miraculously come to you. What would you do if, suddenly, you were given several million dollars? Would you hoard it? Would you be anxious about losing it or someone cheating you out of it? Or would you spend it joyfully, creating your dreams and assisting others to create theirs, knowing that your abundance will keep flowing and there will always be enough to meet your needs and desires?

Now we are not talking about abundance making you happy or giving you a sense of fulfillment or about deserving it. Remember, we are talking about the impartial flow of universal substance, and I am sure you have noticed that many of those who are the wealthiest are some of the most miserable, bored and unhappy individuals. But you must give them credit, they do know how to tap into the universal source with their thoughts, desires and determination. They never waver from their goals. They never let anything or anyone stop them or deter them from completing their missions. They envision, they desire, they believe, they act ... therefore they manifest.

You must begin to focus on the abundance you already have in your life—give thanks for it, be joyful about what you have and the good things in your life. Shift your consciousness away from what is wrong with yourself, with those around you and the world, and begin to see what is right, beautiful and wondrous. You must act as if you are entitled to all the beauty and abundance of the universe and that it is pouring forth in unlimited measure until it begins to happen. We are not saying you are to go out and spend funds that you do not have, but you can begin to see and enjoy the gifts that are available to you ... many which require no exchange of funds or energy.

Your thoughts are more powerful than you know; we keep emphasizing this, but you still allow your minds to ramble and to play, over and over, the thoughts of doubt, negativity, fear, guilt etc., which make your affirmations ineffectual or cancel them out. One moment you believe you can accomplish anything you desire and the next you are wallowing in self-doubt and pity. No matter how conscious you become spiritually, if you do not tap into that stream of consciousness with your mental body and mind that allows you to draw to you the energies of manifestation, you will never become a cocreator of abundance on the earth plane.

First, you must be very clear about what it is you want to manifest ... feel the intensity within your soul-self, not your ego-self. Secondly, you must be sure that your desires are in harmony with your Higher Self; you must surrender to the highest good for yourself and others, realizing that you cannot always see the larger picture, and also, you do not want to limit your Divine Presence as to how your dreams will be manifested. Then you are to listen to that inner voice of intuition—listen for guidance and expect miracles, and then take action as the path is revealed to you. When doubt arises, or your ego begins to play the old feelings of unworthiness or guilt, acknowledge and transmute the feelings and turn your thoughts toward your goal.

Give thanks for the little miracles that take place, making

way for greater and greater gifts to come your way. As you focus more on the positive aspects of your life, you are reinforcing these energies and drawing more of the same to you. You are creating a force field of love, abundance and harmony which no one can disrupt or destroy—only you can do that. And as you seek more awareness and spiritual harmony, you will find great joy and pleasure from your abundance, for you will be in the flow of Creation and in balance with all aspects of Universal Law. That is the secret, dear ones.

Now, let me explain another area of confusion and misinterpretation. It has been said by some that the Earth has moved into the fourth dimension and others say it is just now moving into the fourth dimension. Allow me to explain it this way: everything that manifests in the physical begins to manifest first in the etheric. Just as you are building your etheric Light body, which will eventually create your physical Light body, the same thing is happening with your planet Earth. The Earth's etheric body has moved into the fourth dimension, but the physical planet is still steeped and mired in the third-dimensional experience. However, as the three lower planes of the fourth dimension are cleared, this allows us greater access to and interaction with the Earth and humanity and it allows those of you who have lifted your frequencies into the higher fourth dimensions to tap into that more rarified energy. It is as if you are living in a column of Light—higher frequencies that follow you wherever you go—creating a safe haven, or an island of protection and harmony, while those around you may still resonate within the lower densities, caught up in the illusion of chaos, pain and suffering.

As the Earth accesses more and more of the higher frequencies (through the efforts of all of you, the wonderful, dedicated Light workers) and this energy becomes anchored on the physical plane in greater and greater amounts, it will become increasingly more difficult to remain in the third-dimensional illusion—mentally, emotionally and physically. And so we are asking you, as Light Warriors, to strengthen your spiritual armor and resolve, to firmly envision your path and the goal you are seeking, and to allow no one or no thing to divert you from your mission.

We know that it is difficult to overcome thoughts, habits and traits that you have accumulated over thousands of years, but it is a time of new beginnings, a time to release your old limited viewpoints, doubts and weaknesses. You are MASTERS, you are ascending into a new state of awareness, a new consciousness; you are evolving and returning to your perfected state of joy, balance and harmony, where you will once again glow with the beauty of Spirit as it shines forth for all to see.

Dare to dream, dare to reach for the stars, dare to claim all that the Creator has promised you ... it is yours for the taking, my beloved ones. But remember, you must experience what you create. So together let us, once again, create an Earth paradise where love, abundance, beauty and harmony abound. I AM Archangel Michael and I bring you these truths.

10. A State of Grace Awaits

*B*eloved masters, do you feel a stirring from deep within, an unexplained excitement? Think back to the time of your childhood and how you felt on the night before one of your major holidays, especially those in which there were gifts exchanged, or on the night before your birthday celebration, or some other very special day. Your anticipation was so great that you could hardly sleep or even be still—your imagination ran wild and you had such high hopes, great dreams of what the surprises in store for you would be. Did they meet your expectations? Were you pleased or disappointed after you opened the brightly colored packages and saw what was inside? Was there not a letdown when it was all over, regardless of how high the thrill and excitement of the moment was?

Happiness is a very fleeting thing; is it not? It seems to always be just beyond your grasp. That is because happiness is an emotion of the ego-desire body and it must always look outside of itself for something to bring that sense of satisfaction—someone, something or some event. It perpetuates the feeling of separateness, the illusion that the material world and all its glamour is what brings lasting fulfillment, happiness and joy.

Joy is the emotion of the soul-self. You experience longer and longer periods of joy and peace when you begin to resonate with your soul and the harmony of Spirit. This happens when you begin to attune to the impulses of your Higher Self and derive a sense of en-JOY-ment from the most mundane chores—whether in a crowd or in seclusion, whether everything is going perfectly or it is a time of testing your patience. You will stay in that heart-centered sense of peace regardless of exterior circumstances. True, you may have your periods of doubt or feeling somewhat out of sync with the flow, or you may have peak experiences when you reach a new "high," but you return quickly to that harmonious center where your soul-self is firmly in control. Many of you are tapping into the energy of joy more frequently until this is becoming your natural emotional state, but now that the Light infusions are increasing dramatically as you move to the next rung of the spiral, you are also beginning to tap into a higher resonance, the harmonics of "Bliss." Bliss is the natural state of Spirit and once you firmly connect to this God-created energy, all exterior events will fall into illusion and no longer have any impact on you.

That is the excitement that is building within you, and that is stirring humanity and the Earth from the very depths of the collective-soul memory. You are beginning to get down to the core of your physical existence, dear ones. As you move into the first five years of the new century, a most monumental and critical time, please take time for some introspection. Review the trials and tests of your life and see if you are able to perceive a pattern, almost a tapestry—there is a theme there if you look deeply enough, and you will find tied to these supposed hardships or lessons the secret of your masterhood, your life's purpose, your release from the wheel of Karma. The gift of a "state of grace" is awaiting you, but you must remove the wrappings and ties that conceal the gift.

Know that the old ways will no longer work, that you cannot send out negative or unloving thoughts into the ethers and have them come back years later, or even in another lifetime—often giving the impression that they do not have power or repercussions. Oh no, my dear friends, the circle of thought energy is almost instantaneous—within hours, days, weeks or, at most, a few months. Whether it is claiming your rightful heritage of abundance, love and joy, or projecting feelings of unworthiness, hate or judgment, your thought forms speed out from you and gather like energy and swiftly, like a dynamic boomerang, magnify and return to you.

No longer will you be able to deny the core essence of your true self—both your Christ-self and that part of your core that down through the ages has impacted into a knot of negative memory and experience. Both are clamoring to be acknowledged and brought into your consciousness, into the light of awareness. In order to claim your divinity, you must first freely love the painful, rejected and denied parts of yourself that are creating all the discomfort and chaos, both within your body and in your external reality. This impacted energy has memory and creates multiple sensations of discomfort and confusion.

Why not give yourself the gift of taking an internal vacation, an inner journey? **See yourself firmly anchored to the core of your Mother Earth and surround yourself in the magnificent pillar of Light sent forth from your Divine I AM Presence. Start at your root chakra or energy center and, as if you are a beautiful crystal cell of Light, allow yourself to completely submerge in the memory of that center. What are your feelings about survival, self-preservation, about scarcity; do you feel worthy of the abundance your Mother Earth has to offer? Allow the feelings to flow: sadness, frustration, fear—acknowledge them and if you are ready, state, *"I release you into pure Christ-Light Substance, you no longer serve me."* See the beautiful cell of Light that holds your consciousness divide and enfold** these energies as they are transformed through your love into shimmering perfection. Or, since they have memory and choice just as you do, if they choose not to embrace the Light, see them float free of all your bodily forms: physical, etheric, emotional and mental and out into the ethers to follow their own path. They will choose the Light another time, along with the rest of those who are not yet ready to move forward. Bless them in their choice and know that it is perfect.

Move to the second chakra and allow all the energies of the ego-desire body to come forth: sexual love energy, passion, emotions, and your beliefs about giving and receiving. These energies always come from a sense of lack outside yourself, and they are most often imbalanced—focused on physical attraction or gratification, without thought of mental, emotional or spiritual compatibility. They are the projection of emotion outwardly, toward someone else in hopes they can accomplish what you do not think you are capable of: being loved and feeling worthy of love. All the other games of desire—the ability to give and receive, and relationships in every form, stem from this same deep-seated need to love and be loved.

Why not begin a love affair with yourself? Make a contract with your soul's desire and affirm that you will begin to work with your intuitive nature instead of your instinctual nature. Begin the search for that which brings you into harmony with your true self, your Divine Self. Then you will reach out for relationships and interactions with those who also project a sense of wholeness and there will be a compatibility in all facets of expression: physical, mental, emotional and spiritual. This is a soul-infused relationship, not an ego-based relationship that is doomed to failure. In each instance, follow the same visualization of merging with the energies and sensations of this vortex. See this beautiful sphere of Light infusing love into all the areas of darkness or negativity and repeat the same statement each time, *"I release you into pure Christ-Light Substance; you no longer serve me."*

Move upward to the solar plexus, releasing all the impacted energy in that area that has led you to give away your power, made you fearful of rejection, or instilled feelings of inadequacy. All of the negative emotions of inferiority created by the ego are buried here. Let them go, precious ones. Claim your power once more, claim your creativity, your uniqueness and your divinity. The solar plexus is one of the great energy centers of the future. From here you will send forth the great streams of Light that you access in greater and greater amounts and then, along with other Light Warriors, you will send them forth and infuse the Earth with this magnificent gift of en-LIGHT-enment. Bless, heal and release the energies buried in the solar plexus so that you can, once again, use this center in the way it was meant to be used.

Move up to the heart chakra and sense the shield you have placed in your etheric body to protect you from the pain and suffering you have experienced down through the ages, thereby shutting off the flow of Love/Light both to you and through you. This is the area that builds and maintains your life force, that allows you to access and project the love of the Creator. Dissolve this barrier, please, my beloveds; it is no longer needed. Allow the wondrous Threefold Flame to blaze forth as your spiritual armor and insignia, identifying you as a Light Warrior. Allow this gift from the Creator to be your shield and you will begin to resonate with the love, compassion, wisdom, power and will of the Creator, and never again will you have to suffer the pain and anguish of being cut off from the Essence of Spirit. As you release the restrictions from the heart area, it will also trigger the thymus gland which will once again begin to send out its life-giving hormones throughout your body so that you can rejuvenate or maintain your youth-fulness and vitality—aging, atrophy, debilitation and death are all a result of being cut off from the life force of your Divine Self.

Move your crystal ball of Light to your throat area and feel the restrictions and the congestion that has taken place there. Sense all the untruths that are clogging your vocal chords, or all the times you have not been able to speak your truth that are stuck in your throat, creating a tight-ness, irritation, coughing or problems with the thyroid gland. This is another important power center, dear ones, and it is time for you to begin to exert that power: speak your truth, your spiritual integrity, with discernment and discretion—with nonjudgment and compassion. As you exercise this Divine Right, the thoughts will begin to flow from the deep recesses of your brain and you will begin to use your intuitive nature and wisdom once more. You will say exactly the right thing at the perfect time and you will know when to be silent—both are equally important. So many of you have never spoken about the things that are buried deep within your consciousnesses that have the greatest importance and meaning for you because you are afraid of rejection. It is time to speak and claim your truth and it is possible, if you will clear the pathway of your throat chakra of all the old impacted energies. Let them go—they have served you well as you traveled through the lessons of material density and separation. Release them and once again move into harmony with Spirit.

Move now to the most important area of the third eye (brow) and remove the film from your clear seeing (clairvoyance). See your pituitary gland begin to pulsate and open, sending out vitalizing energy to the lower brain, reconnecting the right and left hemispheres and activating those areas that have atrophied from misuse. This will increase your intuitive nature and bring wisdom and peace of mind as you begin to access and interact with your Higher Self and eventually your Divine I AM Presence. Release the concept of duality and begin to integrate your masculine and feminine energies—the power, will and dynamics of the Father with the love, compassion, creative and nurturing aspects of the Mother. Release what no longer serves you into the Light and move upward, once more.

Focus on your crown chakra, that gateway to the higher dimensions, your Divine Self and the Infinite. See this center open wide and the pineal gland begin to pulsate and revitalize the upper brain as it activates your clear hearing (clairaudience). Know that you are capable of building this bridge, this pathway of Light, to assist you in accessing the inspiration, Divine Wisdom and Spiritual Will of the Creator through your I AM Presence. Release the restrictive energies, release the fear-based emotions and the illusions that have kept you captive for so many ages.

As you clear and balance these seven lower chakras, there awaits you the gift of five additional energy centers that lead you onward and upward to your higher soul consciousness and the higher realms ... this is the path of ascension, dear ones. Reach out for the gift that is being offered you—the greatest gift of all—the gift of wholeness and divinity.

Before you finish this most profound exercise, please let us take you one step further. Sense your inner Essence as it moves up through the higher dimensions and connects with the galactic core. Firmly anchor that crystal gem of your Essence in this fiery core as it begins to draw on that rarified Love/Light of Creation. You are now anchored through your Divine Presence to the pulsations of the galaxy and you are also anchored firmly to the core of your planet Earth. Can you not feel the power of this reconnection? This is the column of power in which you descended into the physical those many aeons ago, and now as you reanchor this column of Light, it will be your means of ascending, once more, into the higher realms of illumination. It does not mean you have to bring to a close your earthly sojourn, it just means you will have access to your Divine Birthright, a love-connection with the Creator.

Begin to share with each other the gifts that really matter, dear ones: love, understanding, support, nonjudgment, encouragement and most of all, your joy and bliss. The expensively wrapped packages are a poor substitute for the real thing—a loving soul and a compassionate Spirit. You are loved and cherished most profoundly. I AM Archangel Michael.

11. A VISION QUEST:
A GLIMPSE OF PARADISE—YOUR HOME

*B*eloved masters, as we come together this day, allow me to take you on a vision quest. Many of you are beginning to remember and accept the fact that the planet Earth is not your home; you are only visitors here—on assignment, you might say. It is not uncommon to hear, "I have never felt I belonged. I never seemed to fit in with others, not even my family." And you have always had yearnings and dreams—nebulous, illusive, just beyond the edges of your mind—out of reach. Even as a child you may have felt a discontent as if there was something you should remember, or that you had to hurry and grow to adulthood, for there was something important you were supposed to do—but what? You had not a clue. Eventually it became a Divine Discontent that pushed you, sometimes not too gently, toward the path of enlightenment and so the journey back home began.

Imagine, dear ones, how it would feel to be in perfect communion with the Creator, feeling such overwhelming all-encompassing love and joy as you are sent forth as a part of the Divine Rays of expression to create and experience at the direction of your Father/Mother God. Envision yourself as a great energy vortex, pulsating with power, sending out great Rays of luminous color, radiating waves of energy and creating symphonies of sound that blend harmoniously with other wondrous beings such as yourself, as you expand out into the universe to do the Creator's will.

Sense how you would feel as the energies you project swirl and solidify, as structure and form become discernible, beautiful and unique beyond measure—your creations—through the power of your thoughts, love/emotions and imagination.

Imagine now what it would be like to experience these magnificent creations—variety beyond measure, fluid, free flowing, perfect and harmonious ... great shining halls, temples, gardens and dancing waters, all shimmering in sunlight so bright and pure that it casts such a myriad of jeweled colors that you would never be able to name them all, much less describe them.

Elegant, beautiful people, male and female, all in their prime—glowing, healthy, vibrant, radiating peace and love, and such joy that you have to smile, and it lifts your spirit just to gaze on their faces as they go happily about their myriad of tasks. There are precious, boisterous, happy young children of every age—playing, studying, creating under the guardianship of loving, patient adults. But you notice that there are no aged, decrepit or infirm beings to be seen anywhere.

You walk through the temples and great halls gazing in wonder at the exquisite, priceless art work and lavish furnishings. As you move past the many open doors you can hear every subject imaginable being discussed by groups of all ages—not just one person teaching, but all interacting, sharing and contributing. Sweet melodies float through the air and you watch as group after group lift their voices in harmony, or play instruments that you cannot even recognize, much less identify, all blending together and creating wave upon wave of resonating vibrations that touch you at your very core.

You move out into the gardens and feast your senses on the beauty and aroma of the flowers and intricate landscape; the crystal waters soothe and cool the air, and you feel such peace and unity with all creation that it seems your heart will burst with joy. You move further along the path until you stand looking out over a great vista, shimmering and glowing in the sunlight, and you know that this is the place where you wish to spend eternity. Here is where you belong and where you will find fulfillment—in this wondrous place you have helped to create.

But after a very long time, you and a vast number of other Beings are called together in the grand hall, a place reserved for only the most solemn, holy gatherings. You are overwhelmed with emotion, for present there are the archangels and many other magnificent ones you recognize. Great, powerful Beings you have traveled and worked with, or had been created by in the dim past. Yes, I am there, as is my lovely Lady Faith, as well as many very important representatives from other far-distant civilizations and universes.

One of great honor and responsibility, a shining, glorious Being, begins to speak to all those assembled. You are told that, if you agree, you have been chosen, along with many others, to be a part of a Divine Experiment on a planet called Earth. I, Archangel Michael, was to be given the assignment as the angelic guardian overseer and director of this experiment, to guide and protect you. You would be called "My Legions of Light."

Now we have told you the details as to what that experiment was to be and how it went awry, but that is not a part of this vision we are giving you, for this is a vision of your perfect past and what, deep within, you are yearning to create again.

You all eagerly agreed, excited and honored to be chosen for such an important mission. You were then given your individual assignments, encoded with your own particular mission, your Divine Blueprint, and then were sent joyously on your way. Planted deep within your soul's memory was the vision of your home, your perfect creations, the shining accomplishments you had achieved in the name of the Creator. You did not doubt for a moment that this assignment would be a great success, as were those in the past.

In the beginning this was true, and the planet Earth was built in the likeness of those perfect paradises from whence you all came. We communed with you, instructed you, encouraged and assisted you in your awesome tasks for years beyond measure. You know what it feels like, deep within your Essence, to draw pure energy from Spirit, from the magnificent Beings who carry the aspects and attributes of the many great Rays. You, as we, were in perfect harmony with the will of the Creator—until all went amiss and fell into a density where we could no longer connect with you, or you could no longer access the energy of your Divine Presence.

The veil of forgetfulness began to form over your memory, and your soul became disconnected from your body, hanging only by a slim silver thread. You were Divine Emissaries sent on a most important mission and you had not failed—you must know that it was not your fault—YOU DID NOT FAIL. There were experiments within experiments—agendas from many civilizations that were not compatible with the original plan. And an experiment is just that—it is not known exactly what the outcome will be—even at the Creator level, for there was the gift of free will involved.

Eventually, a new plan was initiated, a plan to salvage humanity and the Earth, if possible. It was decided to allow those of you who were sent on the original mission to continue with some assistance from the higher dimensions. A decision was made to see if you who loved the Creator so greatly for so many ages past, you who had within you those memories of perfection before you came to Earth, could move into the density and darkness with the rest of humanity and through your love, desire and own efforts emerge into even higher awareness and love, thereby expressing and radiating greater Light than before, and greater wisdom than before because of your many experiences and triumphant victory over the realm of materiality.

It was known that there would be a time when the experiment would have to come to a conclusion, regardless of the outcome—victory or defeat. We are here to tell you, precious warriors, that you can claim victory—it is within sight.

It is now time for you to bring those memories out of the dark recesses of your soul, mind and heart. It is time for you to accept your Divine Heritage, and once again go forward with the task of creating Heaven on Earth. It is time to reestablish The Garden of Eden—not just a particular spot on Earth, but the whole Earth in its entirety, as the paradise it once was—the paradise you transported and rebuilt from your memories of home.

We give you this vision, dear ones, so that you can reclaim it as your own, so that you will know that it is possible. For you have created it before—you know how—you have just forgotten.

Build your vision, my beloved warriors. Start within your own heart center and reclaim that power and magnificence that is your Divine Heritage. Then, begin to radiate that power and perfection into your physical vehicle and outward into your world: your relationships, your work place, communities, country and world. Allow all that no longer serves you to continue on its path of limitation or to join you in the realm of all possibilities. The path toward the Light and the path spiraling further into darkness is coming to a distinct point of separation. You are being forced to face, once and for all, the shadows of yourself—all the imbalances and restrictions that are anchoring you or holding you back from fully empowered self-realization. If you are unwilling to go inward and make the necessary corrections or balance the discordant energies, they will be mirrored back to you in a most dramatic, forceful way through your interactions with others.

Let go, my faithful warriors, let go of all that no longer supports or lifts you toward your chosen destiny. You know ... you all know, if you will just face your own inner truth, those things that are keeping you mired in victimhood instead of masterhood—limitation instead of abundance and health—debilitation, atrophy, aging and death, instead of youthfulness and vitality. Choose the bliss of paradise, choose the joy of once again being cocreators with the great Beings of Light and the angelic realms. Choose the path that will eventually lead you home. And know this, for **we make you a promise, you will never again have to experience the limitations and anguish such as you have experienced on Earth.**

You have earned the Wings of a Master—of "Experiment Earth." Come, help us awaken as many dear souls as possible in the time remaining so that they can join us in our journey ... our return to utopia. But remember, it is always their choice, for you can only choose for yourself. You can show the way and project the Love/Light of the Creator, and by your example and gentle guidance you can ease the transition stages for them, but each must make their own decision to step onto the path. The time is nigh, beloved ones, and your anticipation is no greater than ours. I AM Archangel Michael.

12. WHAT IS YOUR PERCEPTION OF LOVE? WHAT IS YOUR TRUTH?

*B*eloved masters, it is imperative at this time, more than ever before, that you diligently begin to seek your own truth, step-by-step, day-by-day, and that you strive to live in the integrity of that truth. Not your old, outdated programming or what you have read or heard from someone else, but what resonates within you as the truth from your own Divine Essence. You see, there are many truths and levels, or layers, of new truth coming forth now that the quarantine has been removed from your Earth. But each of you must consider your level of awareness and the vibrational frequencies to which you are attuned.

Begin to apply the basic wisdom of love and compassion for yourself and others before you attempt to master or understand the more complex rules and guidelines for those who are further along the path of awareness and integration. You are unique, your lessons and challenges have been and will be fashioned specifically for you in order to assist you in balancing and harmonizing all discordant energies within your physical/mental/emotional bodies. You are not being cast about at the whim of fate, and you are not being singled out to be punished or persecuted. Each person or entity must follow their own particular destiny, their path to illumination and reintegration with their Divine Self. The lessons you are learning and perfecting will be your contribution to the whole. Within these seemingly painful experiences are the jewels of wisdom you will need to fulfill your particular facet of the grand design. So do not judge yourself or your progress by that of any other. Do not look at others in awe and with envy at the talents and gifts they have mastered and manifested, for within you are treasures just as great awaiting discovery—to be brought forth and shared.

This is why we ask you to begin the process of changing your perception of what love is and is not. The energies of love from the vantage point of a Light worker or master are totally different than those still caught in the illusion of the third-dimensional reality. Love is not just a sensation of the emotions, the intense desire to own or possess another in order to feel a sense of wholeness or in some cases, the thrill of conquest and obtaining what seems to be "a great prize" at the time, which, most often, becomes a great burden instead.

Love is not self-sacrifice and victimhood, where you give away so much of yourself that you no longer have an identity of your own. It has been said, you are to love others as you love yourself. We tell you, our beautiful ones, many of you have such low self esteem and disdain of self, if you use this premise, you have little love to project toward others. You must first build the essence of love within you, in your soul center, and you begin by accepting that you are a Divine Spark of God and worthy of love, respect and all the joy, beauty and bounty of Creation. We have said before, it is time you begin a love affair with yourself, where you begin to focus on what is right about you instead of what is wrong. Begin to listen to the whispering intuitive voice of your soul-self (which will grow louder as you acknowledge its wisdom) as it gives you encouragement, insight and awareness of your vast potential.

Love is not enabling those around you to dishonor you and abuse you as they reinforce your own projections of unworthiness. How can you expect anyone else to treat you with respect and love if you are not willing to set boundaries and send clear messages of love, acceptance and worthiness for yourself and for others, as well? The limiting, crippling thought forms of self-sacrifice, martyrdom, suffering, and the denial of the beauty and perfection of your physical vehicle must end. Allow all these destructive thought patterns to be dissolved from your consciousness along with all other third-dimensional illusionary concepts.

Many of you, at the urging of your ego-desire body, have become enamored with the sensations of power and acquisition. Indeed, you came as cocreators to build, perfect and enjoy the material realm on the beautiful planet Earth. But somewhere along the way, you became so caught up in your accomplishments—possessing, owning and hoarding—that this became your measure of love: if you were powerful and influential enough, you would be worthy of love, or if you had the greatest storehouse of riches and possessions, you would be admired and respected.

Focusing all of your energies on these external manifestations creates only momentary satisfaction, as well as constant frustration and dissatisfaction. What happens if your riches and power are taken from you? What happens if you lose your possessions? What do you identify with then? It is as if you have lost all that represents who and what you are. This is why so many lose all desire for life, some even going to the extreme of taking their own life because, from their perception, all that they "loved and treasured" has been taken away, along with their sense of being worthy of love and respect.

Love as an external focus, exterior to yourself, will always bring a sense of vulnerability, always needing constant validation by someone or something. Love as an internal focus projected outward is a constant flow of self-assurance, of self-acceptance, always striving to incorporate and project more of this blissful feeling of unity and harmony with all creation.

Love is the Essence of the God Mind. Love is the Christ-energy pouring forth from the heart center of God/Goddess Prime Creator in great streams of cosmic substance in its never ending desire to experience more of Itself. It is a blessed gift to be used by all Creation—at all levels, from the highest, most powerful, to the lowest, most diminished. It is your birthright to bring forth your own unique self-expression, through loving cocreation in harmony with the Divine Blueprint, which is always in perfect accordance with the grand design of the Creator. How loving are your creations, dear ones? What kind of temple have you created for your soul? Do you identify only with your body and then, through constant judgment and focus on your imperfections and comparison with others, fight an ongoing battle, ultimately assuring failure and validation of your distorted point of view (a love/hate relationship with yourself that keeps you frustrated and mired in self-inflicted misery)?

What kind of world have you built with your constant thought forms of every moment? What kind of example have you been for your children and loved ones? Do you project a sense of pride-in-self, an awareness of how precious the gift of life is? Do you set an example by striving to perfect the myriad of facets within yourself?

There is a path open for each of you to follow, no matter at what station or circumstances you may find yourselves, an opportunity waiting to enable you to assume your power, tap into your creativity, bring to the fore those many latent abilities you have stored deep within your memory banks.

And now, as never before, we are close by, observing, waiting to assist, encourage, create the miracles, smooth the way, and assist you in moving forward.

It is time for all of you, as brave Warriors of Light, to break and cross the boundaries of discrimination, disempowerment and limitation. We dare you, as women of Spirit, to become beacons and examples as "masterful women among men." We implore you, as men of valor and integrity, to become "compassionate men among women." By this we mean, erase and eliminate the lines and barriers between you, offering and accepting the gifts and attributes of each other as you integrate these sorely needed energies into your mental and emotional bodies. Your truth lies in your level of awareness, your assimilation of the cosmic gift of Christ-consciousness. You must integrate the knowledge you acquire, and then you must demonstrate that you have the ability to live by that new level of wisdom. You are judged by your own Higher Self and your Divine Presence as to your readiness to proceed along the spiral of initiation. We have told you that the path of ascension is a very solitary, secular process. Your initiations are designed specifically for you and you alone, for you are like no other. And yet, precious ones, each gain you make that lifts you another fraction, or a step along the narrow path of mastership, also lifts humanity as a whole. You are the "One" in Essence, but "At One" with All.

It is time for each of you to step to the fore, take a stand, and be heard. Begin where you are, at your highest level of understanding, seeing through eyes filtered by love, feeling with a heart filled with compassion and functioning with a mind that is not clouded by guilt, fear or judgment. That is the way you will find your truth, beloved ones. That is the way that your world and reality will be filled to overflowing with love, joy and abundance. That is the way of the master, the way of truth, the way back home.

We honor you for your bravery, we know the way has been long and arduous, but we tell you this, sweet friends, your time of pain and suffering is coming to a close. The time of miracles is at hand. Each day, we eliminate more of the restrictive energies between us, dissolve more of the negativity that swirls in the ethers. We give you our assurance that soon you will have your validation as to what the coming Age of greatness will be like. And you will know, without any doubt, the integral part you have played. We have walked and communed one with another, and that is also a gift that awaits you in the future. With love and profound gratitude, I AM Archangel Michael.

13. LET GO OF THE OLD—MAKE WAY FOR THE NEW

*B*eloved masters of Light, we of the angelic forces, the spiritual hierarchy and all those from other worlds and dimensions who are here to observe and assist you in this great time of transition, wish to honor you and salute you for the miracles you have wrought this past year of earth time (1995). Indeed, although it is not as apparent to you, you have succeeded beyond our greatest expectations. Through your united efforts, the once golden etheric web of the Earth is, once again, beginning to glimmer with Light and resonate to the higher frequencies of the fourth dimension.

The masses are stirring—many more than we ever thought possible are beginning to awaken, are beginning to feel an inner discontent and are slowly becoming aware of their soul's nudgings. And this is largely due to your efforts, precious ones. You, who have steadfastly anchored the infusions of Christed-energy, who have become shining beacons—living examples and teachers of the new reality slowly permeating the Earth and all its dimensions. Although there is still much to be done and our ultimate goal of seeing the Earth return to its pristine beauty and resonance of the fifth dimension is still some years away, we are encouraged and much more optimistic than ever before that this vision will be fulfilled.

So, I come to congratulate you and give you encouragement as to what the future holds for you, the disciples and servants of the Creator, who have steadfastly trod the path of Light and have taken upon your shoulders the burden of assisting the Earth and humanity in its painful rebirthing process. I hereby proclaim, you have been granted a dispensation and now have imprinted on your soul a golden jewel of Light from the Source, which identifies you as an ascension candidate and an earthly representative of the hierarchy. Yes, many of you are ready to take your place in the organizational lineup of future world leaders. Not in the context as you now know the world leaders to be, but as emissaries with solar, galactic, and cosmic credentials—directors of peace, teachers of wisdom, conveyers of hope, facilitators, planners and healers, and, slowly but surely, as government and corporate leaders, scientists and crusaders for freedom and justice, and builders and perfecters of the new Garden of E-Don: Earth paradise.

To assist you in utilizing and making the most of your newly acquired potential in this the beginning of your new year, we will endeavor to bring you to a new, higher awareness of your magnificence. We ask you to let go—LET GO of that which no longer serves you—allow yourself to merge with that wonderful being you call your Higher Self. It is time, beloved ones. Most all of you who resonate to my messages have succeeded wonderfully in accomplishing the soul merge, or reintegrating your soul-self within your physical vehicle. You have brought the ego-desire body under the direction and control of your soul and its wisdom. And because of this, many of you are now in harmony, and yes, even in communication (mostly via intuition—or through telepathic interaction) with your Higher Self. And, there are also a great number who are now accessing directly the wondrous potential of their Divine I AM Presence.

You have experienced the dark night of the soul and emerged triumphant, you have experienced your own unique crucifixion, surrendering all to the will of the Creator. Now you are ready or in the midst of the resurrection process, the donning of your garments of Light.

What do we mean by letting go? Becoming a master means letting go of all expectations as to what being a master entails—what spirituality means and feels like. Let go of judgments of yourself and others. Stop trying so hard to become—just BE. You do not have to be perfect, nor do you have to know everything. Stop being so serious. Remember, did we not tell you that being a master means being joyful, blissful—at peace?

Are you still struggling in your relationships? Why? Are you afraid to state your truth and stand firm in your decisions to become the master of your destiny? Are you learning only to give of yourself what you feel comfortable in giving, and then to take or ask no more than you are willing to give? Are you still afraid of being alone, losing your job, your security? Do you still doubt that you can handle success, power or responsibility? Many of you will be led to the edge of the abyss during these coming years. It will seem as though there is only darkness, a great void or sure destruction before you, but actually it will be your Spirit Self nudging you forward—tempting you to try your wings and testing you to see if you are ready to soar. Being a master is not for the timid or weak of heart, dear ones.

Dare to be bold, firm and assertive when necessary, and yet, gentle, soft-spoken, compassionate and considerate. Yes, you will become a paradox to those around you who do not resonate at the finer frequencies you will project, but do not worry, they will take note. No greater truth can you live by and remember than, "By their works they shall be known." Do not just speak words of love, justice, harmony, peace and joy—become a living example of all that these Divine attributes entail.

For many of you, it may seem as if you have been waiting a long time for your mission to be revealed. To others who have worked so diligently without any clearly defined results or revelations as to what is planned or ahead, we tell you this, it has all been a part of the process—the initiation process, the testing process, the preparation phase, the weeding out and gleaning of those who are not determined or dedicated enough, or ready to accept the responsibility that accompanies the role of a master, a spiritual leader, an advanced Warrior of Light, a member of the spiritual hierarchy in-training.

The time of choosing and making assignments is now in progress. Many of you already know your designated duties, what your mission will entail. Miraculously, others will be led or shown and to some it will come as a great surprise. You see, often, those who have the greatest potential and gifts to offer see themselves as having the least or being the most undeserving. One of the great obstacles a higher initiate has to overcome is lack of self-love and acceptance of worthiness. We are not speaking of self-aggrandizement, but of astute and humble acknowledgment of the attributes and abilities earned and incorporated in one's Being. You must claim what you are and what you are capable of in order to create the reality of masterhood once it has been earned.

For those of you who feel you do not yet fit into the framework of what has been explained above, we give you this encouragement and admonishment. Time as you know it is quickly speeding up or compressing. We know you are all aware of the intensity you are experiencing in your everyday lives, the frustration and uncertainty that is increasing, day-by-day. The reality of your existence is changing whether you agree or whether or not you acknowledge it. You can no longer coast or delay, or procrastinate in choosing your destiny.

Either you continue on the downward spiral of the third-dimensional existence (for it will, and this is not a prediction but established fact, continue to worsen and become more chaotic in those areas still resonating to these lower frequencies), or you will choose the path of Light and begin the upward climb with those who have opened and smoothed the way for you.

All this means is that you will begin to open your hearts and minds to the wondrous possibilities being presented to you in a thousand ways every day. You will begin to hope and dare to dream. You will follow the example of those ready to assist you in healing your bodies, calming your emotions and allowing your mind to break free of its old limitations and restraints. Does it hurt to allow yourself to open your mind to a new vision, to reach out and test the truth and validate for yourself what others have created and manifested for you to see? It is working, my beloved timid souls. Miracles are happening every day for those who have claimed their birthright and learned to use the universal laws of manifestation in harmony with Spirit. They are waiting and ready to assist and gently direct you. You are blessed for you do not have to struggle alone through uncharted territory. The way has been opened and there are footprints of Light for you to follow.

New technology, modalities and scientific data have been brought forth and tested, or are being tested and refined, to assist you in cleansing and healing your body, in releasing the impacted, negative energies that you have carried for so long, in breaking agreements which no longer serve you and incorporating the higher frequencies that will bring you into wholeness. Why do you hesitate? It is the greatest gift humankind has been offered since the inception of life on this planet.

We have told you that the Earth is moving forward on the spiral of evolution and it will proceed with or without you. We do not wish to frighten you or make you uncomfortable, but the first decade of the next century is a time of decision. Where will you be when the Earth bursts forth into its shining perfection and glory as a bright star? All Creation is inexorably being drawn back up the pathway of Light, out of density and separation, into unity and harmony with the majestic higher realms. Your Earth may seem only an insignificant, minuscule fragment of Creation, but make no mistake, it is a precious and integral part of the whole—just as you are. You are a treasure of the universe, a Spark of the Divine Creator, and you are loved beyond measure. I AM Archangel Michael.

14. THE ILLUSION OF FEAR

*B*eloved masters, will you pause with me for a moment and take inventory of your recent accomplishments and what may seem like defeat or failure to you? I would like for you to take a closer look and come to a better understanding as to what the initiation and ascension processes are all about. You are getting a clearer picture of the workings of cosmic law and the magnificence and complexity of your universe, as the veil of forgetfulness is lifted and you begin to tap into the wisdom of your Higher Self and higher mind, but you still have doubts and are confused when you are confronted with some of your old fears and emotions.

All humanity, without exception, is progressing by leaps and bounds—yes, even those who seem to be stuck or mired in victimhood, and karmic interaction of cause and effect, the drama of good and evil, or duality/polarity consciousness. Deep within every sentient being there is a discontent, a yearning, a feeling that changes must be made, that they cannot continue in the same old painful patterns of existence. As you are witnessing, some will choose to vacate the physical vessel, returning to spirit form to await an easier, more gentle time to return and continue the journey of physical expression. Others are becoming bold as they reach out into the unknown and find we are waiting there to assist them—and so, they begin to hope and dream as they take control of their destiny.

Just as you must acknowledge, clear and release all negative memories and energies within your physical/etheric, mental and emotional structure, so it is with your Mother Earth as well. This is the source of the "destruction process" that you all fear so much, but it need not be cataclysmic as has been predicted and you have been led to believe. True, all that is not in harmony with the higher frequency patterns must be transmuted, transformed or lifted, but it can be accomplished by becoming aware of the core beliefs which do not resonate with Christ-awareness. Yes, your Mother Earth is striving to attain her Christ-consciousness just as you are—just as everything that has ever been created is. In order to do that, she is also releasing many core memories placed in her auric field by the masses (called the mass-consciousness), and this is where many of you are having difficulties. You are not yet able to discern which are your own core issues, or those which are carried and projected by different races, cultures and religions which have their origins in many ages past.

As you begin to get a glimpse of or tap into "unity-consciousness," which creates great wonder, joy and a sense of no longer being alone, it also opens the door for you to tap into those ancient memories of fear, failure, betrayal and shame that others also carry in their auric patterns. You do not get just the positive energies, beloveds—part of your mission is to assist all humanity in becoming aware of its self-limiting beliefs, and negative, destructive thought forms and actions. That is why there seems to be so much senseless violence, why so many are lashing out in anger and pain. The world of form seems to be crushing and bruising those who cannot face their own creations and acknowledge that they have, indeed, created their own hell-filled world with fear and suffering. They blame everyone and everything but themselves, for without allowing the soul or Higher Self to assist in the healing process, it is just too painful to face, and the ego-desire body becomes even stronger and more in control of the thought process and behavioral patterns.

That is why we are "pulling out all the stops" you might say, in order to assist those of you who are the vanguard, those who are opening the way or creating the path for others to follow. The process must be clear, it must be simple and not complicated as the ancient wisdom teachings were, which were designed for the select few. Those of you who are the teachers and the Wayshowers have had or are experiencing all the emotions, fears and setbacks that will confront humanity at large. Many of you made the great sacrifice and agreed to pass or experience many tests that were not of your own making (but an accumulation of the memory/energy patterns of other parts of your vaster Being). In other words, many of you came with energies composed of many different facets or expressions which you did not directly experience as a soul, but which you agreed to have placed in your energy (auric) fields so that you would have to balance and overcome these imperfections. So, beloved ones, do not judge a beautiful, awakened soul who seems to have had much more than their share of adversity. Honor them, emulate them, for they are smoothing the way for you.

And so, we ask you to observe the patterns of fear and doubt that are emerging, that which is keeping you from moving on to the next level of en-LIGHT-enment. Each level has its own tests, trials and pitfalls and many of you are hindering your progress because you cannot let go of old deep-core energies. Many are still caught in a "struggle for power," on the one hand, creating and performing great deeds of goodness, but still trying to control or force their truths or ways of thinking on others. Many of those who still feel they must serve and sacrifice in order to grow spiritually are being taken advantage of by those who have not learned that what you take from others unjustly, ultimately, you only take from yourself. Many are still imprisoned in relationships which are hindering and hurtful, rather than supportive and allowing growth and expansion. They are afraid to step out of the status quo or take responsibility for their own spiritual growth and well-being. Ah, so many are afraid to face their nightmares and bad dreams, for they may come to realize they are of their own making and are responsible for their transformation. Stagnation and a sense of futility is the formula for death, beloved ones: death of the emotions, death of mental alertness, hopes and dreams, and eventually, death of the physical vessel.

What are your greatest fears right now, dear ones? What obstacles are keeping you from opening that next door to higher awareness and mastery? Before you can accept and wield the gift of the First Ray of Divine Will, you must face and conquer your fears and demons. We have endeavored over the past months to give you the tools and wisdom to accomplish this, but ultimately the task is yours alone. These next years are critical, and we have said this before, but it is important that you become aware of just how quickly the process of evolution, or the ascension of humanity, is progressing. If you are to stay on track and keep up with the frequency acceleration of your planet and with those who are reaching for the stars on their way back home, you must come to terms with yourself, your fears and your sense of disconnectedness with Spirit.

Allow me to give you a gift, an exercise which will help you break through the restrictive walls of your fears and doubts and help you release those patterns that no longer serve you. We wish to impress upon you how harmful the energies of fear are and how simple it is to move through them—energies which are keeping you from claiming the gifts of mastery.

Stand before a mirror, or hold a mirror in your hand and gaze into this mirror as you bring into your mind that which you most fear. Just as we have taught you to fill your body with Light, I now ask you to allow this fear to build as you create and imagine the worst scenario possible that has to do with this fear. Feel it begin to permeate your body, feel it especially in your heart and solar plexus center, as you move your consciousness throughout your body and feel the restriction, the stress, the crippling energy creep in and permeate your Being. Now look into your own eyes, see the pain, study your facial expression as it changes and ages. Feel the pressure build until you know you can tolerate no more. Now, beloved masters, lift your consciousness out of your crown chakra and draw in the Light of your Divine Self, that wondrous Being who is always waiting and available to assist you through every trial and test. Call on your I AM Presence to fill you with love and the healing frequencies of the Violet Flame and with all your senses become aware as this wondrous gift pours through and around you. Can you hold on to the fear or does it dissolve into nothingness as this magic elixir permeates your Being?

Look again in the mirror, see how soft your eyes have become, how youthful is your countenance. Feel the expansion in your heart and the release of the stress and strain within your body and muscular structure. Fear cannot exist where there is Light, where there is love. Breathe in the gift of life, breathe deeply of the Essence of Creation that is being offered you. When you are in fear, you restrict and cut off the flow of universal life substance. This may seem like a drastic exercise, but in truth it is a great gift, for many of you cannot progress until you face yourself

in the mirror and allow your fears to be reflected back to you. You will become aware that the fear does not originate "out there," but from within.

More and more of you are becoming aware of your missions and how important they are. Do not fear to boldly step out, dear ones. Not only are you healing and resolving the negative patterns of humanity, but as you move forward you will have available to you the wisdom and wealth of knowledge from all the many lives and experiences of your soul companions. This is the wonder of unity-consciousness. Have you not noticed how many teachers and messengers are bringing forth almost identical information; and how many of you are experiencing the same emotional ups and downs and receiving the same thought impulses? Many of you have gone to gatherings where you felt a deep sense of coming home, of being reconnected with long-lost family or friends. Just as many of you no longer feel in harmony with your physical family and seem to have nothing in common any longer with friends of long standing. Do not judge; become the observer—allow your Higher Self to supply you with the wisdom you need to move through or overcome any situation or obstacle.

As you move into nonjudgment and are willing to allow the highest outcome to occur in all situations, you will break free of the bonds of fear, and life will become a constant source of wonder, joy and thanksgiving. Claim the gifts that are being offered to you, precious ones, you have earned them. Move through the fog of fear into the Light of the dawning age. Walk boldly with a spring in your step, a smile on your lips and joy in your heart—those behind you are watching, my brave warriors, do not falter now. Show them, as we have shown you; take their hands and support them, even as we have done for you. Tell them that you cannot take on their tasks or burdens, but you can give them the benefit of your wisdom and experience. You will not have to make claims or state what level you have attained, you will not have to try to impress or dominate; for you know within your heart who you are and that is enough.

I and all the beloved Beings of Light from throughout the Omniverse salute you, dear brave hearts, and we are close at hand to assist you, just as you are there to assist those who are following in your footsteps. I AM Archangel Michael.

15. THE MIGHTY I AM PRESENCE OF GOD
AFFIRMATIONS

We must look to our divinity through God, The Mighty I AM Presence for all good. Through the use of our own magic I AM Presence, we draw all the love, wisdom and power in action of Christ-energy to us, blending and merging with our own Higher Self, and our own Christ-consciousness. Guard your thoughts and what you say, especially when you say "I AM," because you are invoking the power of God. When you say and feel I AM, you release the flow of neutral, primal, cosmic life force energy. Used in a positive manner, you release this power to realize love, peace, beauty, harmony, health and abundance. Use it negatively and you shut the door in the face of this mighty energy, which then creates lack, frustration, fear and misery, thereby allowing these negative influences to rule your life.

Use and say often any and all decrees that fit the circumstances of the moment until the decrees are so firmly planted in your mind, heart and soul that they will come to you automatically at the appropriate time. You must learn to feel the intensity and power of the words when you recite the affirmations—the emotions and feelings behind your thoughts are very important.

1. *I AM the power that creates perfect health, abundance, joy, peace and perfection in my life. I have the power to recognize perfection in myself, everywhere and in everyone around me.*

2. *The Mighty I AM Presence of God dwells within me, and I create only good within and for myself, my loved ones, and in my world.*

3. *I AM slim, I AM trim, I AM healthy, I AM loving, I AM wise, I AM wealthy. I AM God's perfect power in action.*

When you begin to feel a deep devotion and love, and express these emotions in positive words and actions, you create an electromagnetic ring of Light around yourself. Then you begin to generate this love to those around you, and no power can penetrate this force field except Divine Love. Dare to experience this power in action and be silent (around those who are not ready to hear). You will find yourself lifted into a transcendent radiance where all things are possible.

4. *I AM the mighty consuming flame that now and forever consumes all past and present mistakes, their cause and effect, and all undesirable creation for which my outer being is responsible, in this or any other reality. I AM the mighty cosmic energy flowing through, filling, and renewing every cell in my mind and body, now!*

5. *I AM the master of my world. I AM the victorious intelligence governing it. I send forth into my world the mighty, radiant intelligent energy of God. I command it to create only perfection and to draw to me the abundance of God made visible in my hands and for my use.*

6. *The mighty, magic circle of protection of my I AM Presence that surrounds me is invincible, and shields me from every discordant thought and element which seeks to find entrance or intrude. I AM the perfection of my world and it is self-sustained.*

7. *I AM the visible presence of the dearly beloved ascended masters whom I wish to appear to me and whose assistance I desire.*

8. *Divine presence, pour thy radiance through this mind and body, healing, perfecting, empowering and always directing my every thought and action through my own I AM Presence.*

9. *As an individualized spark of the mighty God mind, I AM everywhere present. When my consciousness takes on this expansion of unity-consciousness, I know its energy leaps into action everywhere, in the cells of my body and in those around me, as well as in the world.*

10. *The pure Love/Light of God pours forth and fills me via my I AM Presence. The mighty I AM Presence that I represent is transforming, healing and protecting me and my loved ones at all times.*

11. *I AM perfect health now manifesting in every organ and part of my body. My body of light is radiating forth into the world of form.*

12. *I turn this situation over to my I AM Presence and the outcome is perfect (when something goes wrong or someone is making things difficult for you). My perfect Presence takes control of this situation and resolves all discord and negativity for the highest outcome.*

13. *The mighty I AM Presence of God is the only presence acting in and affecting my world.*

14. *Say often: I AM the consuming power and presence in every bit of fear, doubt and questioning in my outer world. I always make the right choice and take the right action.*

Persistent, determined recognition of your I AM PRESENCE will take you through anything and help you realize absolute certain accomplishment, but you must use it often enough to cancel out the negative thought patterns you have instilled in your subconscious mind. The more you use it and the more power you put into it, the faster you will begin to manifest all the wonderful gifts of God's universe in your life.

15. **I AM in the heart of God and I bring forth ideas and accomplishments which have never before been brought forth on earth. I AM empowered by Christ-consciousness and I will let no one, or nothing, infringe on me or my will for right action.**

16. **I AM a child of God and only that which is pure, good and of love can affect me. I have the power through my I AM Presence to guide, protect and nurture those I love. I AM perfect love in action and I will use discretion and nonjudgment in dealing with those around me. May my God-self shine through.**

May the radiance of your I AM PRESENCE shine forth for all to see.

Love and blessings, Ronna

16. YOU ARE SHAPE-SHIFTING INTO A NEW REALITY

*B*eloved masters of Light, a new day is dawning on your Earth, an era that has been prophesied and foretold for many ages past. The holographic pictures that have formed your realities are shifting, and you feel vulnerable and no longer have an identity that you can relate to, or familiar parameters to guide you.

What is happening is this: you went through the process of releasing all that you thought was important in your third-dimensional reality, surrendering your relationships, your possessions, your perception of what and who you were as you moved into harmony and attunement with your Higher Self—gradually accessing more refined energy, higher frequencies, new information and greater wisdom. Then you eventually became more comfortable with your fourth-dimensional reality as you worked through all the negative emotional energies that came bubbling up from within your subconscious mind, sweeping out and clearing outmoded perceptions. The pulsating, transforming Light frequencies reverberated throughout the depths of your cellular structure and began to break loose all the impacted energies that have accumulated down through the ages—stirring them up, moving them out to be released and replaced with Divine Light Substance. As you began to resonate to a quickened vibration—more of your vaster Being, your soul-self, your Higher Self, your Christ Self began to, once again, take up residency and dominion within your physical vessel.

You had a whole new set of rules to live by, a wonderful plethora of exciting information, and new wisdom to assist you in functioning in this new reality in which you now found yourself. Joy and bliss became the norm and gradually, you began to manifest your dreams and visions and come together with those you recognized instantly as your soul family. You began to share, teach and project this new vision, this new persona you had taken on, and the world began to look much brighter.

Now suddenly, it seems you have taken a step backward. Many of you have suddenly manifested dramatic illnesses that you do not understand. Obstacles are placed in your way, hampering your progress—what you thought was your mission, your gift to humanity. Many of you can no longer find solace in meditation or reach upward (or inward) in order to tap into the loving feeling of Oneness with the Beings of Light. You feel a void, a sense of loss, or at least, a sense of unreality.

Let us reassure you, beloved ones, it is all a part of the process. These are times of great acceleration. We are infusing you with the maximum amount of Christ Light or Divine Substance from the Creator that your physical vessels can contain. In doing so, it has jolted or sped you along the path of initiation, or upward in the ascension process, however you wish to define it. And so, each time you lift your consciousness or tap into a higher frequency and incorporate it in any part of your Being, whether it is physical/emotional/mental or etheric, it permeates the very depths of your Being and releases any corresponding impacted or negative energies that resonate at a lower frequency.

Many of these energies were imprinted in your etheric and emotional bodies during those ancient experiences of your earliest physical incarnations on the Earth plane. They are very powerful indeed and have affected you in every lifetime you have experienced since by adding to and magnifying the negative energies until they held you in bondage, thereby creating pain and suffering.

These are energies that have kept you from having the perfect health you desire, the strong, attractive body you dream of, the abundance, the power, the relationships, and on and on. And so, you see, in order to assist you and keep you from going into "overwhelm," your Higher Self puts you in what might be called a "null zone," or a period of "no time." These are terms that are currently being bandied about in connection with the Photon Belt and are valid concepts, but they also apply to you personally.

Your Earth's rotation is slowing due to the decrease in planetary magnetics, while at the same time the vibrations or frequencies of your Earth (its heartbeat) are increasing. Every human being living on the Earth is being affected by this shift, as well as every other living thing that exists on the planet. At least, each Being is trying to match these new frequencies in order to stay attuned to the Earth, as the old frequencies are no longer tolerable.

Those of you who are the Wayshowers, the Light Warriors, have far exceeded these base frequencies and are functioning from a much higher resonance. Your reality is centered in the etheric-body of the Earth that has moved into the mid level fourth dimension. But, your beloved planet is also progressing rapidly and as it does, your reality must continue to change. All that you thought was your truth, your new way of functioning and being, your new identity, is swiftly melting away. A new holographic picture is emerging, and in your uncertainty you wonder where you fit in this new scheme and what you are to do now. WHO ARE YOU?

Again, precious ones, we say, relax, release, and realize that this, too, is just a part of the never-ending spiral. No longer will you be allowed to stagnate or even stay at a certain level very long—time and the process of transformation are moving too rapidly. Your language is changing, your thought forms are different. The old areas of your brain which contain your past are gradually being refined or dissolved, so it is beginning to seem as though everything that happened before, even last year, is a vague dream. New areas of your brain are being activated and you must learn to think in a whole new way. Light packets of information, holographic pictures of great significance and sacred geometric patterns, will begin to come into your consciousness and you must learn how to decipher these. It may seem as if those whom you are moving beyond no longer understand you, or you cannot find words to carry on the old mundane patterns of conversation. You will also find that you do not need to verbalize every thought as you begin to telepathically pick up the energies and thoughts of those around you. You will not need words and you will not be easily deceived. You will speak your truth with spiritual integrity and you will no longer play the games of the past.

As you don your refined, spiritual Light garments and awareness, be gentle with yourself. You may feel very vulnerable at times; you may feel as if you are losing an important part of yourself, and this is true. But it is a part that no longer serves you, even though you have become comfortable in carrying this old baggage around. It is time to release all that you cannot take with you as you move back into your perfected form of Light.

You descended into a beautiful, perfect etheric/physical vessel, a Divine Body brought forth from the mind of the

Creator. Allow us to give you an analogy of what took place those aeons ago and what is now taking place. Imagine that you are a diver about to descend to the floor of the ocean. You are buoyant and can only float on the surface unless you attach anchors or weights to yourself so that you can descend and walk on the ocean floor or have some means of propulsion that will carry you into the depths. It is the same with your Spirit Being. You had to take on density in order to descend into physicality. And, you took on much more density than was originally planned, making it even more difficult to emerge once again to the surface or what is called the higher dimensions.

So see yourself shedding the anchors and weights that are keeping you walking the depths in the quagmire, the fog and illusion of the lower dimensions. Allow yourself to shed the layers, the burdens that are keeping you stuck or anchored. Allow yourself to soar, once again, into the rarified heights. Are you aware that those of you who have advanced your frequencies and resonance beyond that of the Earth are actually assisting your beloved planet to move higher up the spiral? That is part of your mission, dear ones, to assist your brothers and sisters, but also to be Light Streams that become stronger and more buoyant, lifting the mass-consciousness, clearing the golden etheric web of your Mother Earth so that she, too, can once again claim her Divine Position in the grand drama of evolution.

We implore you, do not become attached to any way of being, any one modality, any philosophy that is too narrow or structured, or buy into any agreement that gives power to someone outside yourself. Discernment, discernment, discernment—I cannot emphasize this enough, for as quickly as an apparent truth comes forth and you incorporate it into your belief system, it may be superseded by a higher truth or a new concept. In looking back, can you not see that much of the knowledge you now accept as your absolute truth was beyond your wildest imagining five years ago, or even a year ago? Be aware that what you are so certain about today will undoubtedly change tomorrow or next week.

That is why you are feeling so vulnerable, beloved ones. You are **shape-shifting** and so is your reality. You are in the midst of an ongoing dream that is fast forwarding at an accelerated speed. If you allow the fixations of the past and those antiquated energies to emerge, to be transmuted or dissolved, and if you do not try to hang on to the old patterns, thought forms or structures, you will not feel so distressed or out of control. You must admit that this is not a time of boredom or stagnation, indeed, it is what you have yearned for since that time long ago when you merged your magnificent Spirit Self into the limiting confines of a physical structure.

Awaken each day in joyful anticipation, with great expectancy, allow the day to unfold in its perfectness, gifting you with new delights, releasing you from shackles of the past. As we have stressed, over and over, stay in the event of the NOW, and in doing so, you are focusing on what is occurring in the moment. Each moment, each thought and event, is of vast importance, for the treasures of new wisdom, new insights, new powers of reasoning and new gifts are pouring forth at an astonishing rate and you must be open to receive them. With each new impulse of a higher vibration, a portion of your existing reality begins to dissolve as the pattern repeats itself time and time again.

You cannot fail. You can only hold yourself back and create

discomfort if you struggle and keep yourself submerged in the old density. Accept these most precious gifts that are being offered. Become your own sacred witness, as you glean, sort, release and refine the information and experiences that move into your awareness. Do not become bogged down or attached to any set pattern or modality as you gradually emerge from the cocoon of physical-humanity into the crystalline form of spiritual-humanity. Allow yourself to ride the crest of the mighty waves of transformation. There is nothing to fear, precious ones, and so very much to be gained. Feel the warmth of our sacred breath as it brushes your cheek and sense the aura of love in which we surround you. We are near; reach out and touch us—we will respond. You are not alone, you have never been alone. I AM Archangel Michael.

17. THE WAVES OF LIFE

The waves of life wash over us,

Tumbling, cleansing, smoothing the rough edges

Until we are a magnificent, shining stone

Of beauty and perfection.

We are buffeted, tossed, rolled around

Until we break free to rise buoyantly to the surface,

Riding the crest of the waves.

A thrilling, exhilarating ride, at last,

Ever free from the rip tides of life,

Free to soar among the stars and taste the

Delights of eternity.

Ronna Herman

18. Mandate for Change

*G*reetings, beloved masters, I wish to give you a mandate for the coming months and for the new millennium. Take heed, if you will, for these are some of the most critical, important years you will ever live on this planet Earth. I have told you that these are years of integration, integrity, and of transcending the illusion of the third dimension. Are you monitoring what you are integrating, what you are allowing to enter your consciousness? Whatever it is, it will be magnified for good or ill.

Many of you are well on your way to mastery, flowing on the currents of the higher fourth-/fifth-dimensional energy and using your creativity in ways you never believed possible, breaking down old barriers and structures that held you in a limited, restricted reality. You have a better understanding of yourself and others as you float through the dance of interactive response, gleaning wisdom and awareness as to what is in or out of balance. Some of you are even amazed at what is now being presented to you via the mirroring process. Your reflection is growing soft, loving, gentle and tolerant.

Mentally, new ideas and concepts are bombarding your consciousness. Nebulous at first, but gradually solidifying as you use your enhanced reasoning abilities to unfold and decode the formulas and inventions of the future. As you tap into the fifth and sixth dimensions, you begin to remember the blueprint of creation: how you assisted in building the structure of the Earth, how to hold a pure thought until it is brought to fruition. You begin to see geometric shapes, sparkling crystals, brilliant new colors as you move through and beyond time and space.

Your bodily form must change as part of this process; it

cannot remain static or be left behind. Just as you transformed your physical body into density with your limited, fear-based thinking many ages ago, you will now transform your physical vessel back into its natural form: a sparkling Light Body, healthy, vibrant, whole and ever youthful.

Make no mistake; in your dream state and meditations, there are those of you who are accessing the sixth and even the seventh dimension, and on rare occasions the eighth and ninth. You are tapping into the vibrations of your Oversoul, the Monadic Level and the dimensions where the spiritual hierarchy and angels dwell. In your etheric body, you have been taken to the galactic core and to the heart of the Great Central Sun to receive a blessing and be given a gift of inspiration, as well as an infusion of Love/Light to hasten your awakening.

It is a time of reckoning, dear ones. Many signs and portents are coming forth from the multitude of messengers on Earth—from unusual astrological configurations and by visitors from both inner and outer space. Regardless of what you may think the comets are or aren't, or who or what they are, know this: in many forms, energy from the Creator Source of this universe is being poured down upon your Earth in greater and greater amounts. These are energies that are exploding and igniting the Light packets of information that are buried and encoded in your brain structure and within the consciousness of the Earth. But the key to unlocking and utilizing this information is love, integrity, truth and a sense of oneness with All.

Those who have used the universal laws of manifestation for their own greedy purposes, for dominance and destruction, will find that their methods are no longer effective. They will find their empires crumbling, and their hoarded riches melting away. Their lessons will be harsh and bitter, but they also will be given an opportunity to change their focus from a strictly material viewpoint to a spiritually inspired point of view.

There are those of you who wish, hope and desire spiritual en-LIGHT-enment and attunement, and you keep thinking, maybe tomorrow I will start meditating or I will start practicing the lessons I have learned. Soon, I will begin to use the creative abilities that are floating on the edge of my consciousness, but I am too busy today.

Time is running out, beloved ones. You must either step on the wave of ascension into higher awareness, or be left behind to wait for the next spiral of evolution—which means you will stay tied to the wheel of Karma and imprisoned in the limitations, fear and futility of the third dimension.

It is a time of wonder, excitement and reward, my beloveds. It is not a time of sacrifice, restrictions or restraint. To the contrary, what is being offered you is mastery of life, abundance, joy, peace and harmony. Anything you are asked to give up will be replaced with gifts so precious, so rewarding, you will wonder why you ever hesitated.

In some areas of your Earth, you are coming into your springtime, a time of new life, a bursting forth of new energy manifested in a wondrous variety of forms. In other areas of Earth, it will be a time for rest and slumber as the cold grip of winter takes hold. You have been in the cold grip of fear and illusion, my precious friends. It is time to allow yourself to burst forth in the springtime of Spirit and new life, allowing the gift of rarified energy from the God Force to take residency within your structure and consciousness. You will be forever transformed.

Many of you have, or are becoming aware, of the importance of the event called WESAK, the time of the full moon in the astrological sign of Taurus. The word WESAK is derived from syllables and energies which are a combination of sounds brought forth from the higher dimensions. Meditate on this word, use it as a mantra and see what emerges from within your consciousness. It is a time of gift giving from the Cosmic Christ, the Buddhic forces and the Christed Beings of the highest dimensions of this universe.

Regardless of where you are physically, you all have an opportunity to partake of this awesome gift, to receive a blessing of the Christ energy via an infusion of Love/Light from the Source planted within your consciousness. Then the next step, if you are willing, will be for you to take these seeds of Christ energy and spread them to others, so that they too will be blessed.

It is a time of birthing the Christ Child within—of allowing your Soul (Solar) Heart to burst forth into full power and awareness. Your Father/Mother Creator desires a reunion of Spirit with you, one of its many precious creations. You have wandered too far from home and have been away too long, precious ones. You are being given an opportunity to return home to the heart of perfection where a dwelling place has been reserved for you.

And so the mandate is this: focus on that which wells up within you as the most important issue of your life. Seek validation from within your heart center and from your I AM Presence. Dedicate yourself to accomplishing that which you desire with all your energy—physical/mental/emotional and spiritual—until it is brought to fruition. Start small, if you have doubts, until you become proficient in using your latent abilities of cocreation. Sweep aside your doubts, and do not listen to others' criticism or admonitions. Follow your own inner guidance; you will not be led astray, beloveds.

This is the time to seek your truth, to once again take control and dominion of your world, to remember you are a representative of the Creator on an important mission called "Operation Planet Earth." Accept your power as a master of cocreation. Accept and activate the gifts you were endowed with that lay dormant within.

I have told you that the First Ray of Divine Will is once again being activated and beamed down upon Earth and its inhabitants. Those who have earned the right to wield this great power will find that their ability to manifest will be multiplied and magnified tenfold. It activates your decisiveness, your will to create; it enhances your desire and ability to focus. It is the Ray that sends forth and births new ideas from the heart of Creation. Its qualities are truth, and faith, and will afford protection if you use its energy correctly and wisely.

The First Ray in unison with the Seventh Ray are the energies which will help you build the bridge to the New Age. The Seventh Ray will be the predominant vibration for Earth for the next two thousand years. However, it must have the catalytic energy of the First Ray to activate the purification and transformation process that is necessary at this time. The Seventh Ray, in unison with the First Ray, gives you the power to activate, transmute, transform, purify and even etherealize energy (return substance back into neutral universal energy to be requalified or purified). Give yourself a beautiful gift and a powerful tool: begin to wield the Divine Sword, symbol of the First Ray's energy, and surround yourself with and use constantly the gift of the Violet Flame. With these tools you can change the quality/vibrations of energy within yourself and the world around you.

You must begin now, no matter how small the endeavor, and we will assist you in every way possible in order that you will realize you have the ability to accomplish miracles.

There is a dream of greatness, beauty, bounty and perfection blowing in on the winds of change. Will you be a part of that beautiful dream, or will you remain in the nightmare of illusion? The choice is yours, dear ones.

We are endeavoring, in every way possible, to let you know that we are available, we are here with you every moment of the day or night. Call on us, we will answer in wondrous ways to behold.

I surround you and enfold you in an auric field of love and protection. I am with you always. I AM Archangel Michael.

19. MESSAGE FROM RONNA

My Dearest Friends:

I would like to share with you an experience I had beginning back in March of 1996. It seems when one of us breaks through to a new level of awareness many others experience the same reality shift. Although for some time, I no longer have felt the need to go to all the workshops or seminars as I did in the past, I was led to attend a five-day seminar in San Diego, called Remembrance of the Solar Heart, given by Drunvalo Melchizedek and six other beautiful, wise Light workers. At the conclusion, there was a ceremony in which we were presented with a small rose quartz stone as a symbol of the Solar-Heart activation. When Drunvalo placed the stone in my hand and embraced me, I felt as if my heart shattered into a million crystalline pieces, along with the shattering of the holographic picture of my reality. I felt different, somewhat disconnected and a little vulnerable. It took me a number of days to assimilate the refined energy infusion I knew I had received.

Lord Michael often addresses issues and situations that I and others close to me experience, and the previous message was a result of my experience. All of what he said held true for me; many of my beliefs shifted and I moved to a new level of expanded awareness. I was scheduled to channel Archangel Michael at the Wesak Festival at Mt. Shasta on May 5 of that year, and I became aware that my beloved friend, Barbara Zimmerman, and I were chosen to take the seeds of love, wisdom and the refined Light Body energy infusion we received at the Remembrance of the Solar Heart seminar to the Wesak Celebration.

Almost 1300 people attended the Wesak Festival, with at

least 12 countries represented. It was a time of great expectancy, joy and celebration. Joshua Stone and the many inspired
presenters did a superb job of lifting us to new levels of consciousness and bringing forth the wisdom and gifts of Christ
energy through all the magnificent Beings of Light. I am sure
that even though many were not aware of it at the time, each
of us received exactly what we needed to accelerate our Light
body activation so we could move into a new level of mastery.

I was given a booth to sell copies of ON WINGS OF LIGHT
and pass out flyers; therefore I was blessed with an opportunity
to meet and talk to many of the beautiful souls in attendance.
As I moved into the auric field of each person and embraced
them, it seemed as if one of those shattered fragments of my
heart took on their Essence and it settled, once again, into the
center of my Being. There was such a perfect, awesome sense
of unity, recognition and love. Sometimes we laughed together,
sometimes we cried—it was joyful, poignant and incredible.

As I stood at the podium to speak and Lord Michael's energy descended into the room, it was more powerful than I
have ever experienced before and I know that there was not
a person in the room that did not feel his presence or receive
the gift of his loving Essence. I was very humbled by the experienced and I felt truly blessed. We were told that the Earth
and humanity were lifted to a new level of awareness and
showered with a refined energy infusion that we will be incorporating for some years to come. It is, indeed, the time of
miracles and we all have an integral part to play.

It is a most wondrous moment when we truly feel the
"ONENESS" of all. Welcome into my heart, dear and precious
brothers and sisters.

In the Light, Ronna

20. TAKING CONTROL OF YOUR DESTINY

*B*eloved masters of Light, it is time for you to take stock, or an inventory of sorts, to allow you to chart your progress, to examine any new concepts that may not serve your highest purpose or enhance your spiritual well-being. Many of you have become too dependent on the knowledge, rituals, methodologies or teachings of others. Answer these questions from your heart/soul center, if you will: do you trust another's channeled information as higher wisdom than your own; do you authenticate or validate all outside information within your own heart/soul center? Do you constantly seek a new method, a new herb, a new elixir or gadget to accelerate your Light frequencies or to jump-start your spiritual awareness without your participation—a magic solution, in other words?

Are you forgetting that allopathic medicine is an important modality of healing, along with taking responsibility for your well-being/wholeness, along with all the wonderful homeopathic remedies and the plethora of mind/body techniques available? There are times when you have reached a critical state within your physical being that drastic intervention must be initiated. You are still in a physical vessel—in a dense material world—and something that has taken years to manifest within your structure to the point it is life-threatening must be aggressively addressed and rectified.

We most strongly stress discernment, but we see that you need to understand more comprehensively what discernment means. Humanity has been in what might be called a "herd" state for thousands of years, and so it is a conditioning that is hard to break. It is easier to follow the crowd and the popular beliefs or trends. It is more difficult to make your own decisions, and through trial and error, begin to trust your intuition even if it means taking radical measures that do not fit within the norm. It is easier to look outside yourself for a quick fix, whereby you do not have to participate or take responsibility for your actions. It is easier and more comfortable to blame someone else. How quick you are to jump on the bandwagon of a new concept that promises miracles. Unfortunately, there are many within the spiritual community that are more than willing to profit from your gullibility/vulnerability. "By their works you shall know them," but sometimes this realization comes after the fact—too late. You must validate from within before you make your decisions.

I do not wish to sound harsh or suggest that you are not making great progress, when in fact the opposite is true. You are making spectacular progress and momentous growth. But many of you are at a critical point in your transition process. You are being sped along the initiation path and new knowledge is pouring forth each day. Even though you have many guidelines and theories out there to choose from, you still are a unique human/spiritual Being whose path is different, whose tests are different, whose perception of reality is totally unique to you. Therefore, what works wonders for another, may do nothing for you. What one affirms as a sure-fire method for healing, balancing, attunement or atonement may be totally wrong for you—even detrimental. Are you going to live by someone else's values, or your own? Are you going to pattern your behavior and project your spiritual truth or be a clone for someone else? You are one of a kind: we tell you this time and time again. The Creator sent you forth with a most precious mission to accomplish, it is encoded within your soul as your Divine Blueprint. Are you going to follow your blueprint or someone else's, thereby leaving yours unmanifested or incomplete?

You are your own physician, but your abilities and insights are still in their infancy. Many of you are taking preventative measures by eating live foods that are as pure and unrefined as possible. Hopefully, you are paying attention and listening to your body and know that your thoughts as well as your actions have dramatic impact on your well-being. You are seeking balance in body/mind and Spirit, but you still are exposed to the stress of family and workplace, or myriad responsibilities. You still must live where the air chokes and clogs your system, and often your water and food are filled with impurities. Slowly these things are changing, but in the meantime, you must be realistic. You cannot retreat from your physical reality, you cannot walk away from or ignore your responsibilities. This is one of the most difficult facets of the ascension process.

You have had a glimpse or a remembrance of the perfection from whence you came. More frequently, you are able to tap into that wonderful sense of bliss and the sense of how it feels to be free of the confines of your constricting physical vessel. You are becoming more and more dissatisfied with your mundane life and the constant turmoil it brings. Even the anticipation and relief you used to derive from recreational activities no longer seem to satisfy. Many of you have a strong desire to walk away from your responsibilities, toss aside your job, or your possessions, which have become more like shackles or a prison. This is not the way of a master, dear ones. You move forward by gradually changing your perception and accepting your responsibilities. You focus on the good, the positive in any situation, person or circumstance. You radiate love and harmony whether you are with a group of spiritual brothers and sisters who project unconditional love and joy, or whether you are in a situation where chaos, fear, rejection, jealousy, or power struggles are present. It is easy to be a master sitting on the mountain top in the serenity of nature, but it is much more important to keep your sense of balance and harmony in the everyday situations of life. Those who cause you dis-comfort and dis-ease within are your best teachers. They mirror to you what is welling up from deep within to be healed. As you change your perception and begin to radiate pure Christ love in all situations, those around you will change, or gradually withdraw from your life. You will have learned the lessons they offered; therefore, they will no longer have an impact on your reality. The more you become in harmony with Spirit, the more harmonious your world becomes—regardless of the chaos that swirls around you.

All that I have described is part of the mutating process, the ascension process which is in progress for your Earth and humanity. It is not a steady, forward-motion process, but an insurgence of energy and new information, and then a time of assimilation, integration and manifestation. Many of the sensations seem more pronounced to you at this time, and you may feel as though you have taken a great leap into the unknown at times or taken a step backward into uncertainty and an intensified sense of vulnerability. By now, you should be somewhat accustomed to the ebb and flow of magnified, accelerated frequencies, but when you are pushed to the next level of awareness, it sets off an alarm of varying degrees in your physical/mental/emotional bodies.

As I have explained to you, there has always been a great surge of magnified energy showered down on Earth and humanity in the months of November, December and May. But as your time passes, these surges of energy will happen more and more frequently, bringing in greater and higher vibrations of Light. This radiant, crystalline substance of Creation has penetrated to your very core and to the core of the Earth as well. Envision a powerful electrical current penetrating your chakra system and any atoms, cells or energy residing there that cannot harmonize to this current being forced out in a great surge. As it resonates throughout your physical vessel, your etheric web, your emotional and your mental bodies, it collects and carries with it the dark atoms or impacted energies that cannot harmonize or attune to this higher frequency. Now envision your auric field and see the distortions this creates as this energy permeates, distorts and clouds your aura, manifesting a sense of being off balance, not in control, and possibly losing your connection to your guides, teachers and spirit helpers, temporarily.

This is why you often feel out of balance, spacey, partly in and partly out of your body. It is important to allow yourself a time of assimilation after you have experienced an initiation or have incorporated a new vibratory level. You may feel the need to retreat into solitude, or spend time out in nature and take a break from reading, seeking or even meditation, in order to allow yourself time to integrate and become accustomed to your elevated sense of awareness.

Many are speaking of the crystalline energy that is being activated within your Earth, in the ley lines and grid system. Many are being led to different areas of the Earth to facilitate and activate these powerful energies. In the past, we have used the vision of a diamond crystal pyramid in healing meditations and visualizations, and others are bringing forth information of great activations of energy around the Earth. Allow me to give you some insight as to what is now occurring. Not only are you being infused with the trans-forming/transmuting higher Rays and the refined Source/God/Goddess energy, but there is an internal activation process in progress within your Earth as well.

At the time your beautiful planet Earth was formed, there were magnificent, sentient crystalline Beings that came from a far-distant universe. They agreed to make a supreme sacrifice and therefore were encoded with the Divine Blueprint for the Earth's evolution and ultimate ascension. They were then installed deep within the Earth at strategic grid points. They resonated frequencies and information from the cosmos to Earth and back again, and also stored vast amounts of information and energy within their Beings.

At the final sinking of the great civilization called Atlantis whereby the Earth sank into density and was cut off from the higher realms by the "Ring-Pass-Not," many of these great crystals were shut down and vacated. You are familiar with those that remained active: Egypt, the great pyramids; the Atlantic Ocean around Bimini; Tibet; Lake Titicaca; Peru; Palenque; Jerusalem/Mt. Sinai; and the Grand Tetons, to name a few. Now, some of these energy centers (which were also portals) have become so dense and clogged with negativity that they have become the focus of much of the conflict on your Earth, particularly in Africa, Egypt and the Mideast. Others have remained radiating energy centers that have drawn thousands of Light warriors to their force-fields so that their internal blueprint could be activated. And those who were led by Spirit, at times through an inner call that could not be denied, went forth to these sacred vortices in order to assist in the healing and cleansing of these crystalline structures so that, once again, they could radiate purely and powerfully the messages of the Elohim and angelic realms, as well as radiate healing vibrations throughout to the core and surface of the Earth.

And so you see, you are experiencing accelerated frequencies from the cosmos, and you are also being affected by the changing patterns from within the Earth as she begins to attune to and resonates to her perfect blueprint. As you know, healing begins from within and radiates outward, gaining power and influence as wholeness is incorporated and maintained.

I explained some time ago about the beautiful crystal pyramids that are being formed in the etheric and asked you to begin to visualize these and use them in your meditations in order to more quickly manifest them in the physical.

I now ask, if you are willing, that you begin to bring forth from your Divine I AM Presence, a diamond crystal pyramid filled with millions of smaller crystalline pyramids. Envision these being incorporated throughout your Being, filling the vacancies left by the dark atoms you are constantly releasing. See them migrating to the areas that are creating symptoms of distress and dis-ease. Place them in all your chakras, glands and organs. See billions of them flowing through your blood stream and filling your body down to the deepest cellular level with pure crystalline Light. These beautiful, powerful crystals carry the codes of your lineage, your heritage, and your destiny. They carry the power, the will, the joy—all the attributes that you seek to incorporate. You can envision them energized with transforming energies of the five higher Rays, or whatever Ray level you are presently incorporating.

These crystal pyramids will create a great impetus for your growth, as well as for the transformation of the Earth. All over the world and especially in the western hemisphere, these great crystalline energies are being reactivated and revved up. These will enhance and accelerate the healing and ascension of your Earth, as well as humanity, with ease and grace.

You must have a burning desire to find your truth, beloved ones, and then you must live that truth with every fiber of your Being. You must insist on justice, justice for yourself and all humanity, and know that it starts with you. You must live in a spirit of cooperation, not competition, assisting others, validating their talents and truth, while allowing others to assist you and give you validation and credence. A sense of personal responsibility will be the cornerstone of the new prototype communities, where all will contribute and benefit, serving the common good. **THY WILL BE DONE FOR THE HIGHEST GOOD OF ALL** should become your creed and motto.

Your spiritual strength and wisdom is being tested, my beloved warriors. You are at a crossroads: will you be a leader or a follower? Will you be satisfied with a glimpse of the New Age, or insist on basking in the full radiance of paradise? We have no doubt as to what your answer will be.

I surround and enfold you in a crystalline aura of love and protection. I AM with you always. I AM Archangel Michael.

21. "Soul Talk"—Creative Language Using the Laws of Universal Manifestation

THINK IT—FEEL IT—SAY IT—DO IT

Words your subconscious mind understands which will allow you to tap into the universal energy of creation with the assistance of your conscious mind and your super-conscious mind.

Thoughts, words, emotions and actions are all forms of energy.

***I AM** = GOD CONSCIOUSNESS · OM or AUM · Sacred sounds of Creation.*

"In the beginning was the word. The word was with God—and the word was God."

***I LOVE** = THE FUEL AND FREQUENCY OF CREATION · Pure love creates perfection.*

The opposite of love is fear (all negative emotions stem from fear).

***I WILL** = RESOLVE · DETERMINATION · POWER to direct your consciousness.*

Self-sabotage = doubt · vacillation · indecision.

***I CHOOSE** = CHOICE · SELECT · DECIDE · PREFER (Using our gift of free will).*

Self-sabotage = reject · refuse · allow someone else to choose for us.

I CREATE = *DEVELOP · FASHION · GENERATE · IN-VENT · ORIGINATE.*

Self-sabotage = destroy · tear down.

I HAVE = *OWN · POSSESS · CONTROL · RETAIN.*

Self-sabotage = beyond · want · need · wish · hope.

I CAN = *ABLE TO · CAPABLE · IN YOUR POWER.*

Self-sabotage = I wish · I want · I'm trying.

I DESIRE = *ASPIRATION · VISION · MOTIVATION · URGE.*

Self-sabotage = indifference · apathy · unconcern.

I ENJOY = *DELIGHT IN · APPRECIATE · SAVOR · PLEASURABLE.*

Self-sabotage = dislike · displeasure · dissatisfied.

Ronna Herman

22. Embrace Your Adversaries and Imperfections with Christ Light

(August, 1996 Message)

*B*eloved masters of Light, let us speak of some of the events that have transpired, which have sent out ripples of shock, pain, disbelief and confusion amongst humanity, creating a great impact on the mass-consciousness around the world. You may not realize how the people of the world are impacted by what occurs in the United States. Those of you who reside in this great country are looked upon with envy, admiration, curiosity, and also with disdain, bitterness and hatred. Whatever happens of major proportions within your boundaries affects all the world, either in a positive or negative way.

First of all, the senseless bombing in your city of Atlanta during the Olympic Games. There is great symbology in the Olympics, and even though it has become very commercialized, it still creates a tremendous surge of hope and inspiration, and instigates great feats of strength and acts of valor. It represents the coming together of all countries and races; the spirit of competition, and yet the spirit of comradery and unity; and it offers the excitement of watching your athletes of all ages put forth their grandest effort. Whether it resulted in being acknowledged in the winner's circle or not, there were no losers present at this event.

Use these enthusiastic, energetic young people as your examples in your spiritual exercises and endeavors. Put forth your greatest effort, work and strive without ceasing, envision your goal and do not let anyone or anything deter you. These young ones know how to stay focused, in their power and in the moment under great pressure and with many distractions. Even when a disastrous mistake occurs that throws them out of the running, they stiffen their resolve, hold their head high and continue through and beyond the test of adversity. Please realize, beloved ones, there were no failures or losers among those who participated. They all came away winners. Some showed great integrity and honor, some showed great bravery and tenacity, and other showed graciousness and warmth as they congratulated those who brought them to defeat. These games are a microcosm of the trials and tests of your everyday lives. You only become a loser if you do not try or if you give up the fight.

We have told you that there has been a great insurgence of energy from the higher dimensions down upon the Earth. You know how it has affected you and created distortion, imbalances and frustration in your personal reality. What we wish you to realize is that it affects your Mother Earth and the mass-consciousness in the same way, only greatly magnified. See great swirls, like whirlwinds, of ancient memory being released from the lower astral planes surrounding Mother Earth and from the mass-consciousness. Do you think it is a coincidence that a bomb was exploded in Atlanta or that a plane exploded over the Atlantic?

As you know, the sinking of Atlantis was a great cataclysmic event that jarred your Earth into the density of the third dimension. She is striving and straining to evolve and move back into her proper place in the solar system. As we have told you, the etheric body of the Earth has moved into the mid level of the fourth dimension, and the physical body of the Earth is trying to follow. Just as you stir up all old impacted memories and energies when you incorporate a higher frequency, so it is with the Earth. Buried within her memory and the astral planes are all the imbalances: the fury and fervor—the destructive forces of violence, fear, power struggles and chaos that have ever occurred on this planet. These are being released in order to be healed, as the Earth moves into her refinement and higher consciousness.

Just as you must experience the changes within your own physical structure, so it is with the Earth. You must focus love, the Transmuting Violet Flame and the refining energies of the higher Rays on this unsettling maelstrom of negative memory in order to transmute and refine it. Have we not told you how much you are needed, how important it is that you become a powerful, anchored pillar of Light, radiating balance and harmony down through and around the Earth?

Watch as more violent scenarios are played out in the key places around the world where there has been so much hatred, war and bloodshed. These hotbeds of ancient negativity need to be refined and transmuted. Many of you who live in or around these areas do so because you were in the cataclysmic events that transpired and remember at a soul level all that took place during and before the destruction. You have returned, vowing to assist in rectifying the horrendous mistakes made, determined to heal the imbalances and memory of failure, and assure that it never happens again.

We also wish to apprize you of the fact that there are beautiful but misguided souls who were a part of the great power struggles and misdeeds that led to the eventual destruction of Atlantis. They have returned carrying within their auric field the same negative energies and are determined, in a last ditch effort, to regain control of as many souls as possible. Many of these are the laggard souls who came from other star systems carrying seeds of hate, greed and fear, with a desire to dominate and conquer.

You will all be confronted, at one time or another, by these powerful ones, but you must not allow them victory. Do not judge them, join in the power struggles or seek to change or dominate them. It is simple, my mighty warriors: stand firm in your integrity, wear your spiritual armor and project love back to them when they judge, criticize or try to malign you. They will not succeed, but they will represent a mighty test, one in which you must show your colors and project your power, will and authority with love and compassion, and move past them in your forward march to victory. They cannot and will not prevail—not this time.

The same situation can be applied to the senseless bombing of the plane over the Atlantic. Do not allow them to tell you that it was not an act of violence, for it was indeed so. We tell you that all those beautiful souls that expired felt no pain and were instantly transported into their beautiful Light bodies in a far more joyous and peaceful place than your Earth. Their deaths will not be in vain. You may not see the larger picture, but each and every one of these violent events stiffens the resolve of humanity and stirs an outcry of indignation of humanity's brutality against itself. Mankind is beginning to acquire a conscience, and you are making inroads, even if your endeavors are, at times, misdirected.

The same rules apply to the Middle Eastern part of the world and other areas you might call "hot spots." The ancient holograms, memories, scenarios and thought forms are re-emerging so they can be rectified and healed, once and for all.

It is time to restructure your past and move forward into your bright new future. Those who insist on staying stuck in these destructive modalities will not be allowed to continue with the planet Earth on her journey back into the joy and beauty of the higher realms.

Many of you are somewhat confused regarding the energies, specifically the Rays which are now accessible to you, that are arching their way down onto planet Earth. You have been influenced by the harmonics of seven for thousands of years: seven chakras (energy centers), seven Rays (aspects and attributes of the Creator carried and projected by the archangels and Chohans), and seven planes and dimensions. As you moved into refinement and expanded your awareness (along with the Earth), you gained access to higher levels of awareness and resonation. This allows you to incorporate five of the higher Rays (eventually more), have access to the higher dimensions, and to activate higher and more refined chakras within your force field, whereby you will begin to resonate to the harmonics of 12 on your journey back into Cosmic-consciousness.

We will give you a different viewpoint as to what these higher Rays mean, and how they are affecting you. There are different theories and descriptions as to the attributes, color and meaning of these five higher Rays. All are valid within a loose framework. The Rays consist of an exoteric or material refinement and color, as well as an esoteric or spiritual refinement and color. The colors of some of the Rays have changed down through the ages, determined by what was needed or not needed at that particular time. All of the higher Rays have a luminescence, or iridescence, to them because of the infusion of pure Christ Light from the Source. These higher Rays are much more potent and effective (you might say, a little goes a long way).

These higher Rays are anchoring galactic and cosmic

energy, intelligence, and transforming characteristics that have not been available to you since the beginning of the third, great Golden Age. You must earn them, dear ones, and then you must use these energies wisely. Just as stirring the Kundalini (spiritual energy) too soon or in too great a measure creates discomfort and chaos, so it is with these higher Rays. These refined energies activate what is imbalanced within you, that which must come to the surface of your consciousness to be brought into harmony and rectified.

Yes, within these great Rays are energies that will facilitate the soul merge, the merger with your Higher Self, and eventually with your Divine I AM Presence. But before this can be accomplished, you must release all the negativity and impacted energies that do not resonate to these more refined infusions of Christ Light. Yes, dear ones, that is what they are: prisms of Christ Light, sent originally from the Creator, down through the Elohim, archangels and great Beings of Light, as gifts for guidance and infusions of loving energy to assist you on your journey out into the cosmos.

Do not be concerned with bringing in the right color; although it is wondrous to feel the subtleties of the different Rays as they pulsate through your body and you become attuned to them, there is no right or wrong way. Concentrate instead on releasing the impacted energies and memories from within. You will never go wrong if you use the Violet Flame to transmute the imbalanced energies within your four lower bodies and then fill the vacancies with pure golden/white crystalline Light Substance.

We often use the colors of the five higher Rays in the activation and healing process. These are powerful, wonderful energies, but we do not want you to get bogged down in ritual and forget the purpose of the endeavor. You are moving into another level of awareness, taking a giant step forward, you might say. Many of you are being catapulted out into the public arena, while others are still struggling to come to terms with their inner and outer pictures of reality. Patience is an important factor, as always, and just when you think you have a clear picture of what is going on, your reality takes another jolting shift. It is difficult to remain complacent, for there is no longer a status quo. You are living multiple lifetimes, in multiple dimensions, while integrating parallel lives and realities and releasing many old fragmented pictures of reality at one time. Is it any wonder that you sometimes go into overload, or feel as if you don't know who you are any longer?

A harvesting of souls is taking place—it is decision time— all must decide whether they wish to move forward with the Earth as she spirals into the higher dimensions, or whether they will choose to leave and return at a later time or move on to another planet of third-dimensional expression to finish their lessons in the physical expression. Many souls will choose to leave the Earth plane as a part of their contract and Divine Mission, and many other beautiful souls are being placed or readied to assume positions of authority, positions of power. They will remain "low key," possibly in the background, until it is time to step forward and make themselves known. They will be dynamic, forceful and carry a new vision for humanity—one that will serve all people and create the foundation for the New Age to come.

Look back over the past few years. What have you accomplished? How have you changed? What has transpired? You are not the same person, you know, regardless of how you see yourself. You will continue your metamorphosis at an ever-accelerating rate, as breathtaking new awareness, visions and gifts are awarded to you. All you have to do, my precious ones, is allow—surrender to your Divine I AM Presence and the highest good of all so that you may be brought into perfect alignment with your Divine Blueprint/Mission. You do not surrender your free will, you only bring it into harmony with the Grand Plan of the Creator/Father/Mother God. Your illumination and return to perfection are the rewards awaiting you, my beloveds.

I surround you and enfold you in my auric field of protective love and Light. You are loved most profoundly. I AM Archangel Michael.

23. EXPAND YOUR HORIZONS

*B*eloved masters, many of you are suffering from the ill effects of the elements, and the harshness and extremes of Mother Nature are being felt everywhere. Your physical vessels seem to be in rebellion and you are feeling weak and vulnerable, or at least, uneasy. There is much talk about the arrival of the Photon Belt, mass landings and visitations from outer space. It is your "Inner Space" that I would like you to concentrate on for the moment, if you will.

Your Earth has shifted to a higher octave or passed through a portal way to the next level of awareness. You might say that the Earth itself, as well as every living, sentient being, is suffering from a molecular flu of sorts—an influx of foreign substance into your bodies—higher energy patterns that are not compatible with your vibrational frequencies as they now exist.

Yes, no matter what level of awareness you have attained, you are being bombarded with higher frequencies—you are being force fed in a sense—so that any incompatible energies within are being stirred up so they can be released. We have said this many times, but it is imperative that you "get it" once and for all. You can no longer remain at the status quo. These past years have been years of transition, of establishing the groundwork, and metering out duties and responsibilities, preparing for the grand debut of the new spiritual leadership and the next turn of world events.

Spiritual awakening is not just the focus of the few any longer, humanity as a whole is stirring and the internal Divine Discontent is reaching a feverish pitch which can no longer be denied. It is apparent everywhere—even those who resist and fear the new paradigm are feeling an irresistible fascination for information about angels, the paranormal, life-after-death, and out-of-body experiences. Any new philosophy, religion or belief system will focus on the radical, extreme and sensational until it gradually settles down to a comfortable, acceptable norm.

You have worked hard and diligently, my brave warriors, and I know it seems as though you move forward to glimpse at the beauty and peace of the future only to be dashed back into the chaos of the present. That is why I ask you to focus on your "Inner Space" when the going gets rough. I ask you to seek the eye of the storm—that calm, perfect place in your heart/soul center. Draw on all the love of Creation that your heart can hold—fill your Being with the essence of perfect peace, beauty and harmony.

Now I ask you to project your consciousness outward, away from yourself and your little picture of reality. Assume an expanded awareness: imagine, if it helps, that you are viewing your life and the lives of those around you from our vantage point, giving you the ability to see the panoramic view of what is occurring from moment to moment. Look back over your year—over several years—take an inventory. Have you not made great strides? Are you not a much wiser, more compassionate, and more enlightened person? Can you not see the perfection or at least the justice in what has occurred in your past? Are you not stronger, wiser for your trials and tests along the way? Observe those closest to you: have they moved forward and expanded their awareness, or are they still stuck on the treadmill of inertia, fearful in their tunnel-visioned view of life?

You view everything from the focus of "I," as if you are the center of the universe. Let us shift that focus, if you will.

For a time, begin to view yourself through the eyes of those with whom you interact. Be as objective and honest in this analysis as you can; it will serve you well. Do you listen to those around you—truly listen to what they are saying, or are you only waiting to make your next point? Or are you a nonparticipant, allowing others to lead you with their thoughts, opinions, and judgments, so that you seem like a nonentity much of the time? Do you offer encouragement and support whenever possible, or are you too wrapped up in your own drama of everyday life to reach out with a kind word or gentle touch?

Do you add a sparkle to the atmosphere, to your surroundings—focusing on the positive, joyful, and beauty of the moment? Or, do you reinforce the negative, adding to the imbalance, the conflict or dissension around you? Make no mistake; every thought, deed and action reinforces, magnifies and adds to its own level of resonance, and you are the ultimate recipient of that magnified energy. You are the one who must live and experience the results, along with those around you who are also susceptible to those frequencies.

Please, dear ones, it is imperative, as never before, that you observe what you are creating and realize how much influence you have on the world around you. Are you still reaching out, trying to grasp that elusive dream of tomorrow that will bring you happiness and contentment—that dream that has been force fed you by your media and marketing masterminds? Many of you are bankrupting your heritage and that of your children as you chase those elusive dreams, when in reality, all you desire has been within your grasp all the time. Look around you, can't you see? Possessions alone are only that—things, things which you think make a statement as to who you are: how important, how successful, how powerful you are, but you fool no one but yourselves.

You contain in that "Inner Space" the true riches you seek. You must realize that from that space springs forth all the riches of Creation, but the first of these must be love. From the well-spring of love pours forth all the miracles you could ever wish for: love of self and all others; a verve and passion for living; a sense of compassion and tolerance, of unity or oneness; a vision for the future. But your focus must be on the perfection of the moment and an unswerving dedication to your mission or destiny, knowing you are an invaluable part of the whole, no greater or smaller than any other. One missing or distorted piece of the puzzle means the perfect picture cannot be completed.

Interestingly enough, as you begin to perceive yourself from another's point of view, you begin to see yourself reflected back through the mirror of life. Down through the years, you have unconsciously projected your own image of reality out into the world and now, with your new awareness, you begin to see what you have wrought with your views and beliefs. You will come to realize, if you are totally honest with yourself, that which is being projected back to you by others is only what you have projected outward in the past.

During this process, dear ones, try not to see or judge anything as good or bad—see it as it truly is, a matter of balanced or imbalanced energy. Focus on that which is balanced and harmonious in your life and see if you cannot expand that energy into the areas of imbalance. Many small issues of ego keep you caught up in situations which could easily be resolved if you would release the need to be right or self-righteous. Is it worth the pain and disharmony?

In that panoramic view you are taking of your life, can you see a plan unfolding, a path beginning to emerge? Are you being nudged to move out of your comfort zone or out of situations that no longer serve you? Many of you will find that certain areas of your life are becoming intolerable and you can no longer put off making changes that you have tried to ignore. It is a time of harvesting and reaping, dear ones, a time of gleaning the wheat from the "chaff." This applies to every area of your life and your Earth as well, and it will continue, expand and magnify as time goes on. This is the chaos you are experiencing if you are resisting the process, or it is the joy you feel if you are allowing yourself to "go with the flow."

The weather patterns you are experiencing will become even more extreme and radical over the next few years, as the Earth accommodates herself to the new frequency patterns. As has been foretold, there are areas of desert beginning to blossom with new growth, eventually to become lush, semitropical gardens of great beauty. Many of the food-producing areas of the world are in distress, soon to become fallow and dormant as the land seeks to rest and replenish itself. The migration of humanity has already begun and the populace of the Earth will mix and meld more and more as time goes on, blending races, colors, creeds and religions. When you see or hear of a cataclysm or tragedy, whether in your own area or around the world, do you see only the negative aspects and feel helpless, angry or resentful, or can you begin to take the higher, wider perspective? It is all a part of the great scheme of things, and out of every adversity comes miracles and good fortune to those who are far-visioned. Offer assistance in whatever way you can, but even as important, send loving energy and thoughts of well-being, peace and joy to those in need.

Many of you will be placed on the periphery of cataclysmic events, not directly involved, but close enough so that your powerful loving presence and energy can act as a stabilizing force and so that you may be an example to those in need of guidance and positive reinforcement. Is it not wonderful how, most often, a tragedy brings out the best in those involved? Traits, abilities and gifts that might not otherwise ever be displayed are brought to the fore.

I will not tell you that the coming years will be the peaceful paradise you seek. No. Not quite yet, beloved ones. But, I will promise you that if you will join me in this expanded way of viewing your life and the world, it will become much easier, more exciting, and you will have a greater understanding of the workings of the Universal Mind. The fewer things you see as negative or bad—the more you view whatever happens as just a part of the process and something to be experienced (a lesson learned), the closer you will be to viewing life on Earth through our eyes.

You are beginning to sense the great love I have for each of you. You are coming to realize that I AM with you always, but will you now allow me to take a more active part in your life—to guide, assist and support you on your journey? I will join you in that "Sacred Inner Space" if you so desire. All you have to do is ask. I AM Archangel Michael.

24. RECLAIM YOUR SOUL POWER

*B*eloved Masters, I greet you this glorious day and send to you, through this transmission, great waves of loving energy and words of encouragement to assist you through these wondrous times of transformation.

Many of you are thinking, "They do not seem so wondrous to me. What am I doing wrong? I am not worthy enough to move forward, to graduate, to become enlightened, as you have promised. Will I be left behind? Why does my world seem to be so chaotic, in such turmoil? Where is the peace and joy you said would be forthcoming?"

Let me ease your mind and help you understand the process. You will not fail. You are exactly where you should be— you are perfect the way you are—you have all the help you need and all the answers to your problems, if you will just allow your soul-self to take over and get your ego-self under control.

Fear is your greatest enemy, dear ones: fear of failure, fear of being unworthy, fear of not being loved or accepted, fear of the dark side and negativity that you think rules your world and fear of the unknown. Fear is the absence of wisdom and love of self. You have been controlled through fear and intimidation for thousands of years and have been enslaved by those fears. It is time to take back your sovereignty and dominion of your destiny. You may wish, dream, hope and envision all you want, but if you do not begin by reclaiming your **SOUL POWER,** by accepting the gifts offered you by the Creator through your Divine I AM Presence, none of your dreams or aspirations will come to fruition.

Remember what we have told you over and over: mentally

envision your greatest dreams, hopes and desires; add the fuel of excitement through your emotions as if your vision had already manifested; surrender your dreams to your Higher Self for the highest and best outcome, and then take action as you are led to do so. These are the basic rules of manifestation, and you must be sure that you include each portion of the formula in order to be successful.

I would also like to ease your mind and clear up another popular misconception. Many of you feel you cannot experience and enjoy all the earthly pleasures of the material world and still be spiritual or "ascend." Nothing could be further from the truth. You came in Spirit as cocreators of Earth. You then designed and assumed a physical vessel so that you could experience all the sensations of physicality. You helped create a most wondrous body which has the ability to register and experience a thousand different sensations. Now you either try to deny yourself the pleasure of physical sensation or you have become totally enslaved and addicted to the pleasures of the flesh.

The middle road or moderation is the answer, dear ones, and your perception or beliefs as to what is right or wrong. You have heard and it is true, Earth is a school and you are here to learn the lessons of the material plane. Do you expect a little one in the first grade of school to act the same or know what a high-school or college student knows? Do you see them as any lesser than or inferior to a student in an advanced grade? Indeed not. Hopefully, you treat them with patience, kindness and tolerance, knowing that their awareness will expand and grow with time and experience.

It is the same with matters of Spirit. None of you who resonate to my messages are novices or beginners at the game of life on Earth. But, you are at different stages and levels of awareness. You must pass through and experience each stage and facet of life on Earth and you should not judge yourself or others by any rigid formula or set of rules.

You experienced the freedom of Spirit many ages past, attuned to and are a part of nature and your Mother Earth— living off the land, hunting and gathering for your sustenance and shelter. You have lived in abject poverty and in opulent splendor, but many of you have not accepted in your consciousnesses the reality that all the beauty, bounty and abundance of the universe are yours for the asking and taking—the secret is you must feel worthy and you must hold your gifts lightly in your hands and allow the gifts to flow forth so they may be constantly replenished. So, my beloveds, do not judge those who seem to "have it all," or those who seem to have even their meager possessions taken from them, time and time again. They are just experiencing opposite sides of the same lesson.

You will finally "get it" when you feel worthy of all God's gifts, but are willing to surrender everything and everyone to the highest and best good or the Divine Plan. Can you not accept the absolute truth: your Father/Mother God want only the most wondrous, perfect life for you that is filled with beauty, peace, and love?

So build your own little paradise, my beloved ones. Create your version of Heaven on Earth and then share it and show others how it is done. Allow them to experience the peace and beauty of your Creation so they will know it is possible, and then help them to do the same: build it, enjoy it, share it and pass it on. That is how your Earth will gradually transform itself back into the beautiful Garden of E-Don.

We have spoken often about your body and your love/hate relationship with your physical vessel. Buried deep within your memory is a picture of the beauty and perfection of form you experienced when first on Earth. Many of you are obsessed with regaining that perfection, and your self-image and sense of self-worth are tied to having a youthful, perfect form. You are not your body, it is only one of the many vessels you have chosen to experience, and it will return to dust as your Spirit is released back into the higher dimensions. You will choose another body, if you return again to the school of Earth, and it will probably be very different, so that you may experience a variety of forms. Many wonderful old souls reside in crippled, deformed bodies (which they chose before incarnating in order to learn a certain lesson). There are many who have beautiful, near-perfect bodies, but are shallow in Spirit and misguided—they too are experiencing a different facet of expression.

I say to you, you chose the lessons you are experiencing in this lifetime. You chose the body and imperfections which you have manifested, so you could overcome or bring into harmony that which is out of balance in your auric field. You carry the memory of all your successes and failures encoded in your etheric body and there they will remain until, through conscious awareness and desire, you bring them back into harmony and balance with Spirit.

You look with envy upon those whom you envision as more advanced or more enlightened than you, but they are no better than you, dear ones. There will always be those a little further along the path, but there are also those who are following behind you, as well. You are most fortunate during these times of great change, for there are many wondrous Beings of Light who have chosen to be on Earth to guide and support humanity. They, too, are here to balance and harmonize that which needs to be rectified, so they may move forward on the path of ascension. They are your examples and teachers and are here to smooth the way for you, if you will allow them to do so. They have trod the same paths as you and experienced the same doubts, fear and pain, but they did not have the wisdom or guidance that is being offered to you.

Time is of the essence and we have made every effort to assist you through this accelerated metamorphosis. It is our greatest desire that as many of you as possible will be able to transcend out of the third dimension, through the fourth and into the fifth dimension with your Mother Earth. But this does not mean that you are to abdicate or turn your back on your earthly experiences or lessons. Make it your goal to balance your emotional nature by eliminating the roller coaster of emotions you experience in your everyday life. Be the observer and allow your Higher Self to assist you in bringing balance and harmony of Spirit into your life.

Begin to practice mind control, or the process of controlling and monitoring your thoughts. Eliminate the worry and fretting that most of you allow to dominate your thinking. Use affirmations to begin the process of reprogramming your subconscious mind and discipline your thought processes until it becomes automatic.

Allow yourself to experience something joyful every day. Give yourself a gift, however simple or small. Gaze at a beautiful cloud formation or listen to some soft, gentle music. Take a warm, fragrant bath and soothe your body with scented oil. Read an inspiring passage or with your consciousness, reach up and touch an angel. Treat yourself as the precious possession you are. Allow the gentle sweetness of your Spirit to emerge, if only for a moment. The wonder and beauty of who you really are may surprise you. We know and see it; why can't you?

So please, see the beauty and wonder of your world and partake of all it has to offer. Envision your dreams, manifest them, live them to the fullest and share them. Enjoy your relationships by loving yourself so much that your love will resonate out from you until it engulfs and surrounds all those around you. Enjoy your uniqueness and allow others to do the same. Know that you can possess no one, you can only share love.

When something happens that is painful or stressful, say to yourself, "This is a test and I will overcome." See only a positive outcome and know that you have the power of angels behind and beside you. You have come so far in such a short time, my brave warriors. Do not despair and do not give in. Take each moment as it comes—perfect that moment and live it the best you know how. That perfect moment then becomes a perfect minute, which builds a perfect day until, soon, you begin to experience the bliss and joy of harmony with Spirit. That is what ascension is all about: one thought, one deed, one expression of love and harmony at a time. I have spoken of the First Ray of Divine Will and Power and how it will gradually be reintroduced on Earth through those who are ready and capable of using this wondrous gift for the good of all. It matters not at what level you are currently expressing or experiencing. You must assume or take back your **SOUL (SOLAR) POWER.** This is the beginning of the reintegration of the virtues and attributes you were given before you came to planet Earth—much of which you gave away out of fear or was withdrawn from you because of misuse.

Once again, you must become a warrior of Light, assuming the responsibilities and gifts you will need to complete your mission.

We watch carefully as you move through the process of transformation, and as quickly as you bring yourself into harmony in any area of endeavor, we begin to enhance or add to your strengths, gifts and power. We are in this grand experiment together, beloved ones. Your triumphs are ours, but we do not see your failures as you do; we see them as steps along the way to success. Please know, beautiful friends, you are not judged. You are not punished, nor will you fail.

I bless you and love you from the depths of my Being. Please won't you love yourself the same? I AM Archangel Michael.

25. You Are Evolving into a State of "Being"

*B*eloved masters of Light, take just a moment to take an inventory of who you think you are and to objectively observe the world you have built around you. Is it a reality that seems to control you instead of you controlling it? Is it a world whereby you react instead of take action, where your physical senses and desires are dominant and take precedence, and where you seem to be tossed around by the whims of fate? If your answer is yes to any one of these questions, is it any wonder that you are feeling so dissatisfied and discontented?

No one or thing can escape the influence or impact of the Divine Energy that is pouring forth from the heart center of the galaxy. You cannot hide from it. You cannot ignore it—it has become too powerful and pervasive. Those who ignore this gift will find all their negative thoughts and emotions magnified and more intense—almost as if they are turning these energies inward upon themselves. Self-destructive impulses are more prevalent among the people of the world, as you surely have observed. The reason for this is that everyone is being stimulated to make a decision—to accept this cosmic infusion as a gift and begin to work with it, allowing the impacted energies within their Beings to be activated, stirred up and released back into neutral Light Substance.

Free will has never been more in force than it is now. For those who do not choose to work with these impulses or energies in a positive way, or choose to ignore them, all of the negativity within their physical, mental, emotional and etheric bodies will still be stirred up, but instead of being released and transmuted, they will experience chaos, both within and without. This will manifest as illness, puzzling symptoms that cannot be diagnosed, depression, great anger, frustration and, in extreme cases, acts of violence brought about by these energies being projected outwardly toward another or inward on themselves.

I spoke recently about the adversarial energies that are the focus for many of you at this time. To explain a bit further, know that these situations are being brought to your attention and into focus so that you may release any memories or impaction of negativity from within that resonate to these lower vibrations. If a situation is presented to you, seemingly from out of the blue, in which someone seeks to dominate or control you, or someone in your life seems to have radically changed their behavior all of a sudden, consider it a gift. Many of you will say, "Now, what have I done to draw this to me?" And you will move into fear or guilt.

Allow me to ease your mind, dear ones. If you will, become the observer when any of these situations are brought into your awareness. If you do not assume a defensive or adversarial stance; if you stand firm in your integrity and speak your spiritual truth as you perceive it without criticism or the need to dominate or control in return; if you will focus on the Christ center of that person (no matter how dim) and not their negative attributes; and if you allow them their beliefs, but do not take them as your own and just move past and beyond the event without allowing it to impact you in any way—then you will have passed the test.

Be self-assertive, not aggressive; learn to set boundaries for yourself and others. Become love-focused and compassionate, but do not allow others to dominate you, control you or take away your power. These adversarial dramas are presenting themselves so that, once and for all, you will emphatically take control of your own destiny without infringing on the destiny or self-awakening of another. However, if you get caught up in the drama and must react by assuming the old posture of self-defense or feel the need to launch a counter offense, then you will know there are still active energies within your Being that must be sought out and transmuted. As a spiritual warrior you will be confident, without deception, and soul-disciplined.

Many of you who are in contact with others on the path, either through counseling or association, are becoming aware of what is happening. Ripples of awareness are continually sweeping your Earth—specific frequencies of energy (not just indiscriminate infusions) are projected to you via the many Rays and Sub-Rays which carry precise combinations of energies having to do with many levels of awareness, both mental and emotional. As a focus is placed on a specific Ray or combination of Rays, it creates a very unique infusion to which each of you are susceptible. You are affected and react in accordance with your level of harmony or disharmony with that particular energy infusion.

This is why so many of you seem to be experiencing the same situations at the same time, the same emotional energies, the same awareness or turmoil. Those of you who resonate in harmony with others receive the beneficial energies of balance and joy that are incorporated and projected out into the etheric body of the Earth. Those who resonate with these infusions negatively also project them out into the astral planes, and they are magnified and picked up by others of like frequencies. Can you see why there is a great division occurring between those who are moving toward the Light and unity-consciousness, and those who are more and more ensnared in the painful illusion of separation, fear, guilt and suffering?

Very soon, I will speak more about using the First Ray of Divine Will, Power and Truth—the Ray of first cause—the will to create. However, at this time, I ask you to concentrate on releasing any residual energies from within that are keeping you from receiving this Divine Gift. Beloveds, please release the need to control or dominate another, either through persuasion or more aggressive means. Your truth is yours alone and you must release, once and for all, the need to change another, to sway them or remake them to fit your picture of reality.

Paradoxically, while it is a great time of coming together, a time of unity-consciousness, a time of remembering the "Oneness," it is also a very private, individual time of transformation, growth and reclaiming all the myriad parts of yourself. It is more important than ever before that you seek, with the assistance of your Divine Self, the forgiveness and resolution of all past infractions and infringements, both by you and toward you. It is as simple as turning inward and allowing your Divine Self to send forth healing energies to each party as you reclaim any energies you have projected and break any agreements you have made (past, present and future).

It is time to reclaim all the fragments of your soul-self, as well as time to forgive yourself and all others. You are not evil or bad, dear ones (and you never have been), you have just fallen short of the perfection of your own Divine Self (which is the true interpretation of "sin"). Have there not been days where you felt all was well with the world, and you were most pleased and satisfied with yourself and your accomplishments? Recapture that feeling and make it the norm instead of the exception. As you focus on what is "right" with you and about you, as well as what is right, loving and worthy about others, you will shift your attention from what is wrong, bad or limiting, thereby reinforcing the positive rather than the negative.

It is true, make no mistake, energies of love, devotion, joy, truth and thanksgiving are the food and nourishment of the angels and Beings of Light. Energies of hate, fear, guilt, control, despair, revenge and dominance are fuel for the negative forces of your Earth and beyond. Which are you helping to manifest, my precious friends?

I ask you, dear ones, to allow us of the higher realms to work with you most intensely during these times of great transition. Be receptive to our nudgings and allow your conscious mind to accept the vision we are trying to project to you. It is imperative that you relinquish those energies within your force field that are keeping you stuck—keeping you from moving to the next level of awareness. Is your ego more important than your divinity? Is pride keeping you from facing yourself and confronting those areas that need correction? Are you still comparing yourself to others—feeling guilty or inadequate when you fall short, or feeling superior or smug when you feel you are more advanced?

Precious ones, a true master does not have to demonstrate their mastery before others, they live it. They do not have to vocalize their level of awareness, they radiate it. They lovingly and quietly go about their mission and their work, leaving love, knowledge and words of empowerment behind. Oh, they may be very visible, if that is their mission, but they are always unassuming, patient, tolerant and willing to share words of love and encouragement wherever they go. By their works you will know them. By their actions they will demonstrate their power and purity.

You too are a teacher, you know. Yes indeed, each of you. Every day you teach by example, by your actions and by your every word. You teach as you learn, you receive as you give— you do not have to wait until you feel you are ready or perfect. You must live your spiritual truth and awareness each and every moment, at every opportunity. Each day is a lesson, a time of testing, maybe subtle, maybe very emphatic, but as you become attuned to Spirit and become what we call a "living meditation" you are always the observer, always in control. You garner the wisdom of a situation without getting caught up in the cause and effect. You do not act on impulse or react to a situation; you create the highest outcome for yourself and others. You speak quietly with discernment, and you keep your own counsel when it is appropriate by not feeding or fueling a situation which is not worthy of your attention.

Be bold enough to move beyond your present boundaries, out into the fullness of Spirit and mastery. The next 10 years will be years of miracles for those who are prepared, for those who are ready to function and operate from a focus of empowerment, love and unselfish service. Now is a time of becoming, dear ones, so that soon you will be ready to move into that state of **BEING,** whereby you will resonate, live and function as a master. You will focus away from self, for you will be the fullness and radiation of true Spirit, continually replenished and supplied with all blessed things. That is your goal, my beloved warriors, so that we may, once again, work together as we did in the past, recreating The Garden of E-Don—Heaven on Earth, where we will commune one with another and enjoy the fruits of our labor.

I surround and enfold you in an auric field of love and protection. I AM Archangel Michael.

26. ENDINGS AND BEGINNINGS

*B*eloved masters, please take a moment to still your mind and find a quiet corner or go into your sanctuaries so that you will not be disturbed as we meet once again. I treasure our time together, just as I sense that you do, and I wish it to become so real that you will feel we are sitting together, communing, interacting, expressing our great feelings of love for one another, reveling in the joyful reunion of Spirit that is taking place at all levels of consciousness.

A new era is on the horizon, and many important cycles of time and foretold events are coming to a culmination. You are only now beginning to perceive how massive and grand, how all-encompassing, this upward spiraling of the cosmos is and all that it entails. We have allowed this experiment on planet Earth to follow its own course for these many aeons—allowed humankind, through the gift of free will, to play havoc and bring devastation to Earth and all its inhabitants, but the time has come for intercession. It is a Divine Dispensation and essential if you are to join the march of all Creation as it begins its upward journey back toward perfection.

Many have spoken of the second coming of Christ, and we have told you before the true meaning of the term: it is the beaming or projection of pure Love/Light from the heart of the Supreme Creator. Down through the ages there have been many wondrous beings who came to Earth carrying a great measure of this Divine Light to show the way, to be beacons and examples for humanity. Now it is your turn to become a Christed Being. The second coming will be your grand event, your turn to reclaim your divinity.

Many of you have experienced what could be termed the crucifixion process, the dark night of the soul, as you painfully and laboriously released all that kept you prisoner in the third-dimensional illusion. Yet, with all you have been subjected to and experienced on your journey toward enlightenment, you must agree your sacrifice has been minor compared to what some of the beloved avatars have had to experience. You will not have to hang from a cross, but will integrate a pillar and cross of Light into your body, transforming you back into your radiance of perfection. You will not have nails driven in your hands and feet, but if you are ready and willing, I will pierce your hands and feet with diamond crystal pyramids of Light, so that wherever you walk you will leave footprints of Light, and whatever you touch will be permeated with healing Christ Light. Allow the Light of Divine Love to radiate from your eyes, beloved ones, and always speak words of truth and compassion. Become powerful in your integrity, masterful in your wisdom and dynamic in action. These are the characteristics and traits of a Christed Being. Your burden will be light if you allow the cloak of Spirit to surround and guide you each moment, of each day. You will be far-visioned, empowered and sure of each decision and action, for you will be inspired and directed by your magic I AM Presence.

Much fear and rage are being stirred up in humanity at this time, at all levels. The darkness within humanity is in its death throes and it will not let go or give up easily. At least, the purging of all that is not in harmony with the higher vibrations of the fourth dimension must be transmuted or released. Each turn of the spiral that accelerates the frequencies of the Earth is putting more and more pressure on those who are not willing to address or acknowledge the impacted energies from within, that are screaming for metamorphosis and integration.

By assuming your earthly garment of flesh, you have taught us much, dear ones. It is effortless to create when in Spirit form, while we now see how difficult it is to hold a pure focus and draw the cosmic energy of manifestation down through all the static and effluvia into the third or even fourth dimensions in order to create harmony and perfection. You have taught us much about emotions: we experience and resonate to the emotions of pure love, but we did not know the pain that ignites and fuels the emotional body in the lower densities when you are out of balance. We know you have been influenced, implanted, duped and misled by those you thought were gods, or at least benevolent beings, and we sense the fear that many of you have that this will happen again.

Let me assure you, my beloved faithful warriors, it will not be so. Those times are past; that is why we say it is time for us to intercede in the destiny of your beloved planet and assist you in moving back onto the path of integration and illumination.

Allow me to give you a new vision, greater access to your Divine Self and a more effective way to assist you in the creation of your bold, new paradise. It will be a different paradise this time, beloved ones. It was most wondrous in the beginning on this Garden of E-Don, but you were innocent and naive, new to the physical expression. Once more, it will be pristine and beautiful, but you will be wise, a seasoned veteran, an equal partner in making the decisions about the future of humanity at large, an active participant in the evolution of planet Earth.

We have given you the vision of bringing down from your Divine I AM Presence a great shaft of white Light, or a laser

beam of Light, and also a diamond crysta.
the energies of the five higher Rays to assis
formation process. This has also helped t.
way or connection between you, your Highe
Divine Self so that you are interacting more fi
nicating more easily as you draw forth and inco.   .ore
of the wisdom and power of your vaster Being.

Now I would like to make that connection even more powerful and real. Instead of envisioning the energies of your Divine Self coming down and merging with you, I would like you to envision the Essence of who you are lifting out of your body and traveling up that path of Light to connect with your Divine Self. Tap into the totality of this wondrous energy, not just a small projection of it; see yourself being bathed in the radiance and magnificence of who you truly are.

After you get the feel and the validity of this action, you can begin to use this powerhouse of energy to help you in all your endeavors and to assist you in assuming your rightful heritage as a master of cocreation. Place any situation or anything that you wish to create, transform or balance in a diamond crystal pyramid, then sense yourself move up the pathway to join your Divine Self. Now see a great fountain of sparkling, golden dust—the transmuting energy of the Twelfth Ray that is bringing forth the gift of Christ-consciousness from the Father/Mother Creator of this universe—pouring forth from your Divine Self, as well as from the core of your Being. See everyone connected to the situation in a circle around the pyramid in which it is enclosed and see this sacred transforming energy permeating each person and problem, bringing all into balance and harmony.

herever there is a glimmer of hope, it will expand and grow; wherever there is a desire or yearning for love, it will be magnified; wherever there is the smallest reaching out for unity and resolution, it will facilitate and help bring it to fruition. But remember, it must be your desire that the outcome be for the highest good of all and in harmony with your Divine Blueprint or Mission. By joining forces with your Divine Self, you no longer surrender to it, you become it. This is the next step, dear ones. Are you ready to assume this awesome power? All you have to do is believe, to dare, and then to claim your birthright.

Beloved ones, you are approaching the time of accelerated activation, of heightened and expanded senses, of reclaiming your sovereignty and of taking dominion and control of your destiny. We have watched you carefully to see if you are ready to reintegrate the power of the First Cause to create: to have singleness of purpose, clear vision and the desire to use this dynamic energy for the good of all. Some are calling this energy the Royal Ray, the Ray of Sovereignty. And it is, indeed, the Ray of rulers, leaders, spiritual warriors and those ready to step to the fore. It is the energy of vitality, initiative and action, and it is needed at this time to break down the old, antiquated ways and make way for the new.

What is being initiated is the integration of the fiery, blazing-red energy of pure creation, Divine Will and Power, tempered by the strength and thrust of blue steel, with a core of pure white which represents purity, truth and honor. It will be magenta in color, and will blaze forth into the bodies of those ready for this dynamic gift—creating brave hearts, bold warriors of Light who will lead in the reunification and transformation of this Earth back into its sovereign status: a peaceful Earth of Spiritkind in human form—all equal and sacred.

Examine your heart and intentions. Are you ready to, once again, assume the responsibility and power of this awesome gift? You used it most dramatically and effectively in those first great Golden Ages, until humanity shifted its consciousness to ego-gratification and a desire to conquer and dominate. It is a two-edged sword, beloved ones. When you accept this gift you must use it wisely, or it will turn on you and bring about your destruction. Never again will humanity be allowed to use this Ray for selfish purposes. If you are willing to take this next giant leap, we will be right beside you to smooth the way.

We bless you for your faithfulness and honor you for your bravery. You are greatly loved. I AM Archangel Michael.

27. It Is Time for Tolerance and Forgiveness

*B*eloved masters of Light, there is a grand reunion taking place on your Earth. Can you not sense the change? That which separated so long ago, splitting into prisms of Light and energy to experience the great diversity of physical manifestation, is once again rejoining, coming together. You, those prisms of Light, as well as every living, sentient thing in this solar system and galaxy are now seeking, reaching out to reconnect with all the myriad parts of yourself in order to return to wholeness. It is a time to unify, not separate; a time to refine that which is uniquely you; a time to reclaim your perfect Divine Blueprint.

You are different than when you first merged with your physical body. You have gained much experience, many battle scars, and taken on imperfections which diminished your ability to cocreate in harmony and beauty. It is time to heal the imperfections, release the memories of pain and suffering you have experienced and claim victory. Only you can decide whether you will join the march toward unification and integration of humankind and Spiritkind—it will proceed at an ever-accelerating pace with or without you.

More and more of you are bringing forth memories and visions that capture your imagination and stir the soul. Memories of how it was in the beginning; visions of your origins, your home out among the vast beyond; a yearning or awareness of what you have lost; and an intense desire to reintegrate into wholeness and full awareness.

Are you able to look at a stranger and sense a comradeship, a commonality, regardless of color, race, religion or cultural differences? Are you more tolerant, patient and compassionate with those around you, sensing their beauty instead of their imperfections? All around the world people are beginning to perceive differently; hope is surging forth to overshadow the frustration and sense of futility.

The rarified Christ Light from the Great Central Sun is beginning to make a remarkable impact upon the people of the Earth. It is a time of tolerance and forgiveness. It is time to release all past painful memories, resentments and judgments that hold you prisoner in a time capsule of third-dimensional illusion.

Do not allow self-righteous indignation to keep you from returning, with love, the negative energies others have projected to you. Do not allow guilt, a sense of shame or the need to inflict self-punishment to keep you from forgiving yourself for all past infractions, all misdeeds or imperfections. To forgive yourself is always the most difficult task.

Many sudden, dramatic events are taking place for each of you. Sometimes these are startling events that change the course of your life, or profoundly change your perception of reality. Look around, dear ones; the change of the Ages is upon you. Bless, nurture and support the blessed souls who chose to transcend into the realm of true reality, leaving the perishable physical vessel behind. They are only lost to you if you cut yourself off from them through misdirected doubt and beliefs or grief. The bridge between worlds is more accessible and the veil between dimensions is thinning rapidly.

Those still functioning in a state of fear or those caught up and controlled by their lower instinctual natures are frantically trying to maintain the status quo—trying futilely to protect their perceived domains. The old rules no longer apply. And, the old methods of operation are no longer effective. That which is built on greed or selfish interests and that which abuses Universal Laws will crumble into dust. You do not have to forcefully participate in the bringing about of their demise; the energies of the new consciousness of the Earth and humanity as a whole will effectively achieve the task. Your duty, beloved warriors, is to live your own truth with integrity, discernment and discretion.

We are most gratified to see some of the religious community coming together to discuss spiritual philosophies and concepts without accusing, blaming or ridiculing those with opposing views. There is a tolerance creeping into the minds of previously rigid and unbending spiritual leaders. Boundaries of dogma and superstition are being dissolved and a new broader viewpoint is becoming acceptable.

You, as spiritual representatives of the Creator, must be allowed to decide for yourselves what are your truths. You must be allowed to determine how you will worship and fulfill your stewardship. Those who still strive to hold you in their grip through fear and guilt are losing their effectiveness, and rightly so. The Creator manifests through freedom, joy, love and beauty. The Creator did not impose suffering, limitation and pain upon you—you brought that about yourselves.

It is time to get down to the real work at hand, my beloved warriors. You have been excited and stirred by the knowledge that ascension is a gift and a possibility for all of you in this lifetime. You have been encouraged and inspired by the vision of mastery—accessing the Universal Laws of manifestation and creating a paradise here on Earth. You are becoming comfortable with the concept that we are real and can interact one with another, that you have access to higher and higher dimensions while still in the physical body. Now it is time to use the gifts for which you have worked so diligently. You will not be allowed to sit back and rest on your laurels or settle for a semi-ascended state. The time for coasting or vacillating is over. You have given dominion to your Spirit Self and it will guide you, nudge you or push you, but you will eventually move forward. Why not allow us to help you make the transition with ease and grace, dear ones?

The reason that tolerance, forgiveness and compassion are so important now is that we are anxious to infuse the Earth with the more powerful energies of higher Creation. It is time to bring forth, once more, the First Ray of Divine Will, the will to create and take dominion. This Divine Energy is needed to reclaim dominion of the Earth for those who walk in Light, the path of loving Creation for the good of all, not the path of greed and oppression. Those who are capable of wielding this magnificent energy of the "first cause" will be the new leaders of the world: the visionaries, the guardians and the servers. They will be the ones who will lead, build, create and serve with love and compassion, always in harmony and accordance with Divine Will. This is when the boundaries and borders will fade, when cultural and spiritual differences will be honored (not scorned or condemned), when all people and all life on Earth will be treasured as a gift of Creation, precious in the sight of everyone.

Many of you are becoming aware that your surroundings, the areas in which you live, are changing. Energies are shifting and refining—a cleansing is taking place. Those beautiful etheric cities and Light communities we have been speaking of for so long are becoming more and more a reality. True, you can not see the beauty or vastness of what is being prepared for the future of humanity on Earth, but you are beginning to feel and sense a difference.

More and more of you will be led to experience different places and energies around the Earth ... your world is becoming smaller in many ways, dear ones. Take the opportunity to sample as many cultures and lifestyles as possible. Connect with the Earth and its history, healing and refining the past with your love and compassion. The more you learn about the Earth and its inhabitants, the more you will see a commonality, a unity, a oneness. Each area resonates with its own unique vibrations, has its own memories, gifts to offer and lessons to teach you.

There are areas around the world that have not been so impacted by negativity or that have not moved so far out of harmony with the Devic and Elemental Kingdoms. These areas are scattered around the world and are noticeable because of the pristine beauty of nature and the unity and tolerance in which the people live together. There are places on your Earth where many cultures live as neighbors, work together and worship beside each other. You will recognize these areas by the beauty of nature, by the lack of barriers and boundaries, by the compatibility and the sense of comradery among the inhabitants.

Fear and greed build fences, barriers and boundaries—structures that end up being prisons. Love dissolves boundaries, expands horizons and allows freedom and unity to prevail.

In preparation for the great infusion of fiery energy that will be available to you in the coming years, I ask you to make a concerted effort to cleanse and harmonize your mental, emotional and physical vessels. Initiate an exorcism of sorts, if you are willing, by allowing yourself to be infused with the rarified energies of the five higher Rays, thereby stirring up and releasing any impacted energies that are not compatible with your newly empowered state. Many of you have for-given others and come to terms with your past, but you still harbor feelings of doubt—a sense of not belonging to the old world—and are still not comfortable or finding a place in the new world you are creating. Allow these blessed energies to permeate your body to its very depths, healing, harmonizing, balancing and attuning you to the higher visions of tomorrow. See a crystalline shower of sparkling, diamond pyramids per-meating your body throughout, down to the deepest cellular level. Then see a sparkling shower of golden energy pouring forth from the highest source of this universe, reconnecting you to that Source from whence you came. This is the path home, beloved ones.

Take stock of your world; what is still out of balance? Lov-ingly direct your attention to that area, not in resistance, but focusing a sense of attunement and refinement on that which you wish to change, thereby gently guiding and nur-turing yourself toward perfection.

It is a time for action, dear ones; the time of preparation for many of you is coming to a culmination. You are being nudged out into the great arena of life as examples, teach-ers, leaders, indeed, Wayshowers of Light.

We encourage you to begin where you are, faithful war-riors, teaching, living, expressing your new wisdom, your reactivated, reclaimed divinity. You are masters-becoming, you are shedding your disguises and assuming your true iden-tity and your rightful heritage. The Earth and beyond are now your domain, the barriers and boundaries between di-mensions and space are being dissolved. Lay claim to your new kingdom, my beloved ones. Let us reign together for the glory of our Father/Mother Creator. I AM Archangel Michael.

28. WE ARE IN THE MIDST OF A "COSMIC MOMENT"

*B*eloved masters, we are all in the midst of a "cosmic moment," a most powerful and wondrous time of change. Beginning in your year 1995, it was determined that your Earth could incorporate a greater level of cosmic energy without creating too much destruction and havoc within your mother planet's structure. After much deliberation, it was also decided that there were enough awakened Light workers, and humanity at large, who had lifted their consciousness to a level where we could safely begin an accelerated infusion of Universal Light Substance—or the rarified cosmic energy from the Creator Source.

The acceleration has been steadily increasing since that time and will continue to increase over the next decade and beyond. Now being activated, both within the Earth and in the physical structure of all humanity, are Light energy packets of information, keys and codes which were placed there aeons ago. They were placed there in anticipation of this time: when you would reverse the process of your descent into the physical and begin the journey back into the realms of Spirit.

It is of the greatest importance that as many as possible are made aware of what is occurring at this very critical time within your physical structures and within the Earth, as well. It is imperative that this vital flow of Divine Energy that is being gifted to humanity and your planet is allowed to flow through you and throughout the ley-line structure of your Earth. As it flows through your physical vessels, it ignites the dormant encodings and Light packets within your cellular structures. Within each of you are also keys and codes needed to activate, purify and ignite the great crystalline structures within your Earth. These portals or gateways make up the chakra system of the Earth, you might say, and as they are activated, the awakening of your Mother Earth will also be greatly accelerated. She will begin to hum with an intensity all of you will sense, as she stirs and lifts herself out of the density back into the Light of Illumination and her true state—the fifth dimension.

As these great energy sources begin to resonate and send out signals once more, the full measure and power of Universal Life Force will begin to pour forth the frequencies necessary to activate the geometric codes and impulses needed for the next level of evolution for you, your planet, solar system and galaxy.

That is why it is so critical that you purify your physical vessel so that the frequencies you relay into the Earth, and then later on, back out into the higher dimensions, will be uncontaminated, refined, and resonate with the highest integrity. What is happening can be likened to humanity and the Earth being plugged into a new, high-resonance power source. You must be attuned to and compatible with this source in order to accommodate and make use of it. You are functioning as the conductor or transducer for this dynamic energy, allowing yourselves to be the energy conveyer for your Mother Earth. She, in turn, activates her own power sources (the great crystal structures within her body), and as these great Beings burst into conscious awareness once more, they begin to send out pulsations of new frequencies—purifying, uplifting, healing energies throughout the Earth's system, and to humanity, as well. You might say, you are being "zapped" from within and from without.

That is why it is so important that you make your physical

vessel ready for, and receptive to, this new influx of energy, especially that of the First Ray of Divine Will and Power and the Seventh Ray of Transmutation and Transformation. As you do so, you become the catalysts for igniting these power centers. With your gentle, loving hearts you will soothe and heal; with your wisdom you will guide and lead; with your power you will stand in your integrity, and you will not let up until the task is complete.

You are in the midst of what might be called the Armageddon/apocalypse/ascension process. As many have predicted and hoped, you will not be lifted off the Earth and out of the chaos you have created on your blessed planet. Each one of you is being forced to face your own illusions, the reality you have formed which creates your own special version of Heaven or hell on Earth. All of what you thought was your truth, all the judgments you have made about good or bad, right or wrong, holy or evil, are cropping up in your everyday situations and circumstances so that, once and for all, you can move into a new, expanded awareness—that of a master. Please listen and take heed, beloved ones; there are many shades of truth, and many paths, but only one destination—back into unity-consciousness with the Beings of Light and the Divine Creator.

Removing old habits and thought patterns from the subconscious mind is no easy matter. Clearing the past involves clearing more than your current lifetime memories; it means balancing and harmonizing all your experiences since incarnating on the physical plane. These memories are all stamped and recorded in your auric field, creating peace and joy, or fear and discord. To clear means to balance and harmonize that which resonates at a discordant level of energy; it means to come to an understanding of and be at peace with all the facets of your existence. Once you have reached that point, the imbalanced energies are forever transmuted and you will not have to experience them again.

The good news is that the process of ascension has been refined, made easier and available to all. Once you are willing to listen to the nudgings of your soul, allowing the new frequencies to infiltrate into your four lower body systems, you become more objective and receptive to new thought patterns. Then it becomes much easier to let go of old fear patterns, the guilt and restrictions in which the ego has held you captive.

In the past, your Higher Self had difficulty getting your attention in order to assist you. It usually took a jolt of some kind, and most often it was not a pleasant experience. Those times are past, beloveds; it will become increasingly difficult to ignore the nudgings of your soul or Higher Self as the veil of forgetfulness is removed and you begin to remember or, at least, feel a "Divine Inner Discontent."

All facets of your Being are resonating to the changes taking place—your emotional body can no longer stand the chaos and disharmony that were once tolerated when it was numb and disconnected from your inner awareness. Your mental body may still be struggling to hang on to outmoded, seemingly safe belief systems, but it is being bombarded with too much new information which either nullifies or shatters old paradigms or moves you into a more expanded point of view where you begin to see events in your life differently. You are no longer fearful of change—you begin to "go with the flow."

Your body is also caught up in the struggle; it is functioning within the constraints of thousands of years of negative input, which manifests as suffering, pain, ill health and death. It, too, is reaching for the healing frequencies of Light, and nothing can stop the penetration of this Divine Life-giving Substance into everyone and everything on Earth. The pain and frustration come to those who resist, who fear, who are not willing to let go of the past or their third-dimensional reality. They will be constantly bombarded until they make the choice to accept the gift of ascension into conscious awareness, or their Spirit Self will see that they make their transition into another realm and another planet of illusion to continue their journey toward enlightenment. The next few years are years of decision, dear ones. What will be your choice?

Now, I would like to clear up an important issue at this time, before I leave you. Many of you are attuning to and focusing on the angelic realms and the archangels in par-ticular as the saviors and the salvation of the world. Beloved ones, please be aware, this is a unified endeavor. We are work-ing in harmony with all the great Beings of this universe, many of which you have heard of or are familiar with, but there are many more Divine Beings of which you are not aware. Just as you are all needed, no matter what your level of awareness, so it is with the higher realms. Every Being throughout the Omniverse has an integral part to play in this grand drama that is so swiftly unfolding, with the Earth as a major focal point.

We of the angelic realms are functioning in the capacity of a transition team, you might say. We are the messengers of the Creator, and in times of great transition we are sent out as the advance guard to relay and transmit the thoughts of the God Mind to all of you in a way you can understand, in a way that is acceptable to every race, religion and culture.

We have always had an intimate relationship with humanity, but you have been at a slumber and could not easily tap into our refined frequencies. We have always assisted you and protected you in whatever way was available to us, or was permissible within the laws of free will, but because of the density of your Earth and your own auric field, you were hardly ever aware of our presence.

And so, beloved ones, call on us and we will answer and assist you, but also maintain or strengthen your relationship with whatever avatar, Christ Being, or ascended master you relate to and resonate with. We know we all have an integral part to play in this grand scheme, and we always work in harmony and synchronicity with each other, just as we are endeavoring to teach you to do.

Do not fear the future, my brave warriors, do not resist the changes that are upon you. Know that what is transpiring is only for your highest good, and will release you from the shackles of enslavement into the realm of all possibilities. It is time for you, the warriors of Light and the champions of truth, to step to the fore—to stand and be acknowledged as Divine Caretakers and Guardians of the Earth, and as healers and Wayshowers for humanity.

We are asking you to remember your heritage, to reclaim the power and perfection of Spirit and physical form which you expressed and manifested when first coming to planet Earth. It is your natural state, beloved, faithful ones. **IT IS TIME—RECLAIM IT!** I AM Archangel Michael.

29. ACCEPT YOUR SWORD OF POWER
AND CLOAK OF RESPONSIBILITY

*B*eloved masters of Light, I welcome the opportunity to once again blend with your consciousness, to fill your heart and soul with love and inspiration and to apprize you of what has transpired since we last met. My desire is that you begin to sense and know that through these messages I am truly with you, that with your permission, I will connect with your Higher Self and merge my energy with yours at whatever level you are able to accommodate.

My beloved messenger has just returned from an adventure into the fifth and even higher dimensions, a most sacred experience and blessed event called the WESAK Festival (April 1997), at Mt. Shasta, California, USA. It was a time of harmony, joy and blending of energies, and a time of great transformation at the deepest, innermost core level. It was a time when many layers of negative energy were dissolved; energies that had been placed around the heart in times past to protect and insulate your emotional and physical bodies from the pain and suffering of the third dimension. The floodgates of the emotional body burst open as these energies were dissolved and the precious gift of the Holy Spirit was once again allowed to take up residency within the heart/soul chamber.

There were Starseed representatives from all over the world in attendance and these blessed Beings carried the seeds of a new awareness with them as they returned to their homes. And make no mistake, those of you who tapped into this wonderful energy from On High in your own locale or at other gatherings were also gifted with an infusion of refined Christ Energy. You were attuned at a higher dimensional level where there is no time or space restrictions or barriers—all were brought to a Oneness in Spirit. All communed with the masters and received a blessing from the Creator. Indeed, the Earth to its very core was bathed in a glorious blanket of Divine Light Substance and every creature was blessed and acknowledged. All are on the path of evolution and transcendence, none is being left behind.

I have encouraged my messenger to share her odyssey, her journey and experiences along the path of awakening. It is important that you all become aware that those who have been thrust out into the limelight or into the public arena are no different than you. Yes, they are special, unique and blessed: but so are you, each and every one of you. They each have experienced the trials and tests of initiation and walked the dark night of the soul into the Light of Illumination. The one trait they all share is their tenacity—no matter how painful the experience, how alone they felt, or how bleak the future seemed to be, they NEVER GAVE UP. They persevered and they overcame until they emerged triumphant into unity and harmony with Spirit and accepted their Divine Mission.

Many of you have integrated a higher awareness. You are accessing new wisdom and feeling a sense of harmony within your innermost self. However, you still have doubts and are reticent to share your insights with others as you fear that you will make a spectacle of yourself, or that you will be ridiculed if you try to pass on what you have learned. There is a Universal Law that states you must not only be an example of your new enlightened state, but you must pass on the wisdom and understanding you have garnered so that you may move upward to the next level. You are a student on the path of initiation, you are a practitioner of spiritual mastery and cocreation, and you are also a teacher with a message to share.

I would like to address another topic for your contemplation at this time and that is a clarification as to how to integrate the higher, beneficial energies of Spirit and how to break the lower energies of negativity that you are striving to release and transform. It is a custom in your third-dimensional reality to honor or pay homage to performers, speakers or entertainers by applauding their presentations. This holds true for spiritual gatherings as well, even after a moving meditation or the bringing forth of great infusions of energy from the higher dimensions. The clapping of hands or loud expulsions of sound is very effective in breaking and releasing negative energy, but it scatters or dissipates the flow of higher energy infusions, as well. It would be much more beneficial if you would lift your arms with palms forward and send love and gratitude to the presenter, thereby radiating an infusion of Spiritual energy through your heart center which will magnify and circulate throughout the room to benefit all in attendance.

Many of the thought forms, habits, cultural taboos, conditioned responses and accepted behavior patterns are being modified and changed. Many practices of the old reality will be looked back on as barbaric and will be seen for what they are: teachings of the unenlightened masses to control, dominate, enslave and conquer.

We are asking you to be bold, innovative, and to step out from behind the shield of mediocrity—a pioneer who dares to be different. This is one of the many facets and phases in the process of accepting and wielding your power, beloved ones. It is easy to follow the masses, to stay within the structure of popular and accepted beliefs, the boundaries and rules set forth by those who have been in control these past ages. Their rule is ending, their power is waning, their day of dominance is coming to a close.

Therefore it is imperative that there be masters of Light, warriors of Spirit, ready to step into a leadership role and take dominion—those who are ready and willing to guide and direct, to hold the focus of the new vision, the new plan for Heaven and Earth, and to see that it is manifested for the highest good of all. You all have an integral part to play. No longer will you be able to abdicate your authority or meekly follow where others lead you. You must take an active part and play the role you were assigned by your Divine Self in order to accomplish that which will be your gift and contribution to the whole.

Remember, my brave warriors, you must draw your cloak of invincibility around you, you must strengthen your resolve and raise your consciousness above the barbs, seeds of doubt and criticism that will be projected toward you. As the masses stir and the chasm between the third-, fourth- and fifth-dimensional awareness widens, the energies of resistance, resentment, and rebellion will be spewed forth by those still in the grip of a third-dimensional reality. They will experience great fear of the changes taking place. They will resent being pushed out of their comfort zone, even if it is a reality of limitation and suffering. They will attempt to discredit and malign you, but you must not waver. You must stand in your integrity, not judging, but radiating loving energy toward all, and take the stance of a master by blessing them and moving on to more fertile fields.

You must not try to change their minds, but teach by your example, speaking your truth at their level of understanding and telling them that there are many paths back to the Oneness of the Creator. Be gentle (but strong in your convictions), compassionate (but do not get caught up in their drama or small story of woe), and stay joyful and enthusiastic so they will begin to wonder what makes you so different. Indeed, they will notice and wonder, and some day they will take heed, for you will have sown the seeds of change within their auric field and hearts. These seeds will not be denied—they will flourish one day as they burst forth and bloom into a Divine Discontent that will nudge them onto the path of discipleship.

And so, beloved masters, I wish to gift you this day with a greater infusion of the mighty First Ray of Divine Power, Will and Authority in preparation for the challenges in the days to come. The time is now, it has begun—that which you have dreamed of, yearned and prepared for from the deepest level of your Being. No longer do you have to exist on faith, hopes and wishes—the proof and substance of humanity's evolution into a higher state of awareness is apparent at some level in everyone and everything on your Earth.

You are learning your lessons well, my sweet friends, and you are well on your way to harnessing your ego-self and bringing it into alignment with your Higher Self. You are endeavoring to govern your thoughts and keep your emotions on an even keel. You have learned that pure love must originate in the wellspring of the heart and it must first encompass self before it can radiate out as a blessed gift to others. You are making great strides at becoming nonjudgmental and objective, as you allow events and interactions with others to flow around you, and you comprehend the wisdom that is to be derived from the moment. You are beginning to sense the serenity and magic of the higher dimensions as you weave in and out of the different levels and frequencies of consciousness.

Yes, there are still many lessons to be learned, and there always will be, but you now have the insight to see the justice and perfection in the dance and drama of life that you experience each day. You are being prepared to take a giant leap forward, beloveds. The time has come for you to take your proper place in this great event: **The Ascension of Earth and Humankind.** Your Light quotient is blazing forth and as it connects with that of other en-LIGHT-ened Beings, it gains strength and momentum, permeating and infusing the Golden Etheric Web of your home planet. You are all moving up to the next rung of the ladder, and into a leadership position as humanity begins to awaken and steps onto the path of initiation.

I sense the doubt and hesitation in some of you as your ego throws blockages of fear and inadequacy into your mind. "What can I do? How can I serve? What do I have to offer?" I hear that small voice of ego whisper within. I tell you, you cannot be faint of heart or timid in Spirit, for the next step on your path toward full mastery is to take dominion of your world, to step forward with courage and determination and reclaim your Divine Heritage. It is waiting for you, my brave warriors, but you must draw forth from the Universal Light Substance the energy that you will use to mold and create your wondrous new world as you become the catalyst and director of your future. You must infuse your vision with emotions of excitement and daring. You must be bold and courageous as you go against the tide of commonality and move out from beneath the stranglehold of mass-consciousness. You must speak words that resonate with the vibrations of success, and you must bear the stance and take the actions of a triumphant winner. You must dare to risk your all as you prove to yourself that when you are in harmony with Spirit, whatever you give freely, with loving intent, will be returned tenfold.

Now, more than ever, you have the tools of manifestation at your fingertips. You must step out of your comfort zone and release all that no longer serves you. You all know where this applies—it has been staring you in the face for months and even years, and will become even more unbearable until you finally relent and release that which is holding you back.

Beloved ones, I offer you that which was withdrawn from you so long ago, that which you have yearned for from the depths of your Being, that which will reestablish your connection with the energies of Creation of the First Ray of Divine Will, Power, Truth and Valor. The veil of forgetfulness is rapidly being lifted and it is our desire that you regain, as quickly as possible, that crown of radiance that is symbolized so beautifully by your great Statue of Liberty. As you integrate and ignite each of the aspects and attributes of the seven great Rays and then progress and claim the five higher Rays of Illumination that are being extended to you, this blazing crown will blaze once again from your brow and you will be forever recognized as a Divine Being, a warrior in my Legions of Light.

I am honored to be a protector of the innocent and a bearer of the Creator Truth. Won't you join me as a standard bearer in this, the advanced phase of expression and learning on planet Earth, as you prepare to move back into the realms of higher consciousness and reclaim your Divine Birthright? Reach outward, beloved ones; reach inward as well. We are waiting to shower upon you all the love and gifts from the Creator that you can absorb. I AM Archangel Michael.

30. SEEDS OF REMEMBRANCE

*B*eloved masters, let us continue our lessons in mind and heart refinement, moving your consciousness beyond a linear, time/space reality to an expanded, yet internal, way of self-expression and viewing your everyday world. First of all, focus on your heart center and feel a warmth begin to build as you ignite and activate the Spark of Creation that dwells within. Sense the love that radiates and fills your physical vessel. This is the fuel and Essence which will revitalize and perfect your bodily form, and will be the catalyst for the miracles that will transform your world, Beloveds.

I have spoken of seed crystals and how many of you had these jewels of Creation implanted within your etheric bodies before you were sent down through the dimensions to join in the game of spiritual/physical expression on planet Earth. These seed crystals carry the keys and codes, the energies, the memories and knowledge of your particular mission and the part which you were to play. You bravely journeyed out into the void—the great beyond—seemingly disconnected and separated from your wondrous Self, so that you could create and express in your own unique way. It has been a journey of joy and wonder, pain and suffering, magnificent successes and devastating failures, but those times are coming to a close, a culmination. The time of living a life of separation (even when surrounded by multitudes), of seeing yourself as apart from others, is being replaced by a unity-consciousness, a coming together, a merging and blending of energies, strengths and wisdom.

Pause for a moment and feel the power and love flow through and around your body as it expands out into the room and down into the Earth, as well. Now, shift your

focus to your brow, or third eye, and sense or imagine a shaft of Light penetrating into the middle portion of your brain. Use all your senses as you move your consciousness into the center of your brain structure—you may have a slight metal taste on your tongue or a slight aroma may tease your olfactory receptors; you may feel an expansion in your head as if a subtle force was expanding it from the inside. Move your awareness into that center space, see if you can feel your skull from the inside—do not strain, there is no right or wrong way to accomplish this. Allow this shift to happen naturally, as if you are now a small, concentrated Spark floating in an expanded sea of consciousness.

Become aware of the serenity and sense of freedom this brings, and how the boundaries of your bodily structure seem to fall away. Sense the energy radiating out from your body as it purifies and expands your auric field, harmonizing and balancing. Spend a few moments, or longer if you wish, to experiment and validate this new connection with Self. When you are ready to proceed, float your consciousness throughout your brain structure until you feel a slight pressure; gently probe that spot and if you feel a sensation in your heart center (a subtle pressure or emotional response) give yourself permission to move into that space. You are connecting to a light packet or jewel of wisdom, an encoding of sacred geometry, or formula that holds the keys and codes to your mastery and your mission.

As you tap into this powerhouse of wisdom, it enhances and speeds up the transformation of your molecular structure and the ability to transmute and balance the negative energies within. In addition, like a radio beacon, you begin to transmit high frequency vibrations which attract those who are also beginning to access and integrate these rarified, refined frequencies. You will act as a catalyst for each other as you enhance and accelerate the release of this expanded knowledge, energy and Light. Herein lies the memories of your origins and abilities, your gifts and your blessed mission. Herein lies the blueprint and formula for the wondrous future of your planet and humanity, and your particular part in the grand design.

Miraculously, you will begin to come together, to be reunited with groups and souls from whom you were separated aeons ago. Your sense of aloneness will disappear as you regain your sense of unity and Oneness. You will add to and complement the talents and gifts of those around you, as they will enhance and strengthen your abilities and wisdom. You will spark and activate the keys and codes within each other as you come together to work, play and fulfill your mission.

Each of you contributes your refined knowledge and experience as you assist each other to heal, purify and integrate your wondrous Light bodies and accept your mastery. You will then be directed to the next level of integration as you become aware that an important part of your mission is to assist your planet in activating the keys, codes and powerhouses of energy that reside within her body. As I explained previously, at the time your beloved Mother Earth was formed, there were great crystalline sentient Beings placed deep within her structure (including a magnificent crystal core), in which the Divine Blueprint for the planet and all humanity from the beginning to the end of time was encoded.

Now, I have explained how many of these great energy centers were shut down as the Earth and humanity sank into density. Only a few major centers were left to radiate the

Light and information to and from the higher realms. These centers became polluted, dense and distorted over time, creating cities of darkness instead of cities of Light. Over the past 20 or so years we, with your assistance as the anchors and transducers of Light, have gradually made progress in clearing and healing these beacons within the Earth, which in turn has helped in cleansing, balancing and refining the ley lines and etheric web of your planet.

It is time for the next step in the grand scheme of transformation. It is time to activate all the dormant power structures within the Earth which harbor the keys and codes, the information and formulas for the ascension of your planet, and all those who are capable of attuning to her accelerated resonance and accompanying her on this "Journey of the Ages."

We are in a time of accelerated growth, an expansion of consciousness and attunement to the refined wisdom of Creator truth. Just as you have focused on the healing and balancing of your bodily structure and activating and harmonizing your chakra system, it is imperative that you now assist your blessed planet to do the same. Your Earth and solar system are gradually coming into alignment with the heart center of your galaxy and the Great Central Sun. You are activating and purifying your own soul (Solar) heart in preparation for the blossoming and bursting forth of your own son/daughter (Sun) ship. The world as you know it has supported and nurtured you throughout the Ages. Now it is your turn to assist and support her in her time of rebirth and renewal.

Your attention and focus will be drawn to different parts of the Earth. You will feel a call and yearning to return to specific places where your memories are buried and where a critical Spark of Divine Energy that you carry within, when joined with others of like resonance, will assist in the activation or healing of the collective consciousness. You will unlock the sacred codes which will fire and fuel these great structures that have lain dormant for so many ages, as they once again begin to receive and transmit the instructions and directions from your Father/Mother Creator in the Great Central Sun.

It is time to heal the ancient memories of pain, failure, abandonment, rejection and betrayal from your experiences in Lemuria and Atlantis. Forgive yourselves for misusing the gifts of power, abundance and cocreation. It is long past time for you to remember that you came to Earth to manifest and experience the physical plane of duality. Are you aware that as you heal your past and realize that you are not judged for your mistakes or misdirected energies, you are refining, balancing and healing the ancient frequencies (memories) of humanity and your Earth? In truth, you do not have to forgive yourselves or anyone else, or ask for forgiveness. For, there is nothing to forgive, but in your present state of awareness, to do so assists you to begin the process of harmony consciousness. Most of you are not yet ready to see and accept that there is nothing you have ever done or can do that the Creator will pass judgment on as "bad" or "evil." True, you have operated under and been subject to the laws of cause and effect or Karma, but you have never been judged or seen as anything less than perfect. It is time to accept that perfection, beloved ones, to stop punishing yourselves.

There will be an increased emphasis on coming together to create a force field of cosmic transformational energy, as you begin to project the unified concentration of Solar Power

(First Ray energy) you are building within. One of those times will be the tenth anniversary of your event called the Harmonic Convergence that occurred in August of 1987 when your Sun began to align with the center of the Milky Way Galaxy, or the galactic equator, and the impulses from the Great Central Sun began to pour down upon Earth and humanity. You all are very aware of what has transpired since that time and, my beloved warriors, if you think there have been miraculous changes since then, we say to you, you haven't seen anything yet.

Just as many beloved Beings have felt the pull and urgency to journey to and experience various sacred sites, holy (and not-so-holy) places, more of you will feel the Divine Call and Discontent to either visit or relocate to strange and wondrous places on your Earth.

The Ring of Fire where many of your dormant and active volcanos are placed around the world hold great storehouses of wisdom and transformational energy. Under each of these resides one of the great crystalline structures of which we speak. In the past, when the negative energies built to an intolerable level, these magnificent energy vortices, under the direction of the Great Devas, spewed forth their fire and frustration, not to harm or destroy, but to make you aware that the pressures had built to an intolerable level and there must be a venting or release. It is time for you to join with the Devic and Elemental Kingdoms, to reunite with sacred intent to purify and release the negative, impacted energies and to activate and harmonize with the Divine Beings whose task it has been to anchor and hold the wisdom and resonance of the Creator within the Earth.

You have worked diligently and faithfully to activate and

heal that sacred place called Mt. Shasta, and it now resonates with a most wondrous Light. We ask you to now heal the other great powerhouses around the Earth, such as the majestic Mt. Haleakala on Maui, Hawaii, the remnants of the great civilization of Lemuria. I ask you to focus on (or make the journey if you are called by Spirit), during the Full Moon in the Fiery sign of Leo, to that sacred place where I will, once more, activate the First Ray of Divine Will and Power, and with your assistance, awaken the great crystalline Being which has slumbered there for thousands of years. You will infuse the crater with your purified intent and help heal the ancient memories of separation and failure, and you will be gifted with an attunement and activation of profound proportions. You hold the keys to unlock and redirect the power within the Earth. In turn, she holds the keys to your unfoldment as a master of cocreation to assist you to return to full partnership as an honored emissary of the Most High, sent on a very special assignment to a place called The Garden of E-Don.

There are many sacred sites and holy places calling you, beloved ones. Does the name Shamballa or Camelot strike a cord of longing within? They are not just myths, but great etheric cities of bygone days. Each of you must attune and listen to that "cosmic call" from within—to that which resonates to the depths of your innermost being. Allow no one to make your decisions or coerce you. Make no journey out of guilt, or out of fear that you will be left behind or left out. Your Spirit Self will give you a clear message that cannot be denied when it is proper and part of your Divine Mission. That is why I gave you the new meditation at the beginning of this message. As you move inward and connect with your innermost Self, you will receive perfect direction; memories will well up and you will feel such a Divine Discontent, such a yearning that you will not be able to deny the impulses. And, if you so choose to follow the nudgings of Spirit, you will manifest, with ease and grace, the way and means to fulfill your mission. Begin to claim your Divine Birthright, my brave warriors. Realize that there is nothing too difficult or impossible when you harness the power and resources of Spirit. Let us move forward together, beloveds, in this sacred dance of cocreation. I AM Archangel Michael.

31. THE PRINCIPLES OF SPIRITUAL POWER

*B*eloved masters, I have given you what might be considered "more advanced" information of late in order to stretch your imaginations and expand your consciousnesses, so that you could gradually incorporate into your reality some of the vastness and complexity of your world, solar system and the universe. At this time, I am aware that many of you are not comfortable with some of the concepts that have been presented and feel they do not yet fit within the framework of what you wish to accept as your reality. This is all proper and we honor you for your discernment. Many of the supposed "new truths" that are being brought forth in various ways are really advanced concepts of Creator truth that goes beyond what humanity has been prepared to accept and integrate. You are coming of age as a race (and here we speak of the human race). Part of the path of evolution in becoming an integrated spiritual/human Being is to allow the old distorted, limiting beliefs to be replaced with ideas and theories which are thought to be revolutionary in nature and often are in opposition to what you had accepted as your truth in the past.

We watch as you ponder over some of the ideas we have presented, and we sense your discomfort as some of these concepts stir up old memories: fear, guilt, frustration, anger and a sense of futility. Have we not told you that the time has come to release all outmoded ideas and perceptions so that you can, once again, accept your mastery? But first, you must believe there is a possibility that you are, indeed, a master, not just a pawn of fate on a never-ending treadmill that leads nowhere.

It is time for you to become a responsible, self-aware,

spiritual adult (another way of saying it is time to claim your mastery), for some of you still do not know what that means or entails. No longer is it permissible to abdicate your future or spiritual growth and transfer the responsibility to someone you think is wiser or more powerful, or has a "connection" in someway to the higher realms of illumined truth. Beloved ones, we are offering you a gift of great value—the wisdom that was lost, distorted and hidden from you so very long ago; the knowledge and wisdom that was only available to the select few who were deemed advanced or responsible enough to comprehend and make proper use of this.

I have said this many times before, but it bears repeating, for these are critical times in your enlightening process: do not accept anything I or anyone presents to you without filtering it through your heart/soul center for validation. If it is loving, empowering or expansive information, as opposed to limiting, controlling or fear-based, then please keep an open, objective mind. If it does not resonate as your truth, set it aside, but do not discard it. Ask that it be validated if it is your truth. Your guardians, teachers and Higher Self will take over from there. You will be presented, in many various ways, with information that will substantiate or invalidate the information so that you will have no doubt as to whether or not it is your truth. In this way, you will gradually expand your awareness into realms, realities and possibilities beyond your wildest imagining.

My faithful friends, please know that the new awareness and knowledge that has been brought forth in this last 20 or 30 years is only the beginning, only a primer you might say, for what is to come. So please give yourself the gift of reaching out into the unknown, beyond the boundaries of safety and certainty, for the walls of your reality are crumbling. That which you once depended on or took to be your security is slowly dissolving into smoke. Even your finest, highest and wisest truths are being replaced or modified by more refined, advanced knowledge of galactic and universal import.

The old beliefs, those so firmly entrenched in the mass-consciousness, and the old ways of functioning are no longer acceptable. It no longer takes lifetimes or years for the harmonious or inharmonious energies that you send spiraling out into the ethers to collect like energy and return to you as validation of your belief structure. Your creations are being magnified and materialize much more quickly so that you can, once and for all, come to the realization that you, and only you, are the creator of your external and internal world. YOU are responsible for your hell on Earth or Heaven on Earth—you and you alone. You were given all the tools, all the gifts to use in any way you wished, as mandated and set down under the Universal Laws from the Creator. You were given the precious gift of free will and told, "Go forth and with your own mental and emotional abilities build a paradise in the plane of materiality so that we may experience and enjoy this new creation together, I through you." This is a difficult and frightening concept for many dear souls to accept. It is easier to blame someone, fate or God, for what happens to you so that you do not have to take responsibility.

Even when someone has good fortune or is gifted with a seemingly unearned "prize" or windfall, it is habit to say or believe "they had a stroke of good luck," or, "they are just lucky." They would not enjoy the gift, no matter what it might be, unless there was like energy resonating in their auric field. At some time or in some life, the person enjoying the "good luck" sent forth the seeds which grew and magnified until the energy returned and they eventually reaped the reward. The reason you are being gifted or chastised so quickly now is that, first, your time/space reality is compressing and secondly, so that you will begin to realize the full measure of cause and effect is in operation.

Let us speak now of fear. Even though we have talked much of this in the past, it is still a dominant force in most of your lives in some measure. I would like to speak of fear along with what we will call **PRINCIPLES OF POWER.** When we speak of taking your power, many of you immediately go into fear or denial. It stirs up memories of being defeated or even killed by someone more powerful than you, memories when you misused and abused your power, or lost all you held dear when someone "overpowered you."

The power I offer you via the First Ray is the POWER of love, the POWER to create and manifest your brave, new world, and POWER and dominion over the lower frequencies which have controlled and shackled you in an illusionary prison of your own weaving. POWER used in its true form is the ability to act with vigor or strength; it is about living your own truth with authority and authenticity, and speaking your truth with valor and integrity. It means being responsible for your own actions and using your influence for the highest good of all, always. It means using the POWER of gentleness and not being afraid to allow yourself to experience the POWER of others; to accept with gratitude that which others have to offer, where their power or abilities are stronger or more advanced than yours, or augment and compliment yours. It is not a contest to see who is the most powerful, or to see who can **OVERPOWER** another. It is an opportunity for you to integrate and utilize the gift of the First Cause of Creation, the universal **POWER** of

Divine Will, in harmony with the will of our Father/Mother God.

Honor each other, beloveds. Honor the beliefs and truths that others present to you, even if they are not totally in resonance with what you perceive as your truth. Allow them to walk beside you and offer a different viewpoint or another facet of truth. Do not criticize or judge; that is the action of someone in fear. Be brave enough to allow others to be different or unique, and be willing to garner wisdom from their strengths and wisdom, for they are sure to have something to offer if you remain receptive and open to change.

Please learn the art of negotiation and gentle persuasion instead of using coercion and force when it comes time to embark on a new endeavor, or with those whom you have chosen to live or work on a day-to-day basis. It is time for all races, religions, cultures, ages and genders to live in harmony and peace, reveling and honoring each other's uniqueness and different ways of self-expression. Demanding others to follow your rules or beliefs stems from fear—fear of being proven wrong or powerless, or unworthy. That which you clutch too tightly or try to dominate will eventually be lost to you. Love-infused power is fearless and means freedom to BE—to express—to create in your own way, and to allow others the same Divine Right.

In order for you to truly use the gift of power that is being offered to you, you must first move out of fear and the need to control or dominate anyone else. I ask you, if you are willing, for the next month, to ponder on the meaning of POWER in connection with the following words:

POWER OF EXPRESSION—Are you ready to freely, without fear, express your beliefs and desires to those around you?

OF EMBODIMENT—Are you ready to envision, ... and manifest your beautiful body of Light, result-... tal health, vitality, youthfulness and well-being?

WER OF COMMUNICATION—The words you use send forth energies which build and create your desires, or sabotage your efforts and weaken you.

POWER OF INSPIRATION—Inspiration is the first step in the formula of using the

POWER OF MANIFESTATION—The energy of inspired thought opens the way to attunement with your higher mind so that you may tap into the wellspring of cosmic knowledge where all things are known.

POWER OF DISCERNMENT—Are you ready to accept the responsibility for your new-found knowledge and powers, to know when to speak and when to be silent, to allow others to find their own truth, in their own time? Those who are true masters know they are only responsible for their own spiritual growth and well-being, and the best way to teach others is by example.

POWER OF BALANCE—Living the middle path, which has been called the narrow path by some, moderation in all things, but claiming and enjoying all the beauty, bounty and opulence of Creation. Balancing and integrating all the facets of your Being, so that you resonate and radiate harmony and peace.

And finally, the POWER OF TRANSCENDENCE—This is the end result in claiming and harmonizing all the other facets of power, dear ones. It is time to move beyond the limitations of the third dimension, to release and transcend your old limiting, controlling belief structures, to advance or graduate to the level of mastery, claiming all the gifts which are yours by Divine Dispensation—you have just forgotten.

What does it mean to be an **EMPOWERED** master, pioneer, or Wayshower? It means treading a path where the meek or weak of heart fear to go. It means climbing the heights and claiming your reward as an enlightened spiritual/human Being and leaping out into uncharted territory, knowing you have the ability and wherewithal to succeed in whatever endeavor you choose to pursue. It means mastering your ego, and bringing your desires into harmony with your Divine Mission—which leads to the peace, happiness and beauty you all seek. All of this assists you in tapping into the **POWER OF TRANSFORMATION,** which leads you gracefully and with ease through the process now in progress, opening the doorway to the higher dimension of illumination and unity-consciousness.

And so, my brave warriors, will you spend some time pondering, meditating on and endeavoring to integrate these **PRINCIPLES OF POWER** I have outlined for you? It is imperative that you are clear as to what the responsibilities are in claiming the gift of the First Ray of Divine Power. It is critical that you use this energy properly, for your highest, purest good and to the benefit of all. The next step will be to assist your Mother Earth and all humanity to reclaim this gift. Through the dedicated focus and **POWER** of you, the few who are bold, brave and dedicated enough to the lead the way, this wonderful gift will penetrate, permeate and transform the Earth and all living things.

I leave you with one last request: I ask you to also focus on the words **JOYFUL EXPRESSION** and what they mean to you. One of the secrets of mastery and claiming ease and grace as you move through this most important process is to approach it and see it as a joyful experience, not a drudgery, or serious task to be endured and conquered. **GOD IS JOY, GOD IS ECSTASY, GOD IS RAPTURE.** When you claim and express joy, you are using one of the most **POWERFUL** tools of Creation.

You have traversed the valleys of despair. You have trod the path of sorrow. You have experienced the dark night of the soul. Now the time has come to claim and reap the benefits of your trials and tests. Claim your **POWER,** brave warriors, and with joy, determination and a vision of the paradise soon to manifest, we will march forward together into the bright future of tomorrow. I will love and support your endeavors with all the **POWER** of my Being. I AM Archangel Michael.

32. MISSION OF LOVE—MISSION OF MASTERY

*B*eloved masters, Solar Hearts, Starseed of wondrous Light, sons and daughters of the most High, I wish to share with you some insight as to what transpired around the world on August 16, 17, and 18, 1997, the celebration of the tenth anniversary of what has been named the Harmonic Convergence. More of you than we ever believed possible answered the call (many of you were not even consciously aware of what you were doing), thereby allowing us to radiate the maximum influx of cosmic energy from the Great Central Sun through you and into and around the Earth, which was then stepped down and diffused to humanity and all living Creations as a whole. It was necessary to have your permission and it was also necessary that you become clear receptacles and transformers for this gift so that it would not injure your multiple body systems, nor become distorted or contaminated. This is why we have endeavored to help you understand how critical this time is on your planet, and for these past months we have done everything within our power to assist you to clear and harmonize your four lower vessels to the greatest degree possible. You have no idea, precious ones, how much loving energy, help and attention has been focused on you and your blessed planet in this, the last decade of the century.

Those of you who were drawn to attend the event in the sacred place now called Maui, Hawaii, answered a call from deep within your consciousnesses, a yearning to return to that wondrous place you once called home, a place you helped create and where many of you had your beginnings in the physical so many aeons ago. The urge was so intense, you could not refuse and once you were committed, the obstacles seemed to melt away as Spirit assisted you to rejoin your spiritual family in this holy quest. It was the same in many other places around the world, as group after group came together to fulfill their particular part of the mission. You all received a gift from the heart center of our Father/Mother God to assist you to remove the veil of forgetfulness, to remember who you are, to accelerate the process of awakening the Earth and all its inhabitants. A new world consciousness is emerging, an inner discontent is prevalent as more people are nudged onto the path of awareness.

This momentous event was celebrated throughout the universe as we watched you move through a portal way of higher consciousness, as you accepted the Flaming Sword of will and power of the First Cause, and agreed to use this wondrous gift for the good of all. What you have initiated, my faithful ones, is a heartlink amongst yourselves and with those of us who reside in the higher realms. This is a heartlink that will spread around the world as more and more blessed ones awaken and begin the process of attuning to their true nature or Higher Selves, and you all reestablish your heart/soul link with the Divine Source through your own Christ-consciousness. You have begun the process of building a web or mandala of Love/Light which will grow and spread until it completely surrounds the Earth, thereby allowing us to accelerate the ascension process for you and your planet, which will eventually radiate out into your solar system, galaxy and beyond.

Our connections with you are being greatly strengthened as more of the frequency distortions are harmonized or removed. Do you not feel more attuned to us and our presence, beloved ones? We of the higher realms are over-Light-ing you with the Divine aspects and attributes of the Creator as you move back into harmony with us. You may feel hot flushes move through your bodies, or ripples of energy flow through you; or you may feel waves of great joy or even sadness wash over you as you adjust to your new higher frequency levels. Your heart may feel so filled with love it is almost painful, as if your body cannot contain the exquisite sensations permeating your Being. Does your awareness seem more focused and do you not view your world with more clarity? Do you not seem to be more in control of your destiny and are you not moving out of doubt and into the certainty that you are "in the flow," and all is right with the world as you view events from a higher, broader perspective? You are donning your cloak of mastery, dear hearts, you are ascending as you allow Spirit to descend and take dominion of your physical vessels.

Over these past years, through these messages and in the gatherings we have encouraged you to attend, we have endeavored to help you realize that the clearing process need not be complicated or painful. It is critical that you process and release all residual impacted energies within your physical/ etheric, emotional and mental bodies by balancing and harmonizing your bodily chakra system (the seven chakras or energy vortices with which you are most familiar). Through use of the sacred breath, toning, visualization and intent, the process is greatly accelerated, thereby allowing your I AM Presence to also activate many of the minor chakras in your bodies, and begin the process of attuning you to the five higher chakras of Galactic Consciousness. This in turn builds your crystalline Light body as you integrate more and more of your Divine Self.

Eventually, beloved ones, you will access and incorporate many more of these higher frequency energy centers which will lift you to a universal-consciousness. But for the time being, it is imperative that you firmly anchor your Higher Self in the physical and learn how to function as a master; how to cocreate and manifest a radiance of peace, love and abundance as your gift to humanity and the Earth; how to focus on the beauty and harmony around you and away from the negativity and chaos, so as to not give energy or fuel to that which is not compatible with the Divine Blueprint for the Earth and humankind. It is all part of staying focused in the NOW, in taking one step and level at a time. You are the examples, the prototypes of the new emerging spiritually attuned humanity, beloved ones. You are blazing the path for others to follow. You are the teachers, the guides, the Wayshowers for those now awakening. What purpose will it serve for you to move so far ahead on the path that no one can relate to you, or if you are beyond the reach and understanding of those whom you are to assist?

Yes, there are those of you who are close to moving far above and beyond the norm, who can realize that dream of fully incorporating your Divine Self, and ascend into the higher realms beyond the illusion and suffering of humanity and the Earth. And yes, we realize the pull and desire is strong and if that is your choice, so be it. There is no wrong choice, but remember, beloveds, you are needed. You promised to assist in the awakening of your brothers and sisters; to teach, guide, and nurture those on the path behind you in these most critical times. That is why it is so important that you do not make the process seem too complicated, too hard to understand or accomplish. Those following your guidance need not know or understand all the complex concepts you have integrated, nor will they have to reach the level of awareness you have attained.

Remember, many of you are being groomed to be the

ascended masters of the future, if you agree to honor your commitment and assume that responsibility. Yes, there are the few who will ascend, taking their physical bodies with them, and others who will leave suddenly as soon as their particular mission is completed. You have all heard of the three waves of ascension, and many have been caught up in that drama and have focused all their intention on being a part of the first wave, second wave, etc., and quite often the ego has been strongly involved in that process of desiring to be among the first. But at this time, most of you who were predestined to be a part of that plan are experiencing your ascension process in the etheric body and you know well who you are. You keep your silence and go lovingly about being of service to humanity; guiding, directing, teaching and gently opening the way for others to follow. It is not yet time, nor are you ready to totally materialize and dematerialize your body/Light body. Do not get hung up on the ultimate goal, beloveds; keep your eyes focused on the mission of the moment.

Humanity at large needs only open its heart center and allow its soul-self to begin the process of attuning its physical vessel to the resonance of the higher fourth dimension. Humanity will then be able to move in ease and grace with the Earth into the fifth dimension when that momentous time arrives. Most of you who have felt the urgency and have answered the clarion call over the past few years are the ones on which the responsibility will fall. It is you who will instruct, teach and lead the blessed beings of Earth into the emerging Golden Age, and when your mission is completed, you will pass the scepter of responsibility to those you have helped realize their mastery, as you go forward to the next level of truth and endeavor.

You have suffered and survived great trials and tribulations. You have emerged triumphant through the valley of the dark night of the soul (or it might be more appropriate to call it the dark night of the ego). You have relinquished and released much, and are now coming to realize that all you have experienced was a part of the process, and the gifts of Spirit far outweigh anything you have experienced in the past.

We have passed the Rod/Sword of Divine Power to you, beloved masters, those of you who have passed the test of love: love of self, love of humanity, love for your precious Earth and all Creation; to those of you who have the ability to access and bring forth your portion of the Divine Blueprint and to move into harmony with your Divine Mission. During the initiation process, which many of you experienced, you were infused with the greatest influx of Divine Energy from the Creator Source that you have received since you took on your coats of flesh—the greatest amount you could incorporate and still stay balanced in the physical.

You are moving to the next phase of illumination, my brave warriors; you have truly earned the title "Warriors of Light" in my mighty legions. I offer you my profound gratitude, beloved exalted ones, and my heart swells with love for you. I am with you always. I AM Archangel Michael.

33. Message from Ronna

Beloved Friends:

My journey to Hawaii and the three-day intensive on Maui were beyond my wildest expectations. I had three book signings with a mini-lecture at Borders Bookstore, two on Honolulu and one on Maui. They all drew standing-room-only crowds, and all the books available were sold, plus a number of orders placed. The managers were all pleasantly surprised, as was I. It was the same here in Reno when I appeared at Waldenbooks and Barnes and Noble. One manager said, "We didn't get this kind of response when we had a best-selling author here." Archangel Michael is certainly spreading his Light. People are so hungry for answers and direction. It was wonderful to see how enraptured and attentive they were; I could feel their sense of frustration and their deep desire to understand what is going on in both their inner and outer worlds. The masses are truly stirring and it is a wondrous time of change.

Sharon Huffman, the facilitator of the Maui event, arranged for me to appear on Channel 9 TV, the KGMB-CBS morning news (6 AM). I was scheduled to be on for four minutes. I am not uncomfortable with TV appearances since I have been on radio and television a number of times, but I was a little anxious about getting any meaningful information across in four minutes. As I often do, I asked Lord Michael to expand time for me and make it perfect. The co-anchor's name was Angela—a beautiful sweet, young woman. She was so excited and talked about her angel experiences right up to the last few seconds before we went on camera. She didn't follow her script at all. Instead, she asked wonderful questions and I was able to address some key points about the rapidly changing times in the world, the inner discontent people are feeling and my experiences in being a channel for AA Michael. We were on for about seven minutes, went to a break and then back on camera for another seven or eight minutes. All the crew was smiling and laughing by the time we finished and I ended up giving "Ronna hugs" all around. It was delightful—Archangel Michael sure performed his magic.

The seminar on Maui was absolutely Divine. The Aston Wailea is a beautiful resort complex with all the deluxe amenities—a paradise setting that is unsurpassed. We had a luxurious ballroom as our meeting room and a lovely private dining room for luncheon each day. There were people from all over the world and what beautiful souls they are—we all made a heart connection that will never be broken. The trip to the Haleakala Crater was worth the whole trip by itself. We went to the highest point on the mountain where we could see the full moon on one side and the rising sun on the other. As we all gathered around (about 150 of us in total), Archangel Michael took us through a ceremony and an infusion of Divine Energy from the Creator that we will never forget. We all knew without a doubt that we had assisted in the activation of the sacred energy within the crater, and we had healed and transmuted many of the painful memories of the ancient past. There was only a gentle breath of wind (it is usually so cold and blustery it is uncomfortable to stay on the mountain for very long), we basked in the glory of the event and the sun's Rays warmed and blessed us as we all stood with tears streaming from our eyes. We did not want to leave as we hugged and shared our own special experiences.

After I returned home, I received a profound and beautiful gift from a dear soul sister, Maxine Appleman from Boulder, Colorado. She sent me an 8 x 10 photograph that she had taken at Haleakala during our sunrise event, while I was channeling Archangel Michael. It overlooks the crater with the mountain and clouds in the background—three of the people in the group are gazing toward the sunrise. Symbolically, it looked like a man, woman and child and there were white halos around their heads. The man was wearing a blue jacket with two red and one white streak across it—the colors of AA Michael's flaming sword. Covering about one-fourth of the left side of the picture is a brilliant oblong shaft of light streaming down with beautiful radiant colors blazing from it. Maxine said her intuition told her that it was our beloved Lord Michael and when I asked him, he validated that he had projected this glowing aspect of himself down into the crater as a gift and physical evidence that he truly was with us. Without a doubt, he and many wondrous Beings of Light were with us at that wondrous event. We all were lifted into the rarified dimensions where angels dwell—we created a miracle and we were all blessed beyond measure.

Wherever you were, or whatever you were doing, know that you too received a blessed infusion from the Divine Source. We are now in a time of accelerated expansion of consciousness and you will find that the manifestation of your thoughts and desires are being accomplished much more rapidly. Happy, joyous creating, dear friends—we are truly ON OUR WAY.

I love you all so much, Ronna

P.S. Maxine graciously gave me the negative of the picture and told me to use it in any way I wished. Since that time, I have sent out hundreds of copies of the picture all over the world. Everyone who touches it feels "angel bumps" rise on their skin. Thank you, Maxine, for following your intuition and turning to snap the picture when Spirit led you to do so.

(The picture is printed on the back cover of this book.)

34. BEAUTY OF FORM—BEAUTY OF SPIRIT

(September, 1997 Message)

*B*eloved masters, much has transpired since we last came together, events which are confusing, disconcerting and painful. Allow me to give you an expanded view and bring you to a greater understanding so you will know that all is in Divine Order. This does not mean that these events were Divinely planned, but it does mean that the precious souls involved agreed to be the vehicles of greater understanding and awareness at this important time.

I am speaking in particular of the violent death of the beautiful soul called Princess Diana and the transition of the beloved saintly one called Mother Teresa. These two precious souls were aspects or fragments of the same great Oversoul who came to Earth to teach humanity two important lessons from an exaggerated, opposing perspective. Princess Diana, born into the elite, titled, privileged class, was gifted with power, wealth and status beyond compare. But what this gentle soul yearned for the most was love and acceptance. She made many errors in judgment, but her loving nature and strong Spirit prevailed and she moved beyond the self-indulgence and self-centeredness of the past to reach out to those in need—to give hope where there was none. She stepped across the boundaries and taboos to touch the untouchable ones, to embrace the helpless and defeated ones, giving them a gift of love and beauty, if only for a moment.

She accomplished her mission by showing the world that all the riches, power, titles and adulation of physical beauty mean nothing without love or a sense of self-worth. In the hearts of humanity, she will remain forever young—a symbol of gentleness, grace and beauty of Spirit.

The beautiful one called Mother Teresa chose a life of sacrifice and penance, rejecting all physical comforts, wealth and status. She became a living martyr, unstintingly serving those in need with complete disregard for her own health and well-being. She had not beauty of face or form, but the radiance that shined forth from within was most wondrous to behold. She, too, leaves a legacy of hope, inspiration, and courage which will forever remain in the memories of humanity.

Do you not see the exaggerated image each of these dear souls chose to present to the world for scrutiny? The opposite ends of the spectrum: Diana totally immersed in her physical appearance for a time, to the point of self-destruction and even a death wish, while surrounded by all of the opulence, adoration of the masses, title and power. Yet, what she yearned for was a sense of love and validation from those closest to her, which really originated from a lack of self-love and acceptance.

Mother Teresa was the living example of the old belief system of self-sacrifice, rejection of the gifts of physical comfort and joy of the material world out of a sense of duty and dedication. She is an example of a belief that in order to be spiritual and to serve, you must turn your back on all the world has to offer in the way of pleasure and abundance.

Can you not see what has transpired, beloved ones? The transition of these two beautiful souls so closely together gives you an opportunity to examine your views and beliefs regarding service and sacrifice: beauty without, versus beauty within, and that abundance and power without love of self and others is meaningless. They played their roles well and left a legacy of great import.

These two blessed souls also provided humanity with an even greater gift. We have told you that time is critical: as the Earth progresses and spirals into a higher frequency it is imperative that humanity at large awakens and moves forward as well. All that is needed is for those at slumber to open their minds and allow their soul-selves to begin to take up residency within their heart centers once more. This will begin the process of lifting their consciousnesses enough to allow them to continue the journey toward higher evolution along with Mother Earth.

Never in the history of your Earth, since the sinking of Lemuria and Atlantis, has there been such a great outpouring of emotion by so many people at one time. Do you not see the perfection in this scenario? Just a few weeks ago, many of you came together to heal the ancient memories of the past for humanity, bringing in wondrous refined frequencies of Christ Light. As this gift spread around the Earth on a golden web of Light, through you it was made available to all humanity. But how were we to get them to accept it? Who else could cause such a great outpouring of altruistic love and emotional release but these two beloved ones? Who else could cause the world's population to focus on their heart centers in unison, and in their pain and sorrow release much of the ancient impacted energies within, making way for the healing energies of Divine Love.

Indeed, a miracle was wrought, beloved ones, and the consciousness of humanity was lifted to a level that was not thought possible. Mourn not for these two precious souls, for they are basking in the glory of reunion with us, their brothers and sisters of the higher realms. They are enjoying the rewards of sweet success, for they are aware that they truly accomplished their mission.

There are other events occurring more frequently which give you cause for concern and alarm. Allow me to help you come to a greater understanding as to what is taking place. More and more of the population is becoming ill from eating contaminated food, and bacteria is becoming more aggressive and mutating at an alarming rate. It is believed that the fault lies in the processing and handling of food, and this is partially true, but you surely must be aware that this not the root of the problem. Food processing, especially meat products, is better than it ever has been. There is more awareness as to proper hygiene and nutrition among the populace and still there are more frequent occurrences of illness due to tainted food.

Turn inward, dear friends, and see if this does not resonate with your new, expanded truth. When you are attuned to the third-dimensional reality and your body functions at that frequency, there is a density, a coarseness, an insensitivity, you might say. Just as an animal can, most often, eat putrid spoiled food and not become ill, the human body in its baser nature develops a tolerance for germs, bacteria and food which carries many impurities. However, as you lift your vibratory rate, clear your auric field and begin to raise your bodily frequencies, you become more sensitive to negativity of all kinds. You become more sensitive to your environment, your and others' thoughts, as well as higher- and lower-frequency patterns. Are you not aware that food has frequency patterns, as well?

We have told you that as you progress along the path of spiritual evolution and if you listen to the nudgings of Spirit, you will naturally begin the process of eliminating certain foods and beverages, as well as habits of a grosser nature with ease. If you listen to your body and your faithful body

Elemental, you will know what is proper and appropriate for your evolving body/Spirit. As you begin to feel a sense of well-being and enjoy greater health and vitality than ever before, you will not feel you are deprived in any sense.

Those of you who have gone through this process and emerged triumphant know the truth of what we say. But those of you who still resist and will not face or listen to your soul's nudgings will suffer the consequences more dramatically and more frequently. This is not an idle threat, my friends, it is the evolving truth as to your responsibilities to yourselves and your budding consciousnesses. No longer will humanity be able to ignore the fact that the world is changing, that humanity is evolving and the old ways of being, thinking and living will bring about much pain and suffering. You are not being punished, nor are you being tossed about by the whims of fate. You are all subject to the same Universal Laws, and these laws are refined and re-structured to a higher degree at each new level of awareness, or as you tap into a more rarified dimensional expression.

It is time for you all to examine your lifestyles, habits and responsibilities to your temples of Spirit, or your physical bodies. Oh, what damage and destruction you have wrought to that perfect, beautiful vessel you first manifested upon your arrival on planet Earth! Many beautiful souls who have caused damage beyond repair to their bodies, realize there is no chance of reversing that damage and are choosing to leave their physical vessels and transcend back into Spirit form. They must return again, at a later time, when they are ready to honor and nurture the blessed gift given them: the opportunity to experience and enjoy the beauty and bounty of earthly life in harmony with Spirit.

Find your truth and create your own path, beloved and faithful ones, as you listen to your own inner nudgings and the intelligence of your body as to what is proper and appropriate for you at any given time. Do not eat just because the clock says it is the designated time to do so—listen to your body's inner messages. Do not be misled by all the tempting advertising and great diversity and complexity of food available to you. Eat simply, purely and in moderation. Gluttony and excess in any area is pure self-destruction and will lead to pain and discomfort in the physical vessel, insensitivity to your soul's and Spirit's wisdom, and is a sure way to retard the process of evolvement.

How can you become attuned to the higher frequencies and vibrations now available if your body is steeped in toxins, dense food, drink or drugs, and struggling to purify itself and create balance? Just as you are becoming aware that you must go inward to find peace and fulfillment—to gain love and acceptance of self—so it is with the desires of the ego body. Make no mistake, this is the source of the constant yearning for gratification, for "sense satisfaction," a constant need for external stimulus to give a false sense of peace and contentment—no matter how fleeting.

Allow us to assist you in gaining the peace and harmony within that does not diminish, but only grows and becomes more exquisite with time, dear hearts. If you experience, only once, the bliss and joy of attunement in body/soul/Spirit, you will forever seek that sense of unity and harmony and everything of an external nature will take on a lesser role in your life.

We are aware that the strength and pull of habits, past conditioning and beliefs are difficult to break and relinquish, and that is why we are bringing forth so much new (old) wisdom, tools and the means for you to move gracefully forward, out of the old structures and constraints of the past. As we have often told you, it is imperative that you stay focused on "the event of the now," which keeps you in attunement with body and Spirit, as all facets of your Being endeavor to give you assistance and wisdom to overcome any trial or adversity. Each time you make the higher choice, you strengthen your spiritual resolve and it becomes easier to walk the path of more enlightened awareness.

Ah, my sweet friends, the gifts we offer you are beyond any moment's gratification you may derive in the physical. We are not asking you to relinquish the pleasures earthly embodiment offers you—that is why you incarnated. We are asking you to allow Spirit to be the guide and director of your desires and actions, and you will find more peace, joy and contentment than you ever thought possible.

Indeed, this past month of your time will go down as a hallmark in the history of planet Earth. The consciousness of humanity and the Earth were raised to a new level and the syncrgy and power of heart-felt love and devotion reverberated throughout the universe. Indeed, you have created miracles, my faithful bearers of Light. Know that I AM with you always as your guide and protector. I AM Archangel Michael.

35. THE TESTS AND GIFTS OF MASTERY

*B*eloved masters, since you still function in and are affected by the concepts of time and space, let us review what has transpired over the last several years from your perspectives and then we will tell you what is taking place from our point of view. We in the higher realms meet continually to analyze what has taken place on Earth and to assess the level of awareness of humanity, both individually and as a whole. Of course, we see you quite differently and measure your progress by Light frequency levels, energy patterns and spiritual awareness, rather than by events, material accomplishments or physical guidelines. You become less conscious of time as you move into harmony with Spirit. Time is registered in the brains of humans as cycles and sequential events. Space is also viewed differently from the higher realms; we see it as a part of an eternal whole, the unmanifested body of the Prime Creator.

Many of you have made outstanding strides and advancements as you move into the level of mastery which allows you to tap into the free-flow of cosmic energy, thereby creating and manifesting your dreams and aspirations. It is a time for many to truly test their discernment and judgment as they, once more, begin to wield the rod of power and take control of their destiny. Be aware, dear ones, that as you gain power, influence and advanced knowledge, that you do not get caught in what is called the "glamour" of the fourth dimension.

Having psychic abilities does not necessarily mean a person is spiritually aware. These gifts or abilities are part of your natural birthright; you have just forgotten how to use them and they have atrophied over the ages. Spiritual insight and attunement with your Higher Self rather than with the desire body of ego is essential before you begin to tap into the awesome cosmic treasures of manifestation.

A plethora of knowledge has been brought forth that has not been available to you for many ages—a wealth of information, much of it inspired and transmitted accurately, much of it distorted unintentionally as various messengers tap into the higher mind of spiritual truth and endeavor to decipher and step down this information into your language and understanding. And, unfortunately, some of the information being broadcasted to the masses in various ways is totally inaccurate and detrimental to your spiritual growth. This is why we repeat, over and over, dear ones, use your discernment. Accept facts and theories only after you have proven them to be your truth. Your monitoring system for validation is now firmly in place, and that is your heart/thymus center. As a disciple of Light, it is imperative that you become the master of your own destiny.

Knowledge is not wisdom, but wisdom is power. As you flex your spiritual muscles and use them in harmony with your Divine Self, you truly step into that rarified dimension where you are the architect and designer of your reality and all that it encompasses: the mental, physical, emotional and material aspects of your immediate surroundings. It also has a dynamic effect on the advancement of humanity and the Earth as your refined, empowered energy joins with that of others and begins to magnify and overcome the negative thought patterns and restrictions of the third dimension.

Take a mental inventory, my brave friends, review your accomplishments and lay out your "Spiritual Road Map" for the important years ahead. It has been a long and arduous journey, but the summit of enlightenment is in sight. Many of you are filled to the brim with knowledge and the desire to serve, yet lack the confidence to step out and proclaim your new truths, fearing judgment or ridicule of "being different."

Others have begun to serve and are creating much good and making a worthwhile impact on the mass-consciousness, but are still caught up in the need for power or control, thereby diminishing their effectiveness. They will prevail for a time, but those around them will soon see that all is not in harmony and withdraw. You must think, act and live in total integrity, beloved ones. As you become more attuned and in harmony with your Higher Self, it will be much more difficult to fool you, and you will become less gullible.

Another pitfall on the path of ascension is impatience. As you begin to remember from whence you came, that the Earth is not your real home, that you are actually wondrous, magnificent Creations of God here on assignment, you begin to yearn and dream of reclaiming all that you relinquished in order to experience the material plane. Be patient, beloveds, it is important that you experience and work through each level of physical expression, balancing and harmonizing the frequency patterns as you gain the wisdom of what you have manifested, no matter how imperfect. Begin an internal review: start with your physical vessel; is it more in harmony and in better condition than this time last year? Are you more in tune with your body and is it responding to your new thought patterns? You cannot send thoughts of love and harmony, one day, and then abuse your "self" or forget that within you is a magnificent creation of Spirit ready to follow your every thought and desire. But you must send clear signals and thoughts and follow through when you get a reply via intuitive nudges, or later on, if you do not listen, by aches and pains. More important than any diet or exercise regimen is your thought regimen. Send thoughts of dissatisfaction, rejection, a sense of unworthiness, or focus on the imperfections of your body, and that is what it will manifest. **IT IS THE LAW.** One of the first great tests on the way to mastery, is to love unconditionally what you have already created and lift your sights to the perfection that is available, instead of what you see before you. See these imperfections as imbalances, not something to hate, fear or battle. This is not an easy task, but you must start somewhere, and what you focus on is what you give energy to. So, why not focus on the grand possibility that you can reclaim the beauty and perfection that are your birthright?

Have your relationships improved? Have you gained the courage to speak your truth and claim your power? Do you dare to be different and allow the new, refined you to step forth? Have you moved ego to the side as you balance and harmonize the energies between those with whom you live, love and interact? As you are learning, it is a subtle dance between laying out a new game plan, setting new boundaries, and yet, allowing others to live their truths and function at whatever levels of awareness they have attained. The danger of self-righteousness is great when you move past those around you in spiritual wisdom. Here again, beloveds, move to a higher vantage point, and allow love to temper your actions and interactions with others. You must be the living, "functioning in the everyday world" example, if others are to learn from you and accept the new truths you offer.

Are you more secure in your world? Has your abundance or sense of abundance increased? As the end of the century grows closer, the predictions of doom and gloom, catastrophes and cataclysms increase. These are some of the distorted and destructive thought forms being brought forth which can only come true if enough of you give them energy. An important part of your mission is to envision and tap into the original, perfect blueprint for Earth and humanity—to focus your enhanced energies of manifestation on reclaiming Heaven on Earth—The Garden of E-Don.

Yes, a cleansing is taking place. The Earth is seeking to purify and reclaim her wholeness, and as a result, certain areas and people will experience devastation, pain and suffering. They are not being punished, dear ones, **IT IS THE LAW.** Those who are not willing or are unable to redefine themselves and come into harmony with the increasing frequencies will have the decision taken out of their hands as the time grows closer for the Earth and humanity to move into the next realm of expression. It is the desire of the Creator and all who are assisting you to move forward that the experience be as graceful and painless as possible, but humanity still has free will and we can only operate within the parameters of Universal Law. The greatest gift of service you can offer is to send the blessed Violet Transmuting Flame to all the areas of your planet in distress and to the beloved people who are trapped in the midst of the power struggles and greed of their leaders.

As you reclaim and integrate the knowledge that you are entitled to all the beauty, bounty and opulence of Creation, you will begin to manifest abundance. Here again, how will you use that abundance? You are responsible for what is entrusted to you. Abundance comes in many forms, not just material wealth, and it is another universal law that you use what is needed and keep the supply flowing outward to be replenished. Even when you are living in integrity, moving in harmony with Spirit and your supply of all good things begins to flow, you will still be tested, dear ones. Tested by those around you who still believe in scarcity, those who still do not trust themselves or their abilities enough to manifest all that is needed through their own endeavors. You will be given an opportunity to stand in your integrity, to claim your power, and yes, also claim what is yours. Being a true warrior of Light means standing up for what is right and honorable at all levels. This is a true test for many of you, for down through the ages you have relinquished your power, your abundance, and even your beliefs and honor to those around you who seemed stronger. You will not err, beloveds, if you stand firm in harmony with Spirit and your inner guidance.

As you redefine what is important and valid in your life, you will relinquish many things that are no longer of importance. Do not fear change, nor hold on to that which fails to serves you. As you grew from childhood into adulthood, you grew out of and let go of many beliefs and habits. You are now moving into your true identity—that of Spiritual masterhood. It takes time to become comfortable with your new identity, so precious ones, be gentle with yourselves.

As I stated in the beginning, our perception of your progress is somewhat different from yours. We see the glow and brilliance of the Light as it increases, resonating from the Earth and humanity. Your radiance is becoming magnificent to behold and it is penetrating deep within the core of the planet, as well as permeating and encompassing the surface of the Earth. You are building a honeycomb of Light, beloveds—a Heart Link amongst you, the Starseed, that is gradually connecting and strengthening until, eventually, it will surround the Earth in a golden web of Light. You are succeeding. You are making a difference. Many more than we had hoped will be able to move into the higher dimensions and harmonize with the Earth's new frequencies, and it is because of you and those like you—because you have allowed yourselves to be the instruments and vehicles of change, the bearers and stabilizers of the refined-Light infusions, bearing the burden and discomfort in order to be the catalysts during these times of transmutation and transformation.

I first gave this gift and assignment to those who took part in the initiation and activation at the sacred Haleakala Crater on Maui during the celebration of the anniversary of the Harmonic Convergence in August. Those beloved ones laid the foundation for this process along with others who were given the same information in various forms around the world. It is now time for all of you to tap into and become active participants in this empowering, blessed ceremony which will spread, accelerate and enhance the integration of the refined frequencies now available to you and your planet.

Beloved sons and daughters of Light, even though you are scattered to the four corners of the globe, you will now make a reconnection, one with another, which will remain intact for time beyond measure. You all made a contractual agreement, many aeons ago, to come together again at this critical time in your Earth's history and evolution. You all carry an integral part of the Divine Plan—in your own way, through your special endeavors, you are the ones who will be the catalysts for the awakening of the masses. You, the blessed servers of the Light, are to be the bearers of the new frequency patterns that are now anchored on Earth. It is you who will receive the visions, guidelines, formulas for transformation, and the ingredients necessary to gracefully make the shift from a dark, limited three-dimensional world to a radiant star-planet filled with beauty, love, laughter and an enlightened humanity.

As a part of your continuing participation in this endeavor, I ask you to come together in the etheric each month at the time of the full moon. At the time of sunrise and moonrise on the day of the full moon, wherever you are, I ask you to move into your sacred space and ask your Divine I AM Presence to shower down upon you the healing, transforming energies of the Seventh Ray, and to activate and infuse you with the gifts of the five higher Rays of Galactic Consciousness. It is important that you participate in this ceremony with the clearest intent, and purest love for all Creation. As the sun and moon crest the horizon and pour forth their life-giving beams upon the Mother Earth, and as the great Rays of Light touch you and pour through your sacred chakra system, they will bring forth a greater infusion of the Divine Ray of the First Cause of the Creator—the energies which carry the perfect encodings and resonance of power, will, valor and truth. The sun will bear the masculine energies of the Creator and the moon, the energies of the Divine Mother.

Allow your own Divine Self to orchestrate your ceremony, but it should include these components: Acknowledge and ask our beloved Father/Mother Creator, all the angelic forces, the great Beings of Light, the ascended masters, the Elohim, and particularly the Elohim Directors of the Elemental Kingdom, and the Entire Company of Heaven and Earth to join us in this grand and auspicious undertaking: THE ASCENSION OF PLANET EARTH AND HUMANKIND.

Face the South, West, North and finally the East and allow the sun's or moon's Rays to penetrate your chakra system. See your pranic tube of Light being illuminated by a shaft of golden white Light from the Creator Source and penetrating deep within the crystalline core of the Earth. Breathe deeply and rhythmically of the Prana of Life and feel a vortex of energy build within your body. Sense a force begin to build, a whirlwind of Divine Power. Center your consciousness in your heart and feel the love for all Creation begin to permeate your Being down to the core level as you build this vortex of cosmic energy within. See this whirlwind filled with the magic Violet Flame and a blazing shaft of magenta, centered with electric blue and a luminous white core—you are now a pillar of Light radiating the pure Essence of the Cosmic Life Force. Move your consciousness to your third eye and then, as we have taught you, move your focus to the center of your brain. You will ignite the keys and codes you carry within which are your gift and contribution to the master plan. Radiate a shaft of Light from your solar plexus and your third eye, see them with your inner vision forming a "V" until they come together before you, approximately three feet above the ground. Watch with your mind's eye as these energies ignite and spread around the globe, connecting with those of your spiritual brothers and sisters. Hold the vision and focus until you hear within your heart center, *"It is done. It is done."*

This awesome gift is yours, a gift to use and share with humanity, and through your combined efforts, the beauty and harmony on your blessed planet will build and grow as others awaken and take up the banner of Light. The enlightenment of all life forms and the Mother Earth is now fully begun, and you, as the bearers of Divine Will, Truth and Valor, will help lead the way toward victory.

Use this blessed gift wisely, my brave ones. You must wield this gift of power with love, integrity and for the highest good of all, or it will turn on you and bring about your destruction. Never again will humanity be allowed to use this gift to dominate, for greedy or selfish purposes.

Blessed ones, be of strong courage, when the doubts creep in or the way is not clear. When you are ostracized or maligned, turn inward and upward—we are near to bolster your courage, to give you guidance and insight, but most of all we are here to love you beyond measure. I AM Archangel Michael and I bring you these truths.

36. You Are Cosmic Architects

*B*eloved masters, let us begin anew as you move into an era which could be called the bridge to the New Age—the era of enlightenment.

Not only has the countdown begun for the transition from one Age to another, but the countdown for humanity's coming of age, for assuming responsibility as cocreative partners in this journey along the cosmic highway to the stars has begun as well. This is a journey which will take you back home to a glorious reunion with your true family.

Because of the gift of free will, the Divine Plan for the evolution of the Earth and humanity has always been subject to change and reevaluation. It has been allowed to take its own course down through the many ages, but that time is quickly coming to a close. The concept of nonintervention has run its course as far as the Earth and humanity are concerned. In the past, humankind seemed to be a pawn in a great game of chance, controlled by outside forces. The greater hierarchy is now taking an active role, has laid down new rules, and new protective barriers have been placed around your solar system and particularly, your Earth. You are being given a golden opportunity, beloveds, an opportunity to take control, and to be the Divine Architects and Directors of the Earth's restructuring and refurbishing. With the help of the cocreative council from the higher realms, you have been given access to unlimited resources, and the expertise of master builders is available for the asking.

We ask you to step out boldly, to take control of your own destiny. Unite with your brothers and sisters—your soul family—in bringing to fruition the wondrous gifts that are being offered you: the beautification and healing of your Earth and the reclaiming of your birthright.

Let us review some of the concepts that have been given to you over the past year, so they will be fresh in your mind. The Earth and humanity are in the midst of a great transformation process. You are retracing the path upon which you descended, as you took on dense physical form. In order to do this, you must release the negative energy patterns within your physical structure to make way for the lighter, higher frequencies. The initiation and ascension process is a gradual progression of accessing new information: gaining new spiritual insight, and then allowing the wisdom and truth of that knowledge to replace old, outmoded concepts and beliefs. This, in turn, changes your frequency patterns, which then gradually changes your world, or picture of reality.

As you already know, this is called building the Light body, which results in your multiple bodies being infused with balancing energies in order to bring you to the maximum level of health, vitality and fitness. It also helps you to tap into latent creative abilities and knowledge stored within your brain structure. We have told you that you have Light packets, keys and codes within your brain that can only be accessed by attuning to the higher frequencies. This is happening on a grand scale at this time, as more of the mass population begin to feel the nudging of Spirit. The veil of forgetfulness is dissolving so that as you bring your emotional and mental bodies into harmony. You also gain the ability to tap into your higher mind and reunite with the many facets of yourself.

We have asked you to go through the process of breaking all agreements, past, present and future, which no longer serve you. This involves forgiving everyone and anyone (past, present and future) with which you have had a karmic interaction, or with which there were dramas and lessons to be learned. Gracefully forgiving and forgetting, or in other words, wiping the slate clean as if the event never happened—this is very important, for only then is the energy completely transmuted within your auric field. It does not matter if the other party involved forgives you or not, or is even aware that you have forgiven them. However, if you are still in a close relationship, they will certainly be aware something has changed between you, because they will sense a difference as you radiate love, and nonjudgment, rather than anger or resentment.

We have also stressed the importance of tapping into the wisdom of your body and elemental body. As you become attuned to the signals your physical body transmits, it will result in you gaining an awareness of what needs to be changed or added in order to maintain or regain health. You will practice preventive health maintenance rather than wait until your body moves into great distress. You will no longer place the responsibility for your good health in the hands of a doctor or health practitioner—you go to them for the wisdom and knowledge they can provide—using their services when needed, but with the awareness that you are the caretaker and ultimate healer of your precious physical vessel.

Remember to breathe deeply and practice the sacred breath each and every day until it becomes natural, dear ones. Deep, rhythmic breathing, or bringing in the golden or white prana of life, is one of the greatest gifts you can give yourself. The golden prana is the energy from the sun or the fire element, while white prana is derived from the element of air. There is also prana which is derived from the Earth, or the earth element, and yes, even prana from the element of water.

These are the vital energies necessary for you to exist and function efficiently in the physical body. That is why it is sometimes called the sacred breath, for it helps transmute and release negative energies within the body. It will also balance and enhance the chakra system, and cleanse and expand the auric field. Concentrate on your breathing techniques until it is natural for you to breathe from the abdomen instead of breathing shallowly from the chest or diaphragm.

If you will consciously practice deep, rhythmic breathing, it will help you to move easily into an altered or meditative state; it also relieves stress and clears the mind as it energizes the body. Deep breathing, with or without affirmations, is one of the best ways to balance and harmonize your energy fields. It is the magic elixir of life.

Your lives have changed dramatically over the past few years, and no one is excluded. Those of you who have stepped on the path of discipleship have experienced many changes and released many things which no longer serve you: possessions, relationships, beliefs and habits. It has not been easy, but as you take on a more expanded view, you begin to see the pattern and perfection of what is occurring. It is becoming easier to allow changes to take place, for you realize that if you maintain the focus of love, and constantly attune with your Higher Self, all is in Divine Order and the outcome will be for your highest good—ALWAYS.

You have learned and are, hopefully, practicing the Universal Laws of manifestation and are aware that words and thoughts have energy. Thoughts, feelings, words and action are the components needed to manifest what you desire in the physical world. Therefore, as you become more proficient in using and accessing the universal cosmic substance from whence all things are formed, be careful to monitor your thoughts, control your emotions, and be deliberate in your words and actions.

Many of you have been told, are dreaming, or getting the idea that you are healers, and many of you deny that this is possible. Believe us, beloved bearers of Light, it is true. There are many ways to heal and you do not have to have an educational degree, a certification, permission or credentials of any kind to spread or transmit healing energy. It is as simple as allowing the pure crystalline Light Substance of the Creator to flow through you and out your heart center to others. It will expand, magnify and enhance your auric field so that others are blessed as you move among them. Ask for, and then feel the diamond crystalline pyramids of energy become active in the palms of your hands. They may pulse or become warm, but even if you feel no sensation at all, know that if you desire to use this powerful energy to help humanity, it will magnify and grow. By a kind word, a smile, a gentle touch, or by sharing and passing on your wisdom and knowledge, you will be doing a great service.

Also, you will find that the way will be opened for you to expand your sphere of influence, and more opportunities will be presented to you as you gain confidence and experience. As you overcome the obstacles and perfect the gifts offered you, you will find your path will become clear and you will know, without a doubt, that you are being helped, guided and supported.

Within the next few years, channeling as you now know it will become an ordinary part of everyday life. It will no longer be unusual, freakish, or a gift for only the few, for everyone who has attained a fourth-dimensional frequency level will be able to tap into and communicate with their Higher Self, their guides, angelic helpers, and yes, even the ascended masters.

Allow me to clarify, at this time, some confusing information or misconceptions regarding the ascended masters and angelic beings. Know that there are more human beings than ever before in physical embodiments who are aspects of, or who carry the energies of the cosmic Beings of the higher realms. Some carry a greater or lesser degree of the energy of a particular Being, but that is all they are, an aspect, or a facet of that great Being. With the exception of the great Avatars, and you all know who they are, no one in the physical expression of the third/fourth dimensions could contain or carry the vastness or entirety of an archangel, or any other cosmic Being. Also, the ascended masters are overlighting and infusing the auric fields of many of their beloved followers. However, except for very short appearances when deemed necessary, they will not incarnate again in the physical body on planet Earth.

When the Earth has moved into a more refined frequency, there will come a time when we will, once again, be visible to you, as we were in the past. Just as we are reconnecting via feelings, energy impulses and channeled messages, we will become even more real to you as you develop clear seeing—or the ability to see multi-dimensionally. This is already happening more often than you realize. You are seeing an expanded light spectrum of colors. There are great signs in the sky via light patterns, cloud formations and unexplainable sightings. Some of you see more clearly than others, just as some of you hear more sharply. These are gifts that you brought with you when you came into the physical. They have atrophied or been forgotten, and it is now time to reclaim them. Believing, or faith in your own abilities and the possibility that what we say is true, is the first step. I ask you to prove it for yourselves, one level at a time, and watch as new vistas and abilities open before you.

Even as we say these gifts are yours to claim, do not get caught up in the glamour of psychic manifestation. Psychic gifts are not necessarily a sign of higher spirituality, especially if used to control, influence or dominate others. Originally, these abilities were a natural part of your physical makeup and will be again in the future. But during these times of transition, your physical structure and mission will determine which abilities you will develop and how quickly they will be made available to you. These gifts have been grossly misused in the past and that will not be allowed to happen again. In the past, it took many years, even lifetimes, for an initiate to develop even the basic psychic abilities. And so, be patient, dear ones, you are being given more help and greater opportunities than ever before. You are making great strides and wondrous gifts await you.

I wish to speak now of your young people. Those who have incarnated in the physical over the last twenty-five years or so are wise and advanced beings. Many are the forerunners of the next race of humanity which will populate the Earth as it moves into harmony and peace. They are more attuned to Spirit and have abilities available to them that you are striving to reclaim. It may not seem that this is so when you see what is happening around the world: the senseless violence, the anger and frustration, and the addictions and excesses in which these young ones are caught up and trapped. Understand that it is not easy for them to live and function in the negativity that they have been exposed to from birth and which constantly surrounds them. They cannot understand, and so they try to drown their pain and sensitive natures in physical sensations of various sorts. They lash out in senseless violence when the pain becomes unbearable. Their senses are not deadened and dulled like those of the older generations. Their mental and emotional natures cannot tolerate the violence and the hate and fear they are exposed to on a daily basis.

Do not blame the young ones, they are only magnifying what is presented to them by the adults around them. If they are to learn respect, they must be respected; to learn unconditional love and to value life, they must be taught that they are worthy, loved and that life is a wondrous gift. If they are to be taught responsibility, others around them must be accountable and responsible for their thoughts, actions and deeds. They are magnifying and dramatically playing out the attitudes, concepts and beliefs of their parents, teachers and role models. They are powerful, wonderful souls, but will continue to be self-destructive, or harm others until they are awakened to their Divine Nature and allowed to connect with their soul/Higher Self. Then, you will see, they will transform before your eyes, and assume leadership roles as they take over and complete the tasks that you began.

Beloved warriors of Light, we consider you our partners in this magnificent cosmic event. You are the actors and directors; we only supply the resources, you might say. But the drama is quickly moving to the next stage, where we will combine our forces even more dramatically. You with full knowledge that you are our emissaries and beloved representatives, and that we are your loving protectors and mentors. We honor and love you most profoundly. I AM Archangel Michael.

37. MERGING SPIRIT WITH MATTER

*B*eloved masters, I bring you greetings and glad tidings from the higher realms to assist you in these stressful times of transition and change. Make no mistake, we are very aware of what each of you is experiencing and the uncertainty you feel as your reality shifts and changes. Many of you are wondering why there is no new forthcoming information— why everything I transmit, as well as other Beings of Light, seems to be a review of what has already been given. The reason is this: you are not ready, beloveds. It is imperative that you make use of and integrate what has been given until it becomes a natural part of your reality. There is much knowledge and new awareness floating in the ethers, but you must grasp it and claim it as your own before you can move to the next level. You must live it and personify it.

You, as well as humanity at large, and the Earth are on the verge of making a leap into the next level of evolution, or initiation. You have integrated and incorporated much energy of a higher frequency and knowledge into your mental, emotional and etheric bodies, and for many of you the status quo no longer exists. We have told you that these next few years will be a bridge to the New Age and this is true. But for the time being you are in what might be termed a holding pattern, a null zone of Spirit, or a time for inward focus and assimilation rather than outward momentum and radical change. Each of you is at a different stage along the path, and so if you look around you will see others to emulate, or those who can give you insight as to what is taking place. The expansion of consciousness is different for each soul, as each has their own Divine Blueprint and Mission, or integral part of the master plan to accomplish. You may feel joyous and in the flow and all seems to be in order today, and yet your perception changes radically tomorrow, for your consciousness is ever expanding into higher awareness.

Just as you, individually, move forward to the next level when your Spirit Self makes the determination that you are ready, so it is on a mass level. You are in the midst of an intense merger of Light with the darkness on Earth and of Spirit with matter. Please do not put a negative label on the term darkness, for it does not mean evil, it only means those portions of the Earth and the souls that are existing with lesser degrees of the Light and love of Spirit. Darkness cannot survive in the Light and humanity cannot survive or move forward without accepting the gift of love that is being offered.

Perfection is not the issue or even the goal at this time, beloved ones. You have the mistaken idea that duality and polarity on the material plane are something evil, or to be denied and overcome. It is not polarity or duality that is holding you back, it is imbalance. You accepted the assignment and were given the opportunity to experience duality. Polarity, or opposite forces, is a part of that process. You came into bodily form balanced and harmonious in your masculine and feminine natures and in the mental and emotional bodies. It was a beautiful melding of Spirit with matter, which is the state you are seeking to recapture and reclaim.

We tell you over and over again that you are here on Earth to enjoy being in the physical form and to enjoy the abundance and wonder of Creation, but it is to be in balance and harmony in all facets of expression. That is why the ascension process is called the narrow path or the middle path. You cannot ignore any of the components or any facet of physical expression. You ignore or abuse your body and it begins to break down and atrophy. If you ignore your mind, you remain ignorant or begin to stagnate and lose interest in life. If you ignore your emotional needs, you begin to feel unloved and lonely. Connecting with your Higher Self and Spirit allows you to tap into the Divine Flow of primal cosmic life substance. This is the energy you used to build your first Spirit/physical form and it is the energy which will help you transform and reclaim that harmony of self.

Many of you are feeling an irresistible urge to step out into the public arena, to begin to flex your spiritual muscles, and yet feel you are being held back. Your Higher Self knows the proper and appropriate time for you to take that giant step out into the unknown. It may be that you have not laid enough ground work, or gained the level of knowledge or expertise that you will need to be effective or successful. Possibly (and this is often the case), the path is being prepared by your guides, teachers and angelic helpers. They will smooth the way, or "prepare a place for you." After you establish your vision and make your commitment and claim victory, it is important that you allow Spirit to take over and bring your dreams to fruition at the proper and appropriate time. Waiting is not easy in the physical, and especially if the ego is in control. Ego thrives on drama, whether positive or negative.

You are all feeling the uncertainty that comes with a dimensional shift. You are learning to exist in shifting energy patterns, in time compression, or a feeling that time is speeding up and out of control. Ask for and take advantage of time expansion. This will give you a sense of slowing down and moving gently and gracefully through your days and nights. Staying in the "event of the now" will assist you in that endeavor, for you will be focused on the moment. Your mind will not be racing forward or spending needless time going over the past. Your energy will be used to create your desires of the moment and you will be much more effective. Maintain an inner focus of serenity and self-control, rather than an outward focus of being controlled by events and the emotions of others.

In the past, we have suggested that you relinquish all the material possessions which are hindering your spiritual growth, which possess you by way of time spent, maintenance or expense. Now, it is time to relinquish the needless activities in your life that are keeping you from coming into harmony with Spirit. What you call television is one of the greatest robbers of time ever invented. It is habit forming and insidious as a tool of mind control. It takes away or dulls your senses so that you have no desire or cannot hear that small inner voice of Spirit that is attempting to make contact. The word "RECREATION"—examine it closely—re-creation of what? How do you spend your leisure time? In needless games that numb the mind and senses, and rob the body of physical activity; or in reading material that reinforces your negative, fear-based picture of reality; or in activities which bring you only frustration instead of satisfaction?

It is time to take a spiritual inventory of how you are spending the gift of life on Earth. You have an allotted time on Earth (determined by your Higher Self) and a specific mission to accomplish. You were blessed and privileged to be allowed to incarnate on Earth during this most important time. Each soul who abdicates their mission adds to the burden of those Light workers who are bravely anchoring the Light (those who are blazing forward on the path, smoothing the way for others to follow).

Oh, you will not fail, my friends. You will eventually listen and come into harmony with Spirit, for that is your ultimate destination. But, when and after how much suffering? That is your choice under the laws of free will. It is said that "time waits for no one," and we add, the evolution of humankind and the Earth will wait for no one. Are you being left behind?

It is important that you understand that all is shifting and changing rapidly, at every level of Creation. You are being asked to stay fluid and flexible, even to hold off in making major changes until you receive strong signals both within and without as to what is appropriate. In other words, you may get an internal nudging or message and it may feel appropriate within your heart center. But during this time of acceleration, before you take action, I suggest that you ask for physical validation as to the appropriateness of the action you are contemplating. Clear signals will be given, but at times, even these will be subject to change. We know this is confusing and frustrating for you, but please be aware that you are taking leaps in years and decades, rather than minutes and days.

This all has to do with the shifting dimensional changes and the fluidity of time. Even from our vantage point, a particular action or event time-line may seem appropriate, only to be nullified by unanticipated events. From our perspective, we view and gauge events by the probable futures that have the greatest potential or carry the strongest energy force field, but now, changes are occurring too rapidly for this to be accurate. That is why it is impossible to predict the future, and why we tell you to place no credence on those who make predictions. We are partners in this great adventure, and we are all forging ahead into uncharted territory. We are at a cocreative expansion level never before attempted or attained, my brave ones, and you are right in the middle of it. It can be an exciting, exhilarating time of great joy and wondrous accomplishment if you will just "stay tuned" to your inner guidance and focused on the moment. Allow your reality to shift and grow, to expand and change direction when needed, thereby taking advantage of every opportunity that Spirit brings your way.

We also ask you to become more attuned and aware of the cycles of the seasons, the equinoxes, solstices and the phases of the moon. We have asked you to meditate and radiate energy down through and around the Earth during the time of the full moon. We now ask you to join together at these powerful times, to unify in a common purpose—that of lifting the consciousnesses of the Earth and humanity. These times are chosen to increase the influx of cosmic energy upon the Earth and all its inhabitants. As more of you allow yourselves to become the receptors and transformers for this refined energy with pure love and unselfish intent, the dynamic power of this energy will grow exponentially. Envision thousands, no millions, from every country, race, creed and color coming together at these designated times with a common purpose in mind and heart: healing the Earth and reclaiming the Divine Birthright for all who reside on her.

Become aware of the power of numbers, as well. With the invention of your digital clocks, it is now possible for your guides and teachers to use this as a method of validating or signaling you that they are with you, or to let you know that you are moving in harmony with Spirit. Also watch what you call your car license plates, as this will also amaze and amuse you as a certain series of numbers is brought into your awareness in a way that is beyond coincidence. I have nudged this messenger to make this information available to you. We will use any means available to let you know that we are with you, helping you to move forward in the right direction.

There is an urgency which is critical and of the utmost importance during this phase that is being initiated, that the knowledge you all take for granted is circulated to the masses, from the lowest to the highest. It is time for the next phase of awakening to begin and on a grand scale. Not the long, slow awakening process that most of you have experienced over the last twenty or twenty-five years. It must and will be, a dynamic, jolting, attention-getting sensation, designed to jar humanity out of its lethargy, to make as many as possible stop and reevaluate their old parameters, old ways of thinking and being, and know that something is afoot. Something unprecedented is happening and it is time to listen, learn and take action. Your loving, soothing, comforting presence and wisdom will be needed and sought as never before.

More facets of your project Starseed Earth mission group will be made known to you. More parts of the puzzle will begin to fall into place as you begin to build a dynamic, powerful, energetic work force with all the knowledge and experience needed to fulfill the Earth's and your Divine Destiny. You have sent out the call on the waves of loving vibrational energy and you are about to be reconnected with those parts of yourself that you feared were lost to you forever. This is just the beginning of the "welcome home" process, dear ones; there is much more to come.

Know that we are as close to you as your heartbeat, and as real as the air you breathe. We salute you for your courage and commend you for your steadfastness. I, Archangel Michael, surround you in love and protection, always.

38. NUMBERS

…omena which are occurring these days to … we are moving with spirit, a way our guides …ave of making us aware of the energies and …f numbers, is the appearance of three or more … number. I awaken very often in the middle of the nig…. and it is 2:22 or 3:33 or 4:44 on my digital clock (occasionally 5:55) or, I glance at the clock and it frequently reads 11:11, or once in a while 12:12.

This information has been compiled from several sources and Lord Michael has validated it.

111   Energy flow · Enhancing whatever level you are at presently.

222   Resurrection and ascension process.

333   Decision number · Either directs you into a phase of 999 completion, or negatively, it puts you in the 666 frequency which throws you back into the third dimension.

444   This is an actual resurrection number · You have just completed an important phase.

555   Experiencing the energy or a level of Christ-consciousness · Very significant.

666   Material world · Third-dimensional frequency · Denseness.

777   Symbolizes an integration of some portion of the four lower bodies with higher spiritual frequencies within the third-dimensional plane, or at the level in which you are manifesting your physical reality on the Earth plane.

888   *Symbolizes infinity · The unified spiral of the physical merging with the Spiritual · Moving toward the completion of the ascension process through the energies of 222 and 444.*

999   *Symbolizes the three levels of the triune or trinity · Completion.*

000   *GREAT VOID · Experiencing a NULL ZONE · Switching or moving into a new energy field.*

11:11 *Beginning of a whole new level or phase of development · Another dimension or frequency of experience · A PORTAL WAY OPENING.*

12:12 *A COSMIC CONNECTION · A bridge to the future · Signifies a level of completion or moving to a new level in the initiation process.*

Have fun with this. I often get validation for a decision I have made or am about to make through numbers. Also, pay attention to license plates.

39. Catching the Wave to the Future

*B*eloved there is a new wave of cosmic energy poised and ready to radiate down upon the Earth and humanity. A Divine Emanation of Light from The Great Central Sun which is a precursor to moving the Earth and humanity into the refined resonance of the fifth dimension. Stargates have been opened and activated, which creates access to the dimensional portals, so that this energy can be focused and directed to the appropriate places. As we have said in the past, the frequencies are too refined and intense to send forth in a blanket effect, as was done in the beginning of your awakening period. You might be surprised to learn that the acceleration process was initiated in the latter part of the 1800s.

As the electromagnetic, cosmic energy was directed to more specific areas around the world in a laser-beam effect, dramatic, positive results were attained, but it also created much pain and suffering. Examples of this are the bombing of the World Trade Center in New York, the riots in the once sacred, beautiful city of angels, Los Angeles, and the devastating bombing in Oklahoma City, as well as the violence and havoc experienced in other areas around the world. The Light frequencies hit the dark and exploded in a dynamic fashion. Out of the chaos and suffering came a new sense of unity, a clearing and cleansing, and an opening of the heart center of those directly involved, creating a rippling effect much as a stone thrown in a pond. The mood and atmosphere in Los Angeles and New York City have been radically changed. Statistics have proven that crime and violence are down and it is much safer on the streets.

In the areas where these violent extremes are taking place, ultimately it brings together a diverse and divided culture, creating a bond and new understanding, as well as an outpouring of love and support. There is still a long way to go, but many agree there is a safer, more gentle aura and sense of community in many of these areas. This same scenario is taking place all over the world. Some are not as dramatic as others, and many are unreported, but change for the better is taking place rapidly. It is inevitable.

It is the desire of the Creator that this process of evolutionary transformation be accomplished with the least amount of pain and suffering for humanity. You have suffered long enough. Therefore, in the future, before the higher level frequencies are beamed down upon a particular area, we are recruiting those of you who have agreed and are capable of being the transformers or receptors for this energy. First of all, we direct to a particular area those souls whose mission it is to open the dimensional portal ways. Then we focus on those whose mission it is to plant the seeds of illumination and bring forth the Light frequencies. You will receive and transmit this energy into the Earth, and via your heart center you will filter and project this gift to others around the Earth. Those souls, in turn, will access and transmit this stepped-down energy at their level of vibrational frequency—Light-seed planting you might call it.

Take notice how often, first one Light worker/leader will go to a city or area and present their message via workshops or spiritual journeys, only to be followed by several others in quick succession. These brave souls usually have no way of knowing that others are also being guided to the same area; they are only following an inner calling that cannot be denied. They each take a different resonance, a different schematic, or what we call Light packets of keys and codes and frequencies to assist in the opening, cleansing, clearing and activation of the particular place.

We have told you that the next few years ahead—the next decade—is a time of transition, a bridge to the next level of consciousness for humanity and the Earth; therefore, this process must be dramatically stepped up. The Divine Plan must move forward and time is of the essence; therefore, the urgency and need for clearing and anchoring these higher frequencies is critical. The areas up and down the West Coast and East Coast of the United States were once wondrous, powerful Light cities in those times of glory, the great Golden Ages of Atlantis and Lemuria. The energies of these magnificent areas, as well as many other wondrous locations around your Earth, have become steeped in fear, greed and negativity as those in power began to use their Divine Gifts for selfish purposes.

Many of you who were born or migrated to a certain area are there because it is part of your mission to heal and transform the negative energy patterns, so that the peace and perfection of that place can be recreated. You carry a memory within your brain structure of how it was in those ancient, bygone days, and a deep-seated longing to recapture the sacredness and beauty of what was once your homeland.

As you know, the energies of the First Ray of Divine Will are being activated once again as a catalyst and tool in the transformation process. It may seem as if all is breaking down, or being destroyed. But in reality, what is happening is that the harmonics of the First and Seventh Rays are now working in unison to transmute and transform old negative energy patterns, and then ignite dramatic new frequencies within the crystalline structure of the Earth and humanity, as well. In this way, the destruction and devastation can be held to a minimum. The dynamic-blue energy of the Divine Will of the Father Creator is merging with the radiant-pink energy of love and compassion of the Mother Creator, thereby forming the Divine Alchemy of the blazing Violet Flame of the Seventh Ray—the over-Lighting frequencies of the New Age.

Envision this: groups of souls are drawn together who have cleared most of their negative energy patterns and balanced their mental and emotional bodies so that they can be clear receptacles or conveyers of these higher-frequency infusions. They come with a pure, unselfish intent and desire to receive inspiration and serve humanity. In various ways, they are led through a gentle process of letting go of old, residual energy patterns, integrating and activating the higher-chakra system, and incorporating the energies and attributes of the five higher Galactic Rays. This makes way for an infusion of the dynamic First Ray of Divine Will and Power, which is needed to activate the dormant, crystalline energies within the Earth's structure. As this energy flows through each person, it activates the keys and codes within his or her brain structure, and this is then added to the whole, as this gift is breathed and radiated down into the Earth. This, in turn, activates the dormant energies within the crystalline structure deep within the Earth. As this energy is ignited, it radiates upward, once again bringing forth the keys and codes of transformation necessary to begin the process of cleansing and healing a particular area.

Each person then takes with them these seeds of transformation. They now are broadcasting or radiating this energy from their heart centers out toward humanity, no matter where they go. And then others who are ready take that energy within and begin to radiate it out toward those around them as well as down into and around the Earth where it magnifies, grows and spreads until it encircles the Earth and touches every sentient Being at some level.

Can you not see the beauty and perfection of this plan? Can you now see how important your participation is in this endeavor? If you do nothing else, beloveds, make yourselves available or state your willingness to be a receiver and bearer of this Divine Gift, at whatever level you are capable of bearing. The strength of your desire to serve humanity and the degree in which you radiate love, peace, harmony and non-judgment will determine the level and power of energy you will be able to access, transmit and utilize. But begin, dear ones. Begin where you are with what you have already been given, and more will be added in greater and greater portions.

This is the mandate that is being brought down from the highest Source as the next step in your awakening. That is why we say to stay focused and flexible, and be ready to change, expand and grow. You are moving out of a linear time/space reality into a fluid, ever-expanding awareness. See yourself stepping on a wave of energy that will shift you back and forth between the dimensional frequencies in which you are comfortably resonating. Now see your future, not as a straight line, but in a circle or oval. You, my brave warriors, as I conveyed to you sometime ago, are going back through the past, healing all the imbalanced energies for your Mother Earth and humanity along the way, as you march boldly toward your glorious future. Humanity at large is still functioning in the third-dimensional frequencies and a linear time/space continuum, wading through the energies of the mass-consciousness, slowly moving toward its destination—but that is the old, outmoded way.

You are being gifted with the solar fire power of the Creator, the blessed gift of the golden Ray of Christ-consciousness, reestablishing that connection with your Father/Mother God. This energy pours forth from the Great Central Sun, down through your own magic I AM Presence. The gift of solar fire is then refracted and projected, via the five Rays of Galactic Consciousness and the First Ray of Divine Will, to your Higher Self, bringing forth new wisdom, gifts and inspiration. As a result, you have been experiencing the gift and initiation of fire by friction: The honing and refining of your physical vessel via the soul. All your trials, tests, pain and discomfort over these past years have been a result of this gift of fire by friction burning the dross (or negative, imbalanced energies) within your physical/etheric, emotional and mental bodies.

You are being honed and polished to the glorious, shining Light Being you were when you first took on the physical body. It is not punishment, beloveds. You may not see it thusly, but it is a wondrous gift. As you learn to harness the fire of Spirit, you will once more become the dynamic, powerful cocreators you once were, for you will be functioning in harmony with Spirit and your Divine Blueprint. That is why I say that many of you are ready to step onto the golden circle of fire. You will soar, flow, expand and glow as you "Catch the Wave to the Future."

These next years of your Earth time are critical in bringing forth and anchoring this Divine Energy within the Earth and making it available to as many souls as possible. The lunar and solar eclipses each year symbolically send out a message to humanity that the radiance of Spirit cannot be held back—that the Light is triumphant over the darkness. And as you experience the spring and fall equinoxes, a day in which the great solar Being of your Earth is positioned equally within the Northern and Southern hemispheres (or when the sun crosses the celestial equator of Earth), please be aware that this is an opportunity for your Earth and humanity to experience an accelerated infusion of solar fire power from the highest source. There are many celestial alignments taking place which are signs and portents, or another way of telling you is that a highway to the cosmos is being formed, beloveds. A bridge to speed you on your way to the glorious New Age where you will express and experience your multidimensional nature, radiating love, peace, joy and harmony.

Commit now, sweet friends, to being a beacon, a tower ready to receive and transmit this wondrous gift of Spirit. You will not only be of great service to the planet and humanity, but it will assist you in attuning to your spiritual/emotional natures, and mentally help you understand the science of spirituality as you perfect your spiritual/human vessel.

There are three words I would like to have you focus on during these coming months: **CREATIVITY, RESPONSIBILITY AND ACCOUNTABILITY.** Meditate on these words. What do they mean to you and how will these words assist you in becoming more empowered and attuned with Spirit? These are words a master takes very seriously and so should you. As creative inspiration bursts forth from within, what are you doing with it? Wishing, dreaming and hoping means nothing if you do not take action. You are responsible for utilizing the gifts being offered—you and you alone are accountable for your deeds at the new level of awareness you have attained. You are being offered gifts beyond measure. How will you use them, and are you ready to accept your assignment as a beacon of Light for the New Age? We await your answers, beloved ones.

As you move toward the **GOLDEN PROMISE** of the future, know that I am ever near to assist you in resuming your rightful place in the Hierarchy of Light. I AM Archangel Michael.

40. RETURNING TO UNITY-CONSCIOUSNESS

*B*eloved masters, at no time during the history of life on planet Earth has it been more important to seek clarity and harmony in each and every moment. Every thought, emotion, verbalization and act is being magnified and cast out into the ethers—that which is building your future and the future of your world. You have asked that you be allowed to become cocreators with us once again— to once more be given the power to tap into the unformed cosmic substance of life, and your wish has been granted. Now what will you do with this gift? As with any gift or talent, it takes practice and time to perfect. At some level, all of you are striving to tap into the knowledge and are searching for the tools you will need to move out of the old paradigm, the constrictions and conflicts of the third dimension, and into the ever-expanding reality where all is possible and attainable.

It is time for you to begin to see yourselves in a different light. Who are you? What title or role do you relate to and identify with? What words would you use to describe who and what you are? Do you identify with your work title, your family name, or as an extension of someone else: a wife, mother, son or husband? Yes, you may be all of these things, but it is not who you are, my beloved ones. Your true identity is so much vaster than you can imagine, and if you could see yourselves as you really are, you would be truly amazed. You are a projection and a representative of a most wondrous Being. You were sent to Earth with many other fragments of your Divine Self to experience, learn and fulfill your particular mission, to contribute your chosen creative talents and knowledge, which are uniquely your own, and thereby add to the wisdom of the whole.

It is time to stop judging yourselves by the standards that have been established by others down through the ages. You are not what your education has made you, or the title it allows you to use before or after your name. You are not your family lineage, nor are you to see yourselves as isolated or bound to just one particular race, creed, or gender. You have experienced many lifetimes, assumed many roles, and donned many disguises and personas. It is interesting to us to see how those still stuck in illusion judge others so vehemently when they have played the same roles and acted out the same dramas. They are judging their own fears and weaknesses that are being mirrored back to them.

The old limited image you have of yourself, or which others have of you, is not who you are. We have stated many times, you are a Divine Being having a human experience. You are not here to seek perfection on the physical plane—it is impossible to attain. It is the ego that is always comparing and never satisfied with things as they are. It is a sense of unworthiness that makes you seek to always gain new recognition, to be more than, or better than those around you. We are not saying that you should not strive to be the best you can, that you should not take advantage of all the opportunities offered you. We are asking you to see yourselves as perfect just the way you are, no matter what your levels of experience, status, life conditions or station.

Just as I explained to you about the life experience you chose before coming back into the physical form, it is important that you begin to see the overview or greater picture of who you are. You decided, along with your guides, teachers and Divine I AM Presence, what was needed for you to return to a state of balance and harmony, what areas you had neglected or avoided. You came with a specific allotment of

talent, awareness and illumination drawn from your Divine
Self, with a mission to accomplish which was in accord with
your overall-life plan. The drama you were to play with others was carefully planned and orchestrated so that you would
have the best opportunity to experience and move through
the blockages and limitations into greater awareness. The
old way is to judge yourself and others by the standards established by those in power or control, or by the popular beliefs
of mass-consciousness. It is time to stop judging with the
mind or intellect and to start viewing others through a filter
of love and compassion.

Leading a spiritual life does not mean giving up the pleasures of the world, martyring yourself or living a life of sacrifice for others. You are on Earth to express **JOY,** to experience
all the wonders and beauty of the physical plane. You came
to express the full potential of your God Essence, no matter
what the level of that expression—from the minuscule to the
magnificent. You came to embody a particular facet of God-
Beingness and each expression is as precious to the Creator
as another. If you will change your perception, stop judging
yourselves and the conditions of your life, and begin to focus
on the opportunities being offered and the joy of the challenge, you will tap into the formula for spiritual mastery.

The next step, and you are in the midst of this now, dear
ones, is moving into unity-consciousness. You must stop
judging your brothers and sisters, and begin to love them
for their uniqueness and diversity. They have great gifts and
wisdom to offer you, as you have for them. They also have
their residual weaknesses and areas of pain that you can assist them to overcome, just as, in turn, they can assist you.
If you judge and see only their imperfections, that is what
you increase or magnify in yourselves. But if you seek what

is right about them in their present state and radiate love and acceptance toward them, that is the frequency pattern you reinforce and what they will mirror back to you.

You cannot see or even imagine how the unified force field of Light is increasing and growing amongst you, the Light Warriors. How it is encompassing, permeating and penetrating the Earth. We call it a Heart Link, but in reality it is the rejoining of Essence-to-Essence, Spirit-to-Spirit and mind-to-mind as you come together in common purpose through meditation, toning, breathing and embodying the magnificent, radiant Spirit of our Creator.

Remember beloveds, Love/Light is expansive—it is active and it lifts up and illuminates. Fear/darkness contracts—it is passive, draws down and constricts. As you come together and offer each other the radiance of your Light and the wisdom of your experiences, you assist each other to move through the illusion and fear of the darkness. You shine your Love/Light out for all to see and allow others to bask in the glow of your victories. You are the examples, with a grand opportunity to assist others and give them the courage to move forward. Those following behind you will see what you have done with your challenges and the rewards you have reaped for your bravery and diligence. You are smoothing the path and easing the way for those who will follow in your footsteps.

You have no concept of your power and ability to change the world when you come together with a unified purpose in your hearts and minds for the betterment of all. When you move aside your prejudices and self-interests, you harness the full force and measure of Divine Light Substance and miracles are wrought. It is time to forge ahead, but as a whole, no longer focused solely on individual endeavor. That is why we ask you to first concentrate on your own growth, balancing and harmonizing all facets of your Being as you come into the realization that you are a Spark of Divine Essence. You then move past the narrow view and concept of the little self, and into unity-consciousness, whereby your focus shifts to that of a master and on the vaster ONE, instead of the small one.

You have all been so eager and anxious to come to full realization, to ascend and attain mastery, that you have forgotten to enjoy the journey and miracles of the moment. Each and every encounter and event has a purpose and contains important information for your growth. If you forge ahead too quickly, you not only make the journey more difficult, but quite often you have to regress to absorb some necessary wisdom or release some outmoded concepts that are hindering your progress.

Remember, you are now in the spiral of evolution, the oval of enlightenment, the ebb and flow of mastery and transmutation. You surge forward, out into the world, in search of new knowledge and information. You must then turn inward in order to assimilate, integrate and utilize what you have learned. You then project that new awareness out into your reality, making it your own and sharing it by example. The process then repeats itself, time and time again.

Many of you are concerned because it seems that you are taking a step backwards, for emotions and energies you thought you had released are emerging once again. At times, it seems these experiences are even stronger than they were before. You are dismayed, you judge yourselves and feel you are regressing instead of making progress and moving into new territory or a new level of awareness. Did we not tell you that you are experiencing the energies and memories of the mass-consciousness in order to heal them and bring them into harmony and balance? Most of these feelings and emotions are not of your own making, but from mass memory of bygone ages. Here again, we ask you not to judge, to move out of the narrow focus on your small self. Realize that you are serving the **ONE** or the whole, along with other dedicated warriors, in healing, balancing and clearing the past memory of humankind and the Earth. The pain, suffering, sense of failure, guilt and fear cannot exist in the paradise that is being formed and manifested in the ethers. It must be transmuted and requalified before humanity and the Earth can move forward and claim that bright new world of tomorrow.

The formula is simple: become aware of your emotions, moment by moment. Sense where within your bodily structure these emotions are affecting you. Be the observer as you examine and move into the area and the emotions, allowing them to express or come fully to the fore. Do not fear, deny or restrict them, my friends. That is the old way. Embrace them, and allow them to give you the wisdom they are offering as you release and transform the imperfections into shining Light Substance. Breathe as we have taught you. Breathe through your crown chakra and down into the Earth, then back up into the crown and down again, forming a figure eight or the infinity sign with your heart as the center focus. Or, tone the energy out of your body and into your auric field and see it being transformed into shining crystalline Light. This is so you do not resonate the imbalanced energy out into your force field which then creates a cause and effect situation which must be rectified. That is the old way. Claim and know that you are entitled to move through this process with ease and grace, not through trauma, pain and suffering as in the past.

I have told you this in the past, but it bears repeating. Each evening review your day. Do not judge, just observe. What could you have done differently? What did Spirit nudge you to do that you did not heed? What would one of the beloved masters have done in each situation that comes to mind? Did you project the unconditional love and nonjudgment of a master? Or, did you miss the mark in some way? After you have reviewed the events of the day objectively, call on the mighty Angel of Forgiveness and the Violet Flame to transmute and harmonize any discordant energy that you may have projected out into the world that day and know that in asking, it is done. This moves you into a state of harmlessness and grace, so that you are not projecting any discordant energy out into the world. As you add your loving thoughts, affirmations, gratitude and vision of perfection for humanity and the Earth, it flows freely, unimpeded and not distorted in any way, joining with like energies. It gains power and momentum as it surrounds the Earth and is catapulted out into the higher realms to manifest and shower blessings down on all who are ready to receive it. This is how powerful you are becoming, my brave warriors, and how wondrous are the times of the present.

Do not tarry or hesitate, beloveds: it is time to take up your banner and sword of Light. Do not miss this grand opportunity to join with your brothers and sisters in a unified endeavor to heal, balance and harmonize, not only yourselves but the Earth, as well. You are ready, you are capable, just as you are this moment. Only you can fulfill your particular mission and add your unique energy to the whole. A golden opportunity is being offered, just as was the **GOLDEN PROMISE** given. The choice is yours; what measure of your Divine Self will you draw to you and manifest? Only you can decide. Know that we see you in wondrous cloaks of Light and in great splendor, and that you are loved beyond measure. I AM Archangel Michael.

41. LIVING YOUR PASSION

*B*eloved masters, as a result of an influx of extremely high-level frequency patterns that are being radiated down to you, you are moving into a new, refined state of awareness. You may not sense this or feel differently right away, but you will—it is assured.

You are beginning to see through God's eyes and your mind and hands will once more radiate with the power of Creation. The connection to your Source is growing stronger each day. Be aware, beloveds, that in each and every moment you are either adding to the glory and beauty of God's perfection, or adding to the imbalanced energies that must be requalified and purified back into neutral, primal life substance, before it can be transmuted into new forms of a higher vibration. Energy, or manifested substance, is never lost; it can only be transmuted or its molecular structure changed into another higher/lower form, or frequency pattern.

We have explained that it is time to bring the science of spirituality into your conscious awareness. There are many wondrous Beings with scientific skills and knowledge now awakened and dedicated to the task of merging the science of spirituality with the theory and emotions of spiritual awareness. This is a most important and critical step in the evolution of humankind. Yes, you must have faith in the future and you must have faith in the perfection of the plan that is unfolding before you. But you are coming into your spiritual adulthood and should now demand and claim the wisdom and detailed information as to the workings of the cosmos and the "why and wherefores."

Blind faith is not a requirement nor a desired attribute of a master. You are becoming responsible partners, cocreators of your future, the future of the Earth and humankind. Your mettle is being tested to see if you can stand firm within the onslaught of negativity, fear and resistance that is spewing forth from those who are not yet ready to awaken. No matter how deep the shadows or dense is the matter that swirls around you, you must remain a pillar of Light anchored firmly on Earth, while tapping into the heights, strength and majesty of your Divine Self.

Many of you are ready to know your origins, from whence you came so many aeons ago, and as a result you will begin to bring forth the wisdom, talents and gifts that have lain dormant, awaiting this time of awakening. The healing sounds of Creation are beginning to resound and echo through your minds—you can no longer ignore or deny them. The geometric patterns of Light and color are beginning to fill your mind's eye and filter out into your reality. You are remembering that you came as crystalline pillars of Light made manifest in solid matter, gradually taking on the physical form of body, mind and emotions. As you reclaim the fragments of yourself and heal the memories of the past, you will, once again, come into mastery as your life and all around you begins to sparkle and glow with the purity and power of Spirit.

Allow me to give you another taste of the wisdom and insight that awaits you as you tap into the higher wisdom of Creation. You have become familiar with and aware of the colors of the chakra system (both the colors of the physical realm and their resonance, and the transforming higher frequencies and colors), as well as the Rays, their colors, aspects and attributes. Your interest in crystals, precious and semiprecious stones, minerals and the Earth's treasures such as gold, silver and copper has increased dramatically—and not just for their ornamental value. There is an esoteric meaning (hidden wisdom, or intended for the understanding of initiates or disciples) behind this which you have forgotten. When you agreed to leave your home in the higher dimensions and journey into the density and limitation of physical form, we wanted to make sure that you did not forget the magnificence of your origins and the beauty of who and what you truly are. Therefore, the golden and silver radiance of the Great Central Sun was deposited in solidified form throughout the Earth, and great caches of gem stones and beautiful minerals were strewn where you might easily find them. Humanity has sought and coveted these treasures down through the ages without knowing or appreciating their true significance.

Each of you came into conscious awareness as you were breathed forth from the Essence of the Divine Father/Mother God. You were a blazing white beam of Light which then refracted into a gold and silver beam, the duality which was to be experienced on the Earth plane—the gold bearing the energies of the Father aspect and the silver radiating the Mother aspect of the Creator. Just as the life-giving sun represents the power of the Father, the silvery moon reflects the love, beauty and purity of the Mother. The great variety of gemstones are symbolic of the refracted Rays that were projected from the core of their creative Spirit and infused with the virtues, aspects and attributes that were to be incorporated by you and all humanity. The chakra system was then attuned to these virtues, aspects and attributes—originally in perfect harmony. Only after many ages did you lose your connection to these harmonizing frequencies as your chakra system became distorted and imbalanced. Copper has acted as a stabilizer and conduit for anchoring the higher frequencies on and through the Earth and has played a secondary, but an important, role.

You think you covet and desire gold and silver because of its scarcity and beauty, but that is not the only reason. As you lift your frequencies, balancing and harmonizing your four lower bodily systems and the seven major chakras (and many minor ones) available in the third dimension, you can magnify and once more ignite the frequency patterns in crystals, gemstones and precious metals. This, in turn, allows you to tap into and access the Galactic Chakra system and the five higher Galactic Rays and activate these within your physical and etheric body. There is an exoteric (material or external) meaning, as well as an esoteric (spiritual) meaning for each Ray. The colors have changed or blended at various times throughout the ages, depending on the lessons to be learned and which attributes most needed to be incorporated by humanity. The colors were determined by the Creator and whether the aspects and energies were being projected from the Great Central Sun or from one of the lesser suns.

If you seek to claim more of the Solar Fire Power of the **First Ray,** wear a red gemstone, or to soften too much aggressive use of the First Ray, temper it with a sapphire gemstone. To tap into the Illumination/Wisdom of the **Second Ray,** wear a light-blue stone, or a yellow topaz gem for enlightenment. Yellow may also be worn or used to refine the Intellect aspect of the **Third Ray,** or luminescent pink for Divine Love. Green is the desired color or stone to create Harmony and Balance, or the white diamond, symbolic of Purity, and is the focus of the **Fourth Ray.** The **Fifth Ray** color on the material plane is orange, and radiates the aspects of Science, Healing and Logic; however the esoteric or spiritual color is green and, therefore, the jewel to wear is the emerald in order to attune to the higher frequencies of this Ray. The **Sixth Ray** carries the energies of Service, Devotion, Mercy and Grace. Its color is indigo, but the gemstone is the ruby, which symbolizes the sacred blood of the Christ-energy which flows through your veins, or the Creator made manifest in the physical. The **Seventh Ray,** the Ray of Purification, Transmutation and Freedom is the most active Ray on Earth at this time, along with the energies of the First Ray of Divine Will. It will be the predominant vibration on Earth over the next two-thousand years. Its color is violet and the gemstone is amethyst. It radiates the Flame of Forgiveness and the Divine Alchemy which reconstructs and perfects energy.

The five higher Galactic Rays are infused with the luminescence of Christ Light from the Divine Source. The **Eighth Ray** is aquamarine, or seafoam green tinged with the Violet Transmuting Flame; it will facilitate the cleansing of the four lower bodily systems and bring clarity. The **Ninth Ray** is magenta in its exoteric form, yet now radiates refined energies the color of a turquoise gemstone, which is anchoring the new combined heart/throat chakra and reactivating the life-extending thymus gland. The **Tenth Ray** is a beautiful, pearlescent white tinged with gold (whereby you are now accessing the golden richness of the Creator which increases and magnifies with each succeeding higher Ray). You are beginning to anchor the Light body and tap into the eternal Peace and Joy of the Creator. The **Eleventh Ray** is an iridescent peach, or pink tinged with gold, which is the rainbow bridge to the higher-causal mind, or reconnecting with your Divine I AM Presence. Finally, the magnificent **Twelfth Ray,** which is the Golden Solar Ray, radiates an opalescence of great beauty. The gemstone is the shimmering opal and is symbolic of Transformation. It is the Ray that will anchor the Christ-consciousness on Earth and is a combination of all the other Rays. Or to put it another way, all the other Rays are refractions of the Twelfth Ray.

I have endeavored to refresh your memory and bring into focus the true meaning and purpose of some of the precious gifts given to you by the Creator. These wisdom teachings are as old as humankind; you have just forgotten. Allow your own inner knowing or Higher Self to assist you in determining which Rays or attributes you need to focus on, integrate and perfect. Then, wear the corresponding colors and meditate with, or wear, the appropriate stones.

I remind you, the information given here and the use of these tools must have the catalytic power of loving intent to activate them, and you must use discernment by allowing your intuition to guide you as you move along the path of illumination. Remember to claim and express the Joy of Spirit each day as you fully live in the present and boldly move toward the future. As you move deeper and deeper into the meaning of, and in harmony with, each Ray, you will be more empowered and yet, more gentle. Knowledge will transmute into wisdom as you tap into the Divine Mind where all things are possible.

Your abilities to heal yourself and assist others to do the same will increase and you will come more fully into balance and harmony both within and out in the world. Your creativity will flow and you will manifest works of great beauty. You will become more godlike, and at the same time, more childlike, as you celebrate life, live in wonder and appreciate the magic of the moment. You will radiate love and feel an exquisite connectedness to all. The Earth and all living things will become sacred as you live in reverence and become aware of the divinity in everyone and everything. As you claim your mastery, you will feel a great sense of self-worth, acknowledging the sacredness within you, and you will radiate that gift through your eyes and hearts to everyone you meet so that they, too, may know they are Divine Beings.

You will live in peace and harmony with all those around you no matter what challenges or lessons come your way. You tap into the wisdom and strength of Spirit as you utilize and activate each gift and attribute until the band of Light on your brow radiates fully and harmoniously the full spectrum of the Twelve Rays. **As it was in the beginning, so will it be once more.**

It is time to reclaim your passion with life and Creation. Let go of the memories of failure and recapture the vision of your original mission on Earth. Yes, you must integrate all the facets of expression that the Twelve Rays represent, but you have within your memory bank that special, unique desire waiting to be brought into manifestation on the Earth plane. Within you, waiting to come forth, is a wondrous gift which was offered by the Creator and claimed by you. Within that passion to create is the formula in which you will fulfill your contract and complete your part of the Divine Plan.

Do not tarry, beloved ones. Take up the **Flame of Creation** once more as we blaze a trail together, back to the glorious temples of Alpha and Omega. You are loved beyond measure. I AM Archangel Michael.

42. INFINITE MOMENT

Every moment in time is written on an infinite line

Of emotion, thought and deed.

There is always an intrinsic need

To leave a trace of ourselves,

An indelible color, sound or impression

Of who we are, so that others will not forget

That we were there before them.

The past weaves its memories,

And the future holds a glimmer of bright promise,

But only the present moment is magical,

For that is when we can feel the breath of God

Stir within our soul,

And we know we, too, are infinite.

Ronna Herman

43. THE JOURNEY HOME HAS BEGUN

*B*eloved masters, I ask you to take a moment and allow yourselves to lift your consciousnesses out of your physical vessel as you read my message. First, feel your heart expand to incorporate the vastness of the love I radiate to you. Go within your brain structure as I have taught you and feel the Light packets of wisdom ignite and begin to pour forth. You may feel a slight pressure as if you have a band around your forehead, but there will be no discomfort. Now, sense a pulsating, radiating, golden halo begin to form about eight inches above your head as I send down a shaft of loving energy to enfold you. Allow the Essence of who you are—the true you, a Spark of the Divine, to burst forth and move up and beyond the confines of time and space, into the rarified realms where we dwell. We come together during your sleep time, and we answer your calls during meditation or times of distress or sadness. Now it is time for you to realize that you have the capability of reaching us and communing with us during your conscious, awakened state and that we are not "out there" but only a thought away. We resonate at a higher vibrational frequency, and presently most of you cannot see us, but we are real—more real than you in your physical overlay of matter.

I will endeavor to strengthen your connections to the higher realms and to ease the distress many of you are experiencing at this time in your physical vessels. Most of you are in the process of releasing the residual impacted energy within your bodies from a deep-core level. You are experiencing facets of yourself which have been unavailable to you for hundreds of thousands of years. All of those imperfect fragments you have projected out into the ethers down through the age, as you endeavored to recreate the perfection of your first embodiment, are streaming back into your conscious awareness. Those energies have emotions and frequency, and they trigger responses and reactions within your physical vessel—wherever those memories are stored and impacted. That is why it is so imperative that you become the observer of this process. Register the emotion, observe where in your body it causes a reaction or a stressful response and move into the energy. Do not fear it, it is a gift. What awareness or wisdom is to be garnered? What lessons to be learned? Your Higher Self will give you the insight of the experience if you will allow your intuitive mind to flex its muscles and become your mentor and teacher. Breathe the healing, transmuting Violet Flame throughout your body and see the impacted energy dissipate. Or, see the spiraling radiance of the luminescent five Galactic Rays spiraling throughout your body as they continually requalify, balance and harmonize the third-dimensional thought patterns which do not serve your highest good.

Many of you feel somewhat out of the flow. You are weary and feel the need for more rest and may need more hours of sleep. Your eating patterns are erratic—you may have a craving for foods you do not usually eat, or your appetite may increase or wane. Many of you have put on additional pounds without changing your diets and you are wondering, "What in the world is going on?" It matters not what you eat at this time; you might say you are reversing the process that brought you to this point, that made you who and what you are today. You are releasing old energy patterns and thought forms from your ancient past and even your ancestry through your DNA patterning. Allow, beloveds. Allow. This too will pass. Be gentle with yourselves and as I often tell you, listen to your body elemental. It is once again becoming your friend and partner. It will help you to reclaim your health and vitality if you will allow it to do so. Stop before you put sustenance in your body and ask your body elemental if it is proper and for your highest good. Become conscious as to whether you are eating for emotional nurturance or to give your body fuel. If your body is overloaded with food, which must be processed through your digestive system, that is where the focus of your multiple bodily systems will be; for your mind will feel sluggish and your senses will be dulled so that your creative Spirit cannot effectively work with and through you. Your energy level will drop and the focus of your existence at that time will be on processing the material frequencies you have ingested, changing them either into dross or refined energy.

Your Mother Earth is experiencing many shifting, radical energy patterns as well. Many places around the world are experiencing the elements of water and wind, as these powerful forces attempt to heal and balance the emotional frequencies and negative thought forms with which humanity has impacted these locations. Also, through the element of fire, many other areas are being given a golden opportunity to heal the anger, fear and desire for power, control and domination brought forth in the memory of many from their lives in ancient Atlantis. It is not by coincidence that they have reincarnated in areas where it is of major importance that they endeavor to heal the negativity they helped to create. There are also many brave and wondrous souls living in these diverse places who are attempting to anchor the Light, to lift and harmonize the frequencies, but the population at large is still in denial and resistance. Therefore, the great Devas using the element of fire are attempting to instill awareness as to the urgency of the times, not as a punishment, but as a wake-up call. Those who need these cataclysmic events to shock them into awareness will be greatly impacted and affected. Those who are endeavoring to allow Spirit to flow forth and magically clear the way will find they will be kept safe and not have to experience the destructive effects.

Remember what we have endeavored to instill in your consciousness these past years; all that is not in harmony with the ever-increasing frequencies of the Earth must be restructured and requalified, either willingly or through the laws of cause and effect, known as Karma. A most wondrous gift is being offered to humanity, but many are still ignoring the warning signs, the predictions, the nudgings of Spirit. Negative predictions are brought forth so that, through the gift of free will, you may change and requalify or negate the energy patterns from which those predictions were made.

Remember, beloveds, all that is transpiring is part of the ever-evolving process of ascension. The imperfections must be brought to the surface and requalified, thereby making room, or preparing a place, for Spirit to once more descend and take dominion.

Those of you who participate in group meditations, or on a grander scale, the worldwide, unified meditations, or who actively take part in opening the portals or galactic stargates are providing a great service. Your synergistic endeavors are much more powerful than you can imagine. It is the beginning of the return to unity-consciousness, as you all focus on one particular project, sending loving energy to a distressed area or a group of suffering people. Or there are those of you who, through your unconditional loving intent, establish the refined pathway for the higher resonance of Spirit to descend to Earth. You are becoming aware that you are not an island unto yourself. Your negative energies resonate out into the frequency highways that surround the Earth and affect every sentient Being—just as your loving thoughts and energy Light-en the thought waves and give hope and inspiration while lifting the consciousness of the masses. Never underestimate the power of your thoughts, deeds and words you speak. The golden etheric web of the Earth has been reconnected, refined and is fully functional and operating as it was in the beginning. You are becoming more telepathic and empathetic as the thought patterns from within the Earth, the higher realms and humanity begin to flow through this web of Light. That is why you can no longer ignore what is happening on the opposite side of the Earth. The thought patterns and frequencies surge forth and sweep around the Earth in moments and affect each and every one of you. If you have the same frequency patterns within you, negative or positive, they will impact and affect you in very dramatic ways. You cannot hide or go into isolation—those times are over, dear ones.

I will give you another vision of the perfection of the grand plan for you to ponder on until next we come together. The Creator's directive for this universe was that there would be many unique, detailed and focused Creations brought forth, whereby those of you who were drawn to a particular world and culture would become experts in one specific aspect or attribute of Creation. Whatever your focus was: mental, emotional, scientific, medical, historical, creative, teaching, nurturing and serving, leading and directing, then those particular aspects and attributes were integrated into your Divine Blueprint/Mission through the energies and overlay of the energy patterns of the great Rays. That is what you have endeavored to do throughout the ages, to bring to the fore and perfect.

See the vast multitudes of Divine Sparks of consciousness flowing out into the universe via the energies of the great Rays from the heart of the Father/Mother Creator of this universe to the Cocreator Gods, the Paradise Sons, the Elohim, the builders of form, the angelic realms, the great Beings of Light and ultimately, **YOU.** Envision yourselves among these blessed, brave ones as you surge and flow, experience, create and grow in knowledge and expertise. Aeons later, the next part of the grand plan was put into effect and the vision of a small, special planet was brought forth—a planet which would be beautiful beyond measure, for all the wonders of Creation would be brought to this one, small place within the outer limits of a galaxy, at the farthest edge of Creation.

The process of bringing this miracle of Creation into physical manifestation in one place began. After being scattered throughout the universe, all was gradually brought and recreated on planet Earth: all the diversity, all the uniqueness, all the expertise and wisdom garnered throughout the long journey since the inception of the grand plan. You all traveled down through what is called the seven spheres of experience, or the realms of the seven Rays of expression, which contained all the virtues, aspects and attributes you would eventually incorporate. You stayed the longest in that place with which you resonated from within, the place which was attuned to your Divine Mission. And there, you stayed in the form of your great I AM Presence, who then projected you down in many fragments which would become known as your "soul family."

You kept a portion of your "cosmic memory" intact for

many ages, until the Earth and humanity sank into the density of the third dimension. The veil of forgetfulness was gradually drawn across your memory and the Ring-Pass-Not or quarantine was placed around the memory of Mother Earth's consciousness as well. You have journeyed throughout the past thousands of years feeling alone and disconnected from us, the Beings of Light, and from your own Divine Self. You were sent forth, alone, to experience, create, gain wisdom, and share the expertise and knowledge that are uniquely yours. You had to learn what it entails to create on the physical plane, in a physical body, to remember as you perfect your earthly skills—that you are a master.

Your "cosmic memory" is returning as you clear and balance all the energies created through the mistakes, trials and errors made down through the ages. All was part of the overall grand plan, my brave ones, but it was not known how the drama would play out until it was brought forth and implemented, and free will was granted as the ultimate test in cocreation.

Just as you burst forth from unity-consciousness—separating and fracturing into fragments of many sizes and resonance, weaving your way down through the dimensions and through your many lives and experiences on Earth, seemingly alone—you are now reversing the process. You are healing and integrating the fragments of yourself. You are balancing and harmonizing your force fields so that the multidimensional aspects of your Being can also begin the process of reintegration. Many of you are now in harmony and attunement with your Higher Self and are well on your way to integration with the power, love and wisdom of your Christ Self or I AM Presence. In addition, you are merging into unity-consciousness with your "companions on the journey," the multitudes of brave souls who stepped forward with you in answer to the clarion call and agreed to traverse the unknown as a participant in this "grand experiment."

How wondrous it is to watch you, precious, brave ones, as you remember, and as you recognize those who are your companions-in-Spirit, those from whom you were separated and have missed so sorely. We revel in your excitement and joy as you lovingly reunite and share the experiences of your journey, as you bring forth and share the wisdom you have garnered, and allow others to help you reclaim and integrate that which you lack.

Indeed, it is a time of great change, a time when all the facets of Creation are striving to return to the harmony of unity-consciousness from which it sprang. Those who remain on the fringes and those who are unwilling to begin the process of awakening and integration will feel more and more isolated. The sense of being alone and cut off will increase until they cry out in anguish, and reach out to those of you waiting to lovingly assist them back on the path and the homeward journey ... eventually to rejoin one with another in the heart of our Father/Mother God from whence we all came.

We are awaiting the opportunity to assist you to leap beyond the obstacles and boundaries which keep you ensnared in anything less than perfection. You no longer have to journey alone, beloved ones. We are here to offer guidance, assistance, wisdom and all the Love/Light you can integrate and pour forth from your Being. I AM Archangel Michael and I bring you these truths.

44. THE MAGIC DOOR

*B*eloved masters, imagine if you will that we are all seated together in a great circular room, reclining on soft pillows. There are gentle breezes blowing an exquisite fragrance through gossamer curtains and soft, sweet music playing in the background. We will call this place the Temple of Reunification and Harmony. Envision the marble pillars veined with gold, and see the magnificent crystal which hangs suspended from the center of the domed ceiling, radiating and refracting through its prisms all the colors of the Twelve Rays. Fill this temple with all the beautiful treasures you can imagine, everything you will need to return to the paradise of the heart, that wondrous place you left in order to fulfill your mission, journeying through aeons and light years to the physical realm on planet Earth. Know that this temple is a safe and sacred place, and as you bravely delve within and face all the shadows that you fear so much, you will see them miraculously disappear. They will be replaced with hope, inspiration, vision, courage, and the power and wherewithal to create your greatest dreams and desires, as long as they are in harmony with your Divine Blueprint and for the highest good of all.

Your soul family is awaiting you in this sacred temple, as are your guides, teachers, and we of the angelic kingdom who have journeyed with you down through the ages. The masters you have worked with are there, and most importantly, your own beloved I AM Self. Believe me when I tell you, this is not just an exercise. It is the beginning of a new phase in your awareness; allowing you to bring into your awakening consciousness the realities of what takes place in your astral journeys while your physical brain and body are at rest.

What we will endeavor to do this day is to make you aware of how deeply the fear of death and survival are entrenched within you and how it is still affecting your life in every facet of existence. When you were cut off from your soul family and the Source, via your Higher Self and your I AM Presence, and began the journey of aloneness—a feeling of being separated and apart—you forgot that you are immortal and had only assumed a disguise in the form of a physical body. You began the journey of duality and learned to play the game of polarities.

All of you (and none who are in the physical body are exempt) have played the game of victim and victimizer, at one time the one who exerted power, and then at another, the one who was overpowered. You have experienced riches and scarcity, beauty and bounty, as well as lack and limitations. You have squandered your gifts and you have used them to bring a modicum of paradise to Earth. You have cherished and nurtured those around you, and you have lived lives of great selfishness, focusing only on yourself. These are all issues of survival and the deep-seated need to claim what is your birthright. But, most often, you have gone about it in the wrong way, either demanding or claiming what belongs to others, or allowing others to enslave you and take what is yours. You have forgotten that there is enough love for all, a never-ending supply of all that is required for you to live a long, fruitful, bounteous and joyous life on Earth in a healthy, beautiful body.

As you disconnected from your Higher Self, you moved into a modality of survival and scarcity, focusing on the limitations of the physical body without the awareness and wisdom of Spirit. You began to feel "less than" and therefore, imperfect and inferior. As you projected all these thought forms out into your etheric body and the ethers, they gained strength and momentum down through the ages, until you created a world that reflected your worst fears and obsessions. Each lifetime you were given an opportunity to rewrite the script, change your perception and erase the source of your heartache and lack. It has been a long, painful journey, my friends, and we are well aware of how you have suffered, for we have had to stand by and watch. We were limited as to how much assistance we could give for we could not infringe upon your free will. All you had to do was ask and give us permission to assist you, but most often, you did not. You have forgotten that we promised to answer your every beck and call, and so you struggled alone.

Those times are coming to a close, and once again, you are remembering and reaching within and beyond what you can see in the physical. You are starting to trust your intuition, the nudgings of Spirit—that wondrous, wise wellspring of knowledge and strength that will lead you unerringly onto the right path and toward the right action.

While you are in this sacred space, let us assist you in releasing those survival issues which are keeping you from claiming your power, your mastery. Suddenly, many of you find yourselves in transition, or a forced change is looming with regards to your health, work, relationships, home and family. We have told you that the status quo no longer exists, all is in a state of change—an evolution. All that does not resonate to the refined frequency patterns that are bombarding you and your world will be stirred, stimulated and brought to the fore to be faced and rectified. Sit quietly and focus on each situation that is being brought into your awareness (your work or job, for instance). Does it bring you joy and satisfaction? Are you using your creative talents and able to express who and what you are? Or, are you stifled in an atmosphere that you have outgrown, no longer able to relate to those around you? From deep within have you longed to make a change and find a position which would supply all your needs: financial support, as well as emotional and mental stimulation and reward? Many of you hesitate and vacillate, afraid to make a decision, until seemingly fate steps in and forces you to make the change by removing that which you have outgrown or does not serve your highest good. Spirit will assist you in attaining that which you desire if you are brave enough to build your vision and then grasp the dream when the way is opened.

Your relationships and home environments are a wonderful testing ground and have the potential to help you move forward rapidly in your spiritual growth. Your loved ones are mirroring to you that which you need to address and resolve—your own fears and inadequacies. Are you playing the power game? Are you giving away your power, trying to reclaim or assume your authority; or are you fearful of not being in control so that you have to control everyone and everything in your life? Do you focus on all the imperfections of those around you, or do you see their beauty and uniqueness, thereby reinforcing that which is positive and loving? It is sad to observe that so many of you project onto your loved ones the blame for your sense of unworthiness and your fears of failure. Some of you have outgrown relationships/partnerships and are feeling stifled and restrained. Are you aware that if you focus on the positive attributes of those around you, giving them an opportunity to be their best, while being a loving example, firmly living your truth and integrity, there is a great possibility that they will begin the process of transformation—awakening to the nudgings and inspiration of Spirit? However, if they do not, you will have fulfilled your obligation to them and if you ask and remain heart centered, claiming the highest good for all, Spirit will take control and resolve the dilemma for you. No one or thing will be allowed to deter those of you who are dedicated to your missions and the paths of enlightenment. When you have learned the lesson or garnered the wisdom of a situation or relationship, it will be transmuted or resolved.

Does this stir up fears of failure, responsibility, or of losing those around you via the death process? Many have made the decision not to remain in the physical during these times of great turmoil and change. They are afraid to face themselves and what it would take to move forward to the next level. Those of you who are reading this message and taking these words to heart most likely do not fear the death process for yourselves, for you know it is a transition into another realm of awareness—going home and being welcomed like the prodigal son/daughter. Can you perceive the vaster picture, the greater plan? Are you not aware that there are worse fates than death for those trapped in the pain and illusion of the lower dimensions? If you have absorbed what we have been trying to convey to you over these long months and many messages, you will accept the reality that death of the physical vessel is a new beginning. It is the end of pain and suffering and an opportunity to start anew.

For those you love and treasure, know that it is not a separation and they will not be lost to you. The veils have been lifted and cleared between the dimensions and so, it is becoming easier all the time to maintain contact and sense the loving presence of those who have transcended. You have a wondrous opportunity to assist your loved ones who have chosen to leave the physical plane. Talk to them and ease their fears of death. Help them to forgive and resolve all remaining issues with loved ones and most importantly, make them understand that they may ask for and receive forgiveness for all transgressions. Give them the gift of awareness by telling them that there are wonderful angelic beings or loved ones waiting to assist them on their journey into the beyond. And if they are open and willing to accept the truth, help them to know that there is no hell or damnation awaiting them on the other side of the veil, only love, joy and Light. What a great and loving service you can offer those you love, and you can also assist others who are facing the possibility of having to experience the loss of their friends or loved ones through the death process.

As you face each issue, trial and test, move into your temple and bring it into your conscious awareness. Allow the unified energies of Spirit to heal, transform, transmute and release all that is holding you back, whatever is causing you pain: discomfort, fear, or emotional distress. As you objectively observe the process, you will come to the knowledge that no one is to blame; each person is attempting to stifle or remove their own pain. As you claim your own fears, pain and sense of unworthiness and stop projecting it toward others, something miraculous happens. They become manageable, new insights arise and you begin to feel a sense of power and in control of your destiny.

It is called facing yourself and your demons, beloveds. Your demons cannot survive the emotion of love, or the wisdom of Spirit. As you begin the process of reclaiming your spiritual sovereignty, you will move into and begin to function within that Temple of Reunification and Harmony. It becomes a real and tangible place for you, and your perception of the world and its workings will be forever transformed.

What we are endeavoring to do and to help you accomplish, dear ones, is to make the higher dimensions real to you, to assist you to tap into that spiral of higher awareness so that you will constantly be buffered from the turmoil of the masses by the gentleness and love of your Divine Self. It is a gift that is offered to all, but each one must be a willing partner and take his or her share of the responsibility so that we can open the magic door that leads to reunification and harmony. Step through that doorway, my brave warriors, and show those who follow behind you that the journey is not so difficult and the prize is attainable.

We await you in this place of beauty, love and harmony. You are the guests of honor and we cannot begin until you arrive. Join us, precious ones, and let us move forward on this great adventure together. You have earned your place among us and you have been sorely missed. You are loved beyond measure. I AM Archangel Michael.

45. YOUR INNER-HARMONIC CONVERGENCE

*B*eloved masters, what may seem to be chaos and turmoil within your own physical vessels, on or within the structure of the Earth, is actually an attempt to bring all facets of physical expression into balance. The intense and dramatic weather patterns which are breaking all known records, causing everything from extreme discomfort to total destruction and even death is not just coincidental. Upsetting, life-changing events are occurring at every level: nations experiencing not only cataclysms caused by the extreme forces of the Elements, but monetary uncertainty, governmental and corporate concerns, as well as many individuals being thrust out of what they thought to be solid relationships, or positions with a secure future.

All are being held accountable, from the lowest to the highest. Spirit is at work here, agitating, stirring up and exposing that which is not in harmony and balance, that which is fear-based, or does not come from loving intent. No longer will it be possible to hide or shield those energies brought into manifestation through greed, desire for power, avarice, selfish intent or self-aggrandizement. The laws of cause and effect, or Karma, have never been more active and visible. No longer does it take lifetimes to see the result of your actions, positive or negative. They return almost immediately, or within a very short time, so that you will be able to compare and see the result of your actions—that you truly reap what you sow. Positive, loving actions bring harmonious, loving, beneficial results. Negative, fear-based actions result in stress, pain and suffering.

True, there are many of you who, through your loving intent and conscious endeavors, have moved beyond the laws of

Karma. You are enjoying a state of grace whereby, with the assistance of your Higher Self, you can gain the wisdom from the events in your everyday-life situations, rather than having these mirrored back to you through painful experiences.

As you move deeper into the process of letting go of all the old energy patterns within your physical, mental and emotional bodies, it may seem as though you are regressing in your spiritual growth. Many of you have that concern at this time. Be at ease, dear ones. This is not the case. Accept the temporary discomfort as a gift of Spirit. An opportunity to, once and for all, release all that which does not radiate love, health, joy, or your **God Essence.**

As the Earth spirals and resonates to a higher frequency, all that cannot attune to these higher vibrational patterns must either harmonize and adjust to these frequencies or fall into chaos. That is what your Earth is experiencing and that is what each and every one, and every thing, on the earth plane is experiencing. We have spoken often of the Violet Flame of Transmutation which is coming more and more into focus and strength on your planet. It will assist you to balance and harmonize or change the qualities of any energy less than perfection—it acts as a catalyst in the process of purification and facilitates the redemption or harmonizing of misqualified energy. It is the Flame of Forgiveness where all is brought into alignment through conscious intent. It is the Divine Alchemy which resurrects and perfects through the power of visualization and affirmation. It is a glorious gift that has been given to the Earth and humanity during these times of great change.

Remember, everything on Earth resonates at a distinct level of vibration or frequency. Through your thoughts, actions and deeds you create the frequency pattern within which you live and function. When you bring your mental, emotional and physical bodies into a state of balance, you begin to resonate at an ever-increasing or refined frequency level, thereby living within the various planes or levels of the fourth or fifth dimensions, rather than the oppressive density of the third dimension. This is when you truly begin to experience Heaven on Earth, or a paradise of your own making.

Allow me to give you some brief, concise guidelines to assist you in attaining and maintaining a state of grace, to help you become attuned to the wisdom of Spirit, as you accelerate the transition process on your never-ending journey along the spiral of illumination:

You must **CREATE, CLAIM AND LIVE YOUR TRUTH.** Process all new information through your heart monitor. Remember, that which resonates with love, self-empowerment and for the good of all comes from Spirit or higher truth. That which controls, diminishes or is fear-based is not of Spirit and should be discarded. Do not accept the old limiting thoughts of the mass-consciousness, "We are heading for a depression—Armageddon is here, or there will be world cataclysms." Do not heed old concepts about illness, relationships, mass karmic events, predictions or tales of mass destruction. You have free will and are more powerful than you know. If you are willing to claim and live your own truths of self-empowerment, abundance, vibrant health and joyous living, then you will truly have moved beyond the level of the mass-consciousness and mass Karma.

INTENT · INTEGRITY · INTUITION · Be focused in your intent—as we have taught you; lay out your future plans in great detail in all aspects of your life: physical, mental, emotional and spiritual. Then turn the plan over to your I AM Presence so it will be in harmony with your highest mission and Divine Blueprint. Add the fuel of emotions: sense and feel how it would be to live and function within the world of your own desires and perfect Creation as manifested through Spirit. Then you must take the steps or go forward as Spirit guides you, via your intuition. Listen to the small nudgings of your soul-self as it gently guides and directs you along the Path, knowing that all is in perfect, Divine Order. Live your integrity, or the truth as you know and accept it each and every moment—not someone else's truth or understanding, but your own. "To thine own self be true," is a most important and profound statement. There are many levels, variations and layers of truth and many paths back to unity-consciousness and the profound truth of the Creator. You are a special voyager on a journey and assignment of cocreation who must seek, claim and live by your own unique version of truth, integrity and conscious manifestation.

CREATING AND CLAIMING BALANCE AND HARMONY · This means in all levels of expression: physical, mental, emotional and spiritual. An overemphasis or focus on one fact or endeavor leads to disharmony. Many of you feel that if you concentrate enough on your spiritual growth you can forget or ignore the rest. You know how to live as and be SPIRIT. This is your natural state, remember? Your assignment was to allow Spirit to experience the realm of physicality. You are to love, embrace and honor your physical vessel, while allowing Spirit to radiate forth in all its glory from within. As you love, accept and endeavor to improve your physical structure, nourish and discipline your mind, as well as nurture and heal your emotional wounds, Spirit will begin to radiate joy and vibrancy through you and all will be brought into harmony once more. Do not neglect or deny any facet of your Being, beloveds. Love your imperfections and watch as they miraculously transform back into perfect expressions of Spirit.

CLAIM YOUR POWER · ESTABLISH BOUNDARIES · As you claim the right to live and speak your truth, set boundaries and live your integrity, you must give others the same right. Know where your responsibilities begin and end. You are not responsible for anyone's spiritual growth but your own. You are to teach by example and only offer information and guidance when asked. This is difficult when those you love are suffering and will not heed the nudgings of Spirit. You cannot take on another's burdens or problems, and you are doing them a disservice if you try to "fix" negative situations for them. Children especially will never learn the ramifications and results of the law of cause and effect if you continually intercede, cover up, or try to correct every problem situation in which they find themselves. Move into the position and expression of a compassionate observer, radiating love and encouragement, offering words of wisdom when appropriate, but standing firm in your commitment to allow each person to live his or her own truth, at whatever level that may be, and to be responsible for his or her actions or their Creations.

PRACTICE SPIRITUAL BODY BUILDING · Via toning, sacred sounds, gentle body movement and ancient breathing techniques you will enhance your vital life force energy and your body will become a more suitable receptacle for Spirit. The breath has been used as a vehicle for spiritual enlightenment and physical health for centuries. Deep, rhythmic, diaphragmatic breathing releases stale, stagnant air, and allows the healing life force energy, or prana, to enter and fill the body, energizing the brain, and revitalizing the cells and organs. Adding affirmations to your deep, rhythmic breathing techniques allows you to slow down the brain wave activity and attune to your subconscious mind where all emotional and mental traumas are stored. It is time to awaken the subconscious mind and make it a conscious partner in this journey toward unity-consciousness. There are many levels of conscious expression, beloveds, and they must all be brought into balance and harmony.

CREATING AND LIVING IN YOUR SACRED SPACE · We have taught you how to protect yourselves and to harmonize with Spirit each morning by calling forth a crystalline pillar of Light from your Divine I AM Presence to surround and enfold you, and anchor in the core of the Earth. We have taught you to ask that your Higher Self act as a Sacred Witness, observing, guiding and directing all your activities of the day, thereby assisting you to live in integrity, honor and with the intent that all your actions be for the highest good of all. If possible, create a small, sacred place within your home where you can place those objects and loving symbols of Spirit that touch your heart, or come to you to inspire and support you. Here you will be drawn in your times of need, when you wish to express gratitude, or when you want to magnify the love, strength and support of the Spirit realms. We will join you there, beloveds; just call or radiate your loving intent and we will answer. As you gain spiritual strength, it will be possible to tap into and access a rarified beam of Christ Light from the Source to anchor and build an ascension column within your sacred space, and as you become more proficient, you will radiate that energy throughout your home, neighborhood, and across the land. This is yet a different way to draw on the magnificence of

Spirit, to bring it down to the Earth plane, anchor it and bring forth its healing radiance to all those around you.

It is once again the anniversary of that momentous time called the Harmonic Convergence. The power and magnificence of our Father/Mother God were showered down in great force on all the Earth and its inhabitants during the month of August, in your year 1987. This Divine Frequency has become more and more refined and more difficult for humanity at large to access and integrate as the years have passed. The carriers, or receivers, of this gift must be attuned, or balanced and in harmony within to a certain level, in order to accommodate and integrate this energy. This is why we say you must heal and harmonize the physical vessel, control and expand your mind, ease and soothe your emotions in order to make yourself a suitable receptacle for this blessing from the God Source.

Allow the power, protection and initiative of the First Ray to inspire you. Incorporate the illumination, wisdom and perception of the Second Ray, as you radiate the love, tolerance and gratitude of the Third Ray. The Fourth Ray will help you develop your artistic abilities, while giving you clarity of action, humility and a purity of purpose. The Fifth Ray will help you claim your truth, bring forth scientific knowledge, and enhance your healing abilities, while the Sixth Ray will strengthen your willingness to forgive, your desire for peace and will to live in an atmosphere of devotion, faith and gratitude. Over-Light your existence in the magnificent Violet Flame of the Seventh Ray. See it blaze up from beneath your feet and completely surround you in the Divine Flame of Transmutation which will allow you to change the quality of energy at will. Become a magnetic center for Spirit, so that it may radiate through you, and project from you out into the world this wondrous energy from the Heart of God.

My beloved ones, as you focus on and radiate love, we will enhance, magnify and increase your efforts a thousand-fold. We await with you, ever at your side, as the next miraculous step in this great adventure unfolds, as the excitement builds and the wonder grows. Our eternal love and gratitude we shower down upon you. We are with you always. I AM Archangel Michael.

46. Highway to Heaven

*B*eloved masters, shall we gaze into the future—your future—and see what is in store for you over these coming months? As you are aware, it is a very important time. The decisions you make now, or the energies you radiate out from you to create the force field within which you live, will determine your reality and how you will move forward into the new millennium. It is time to decide whether you will move forward on the spiral of ascension through the gift of the life process, or the old energies of the death process. Make no mistake, every human being on the planet is in the midst of this process, at some level and some form, whether they are aware of it or not.

You are reversing the process that you initiated thousands and thousands of years ago, as you descended into the realm of materiality and began the process of building a temple of flesh in which to contain your precious gift of life, your Spirit self. You have forgotten that in past ages, you transcended and moved into the higher realms of expression by moving through the blessed Violet Flame of Transmutation, whereby the dross was transmuted and refined and you were, once again, a shining, perfect Being of Light. It will take some time to accomplish that miracle of Creation or re-Creation again, but we can help you to make the process less painful and more expeditious.

It is time to closely examine your beliefs and what you have accepted as your truth, for that is what you will have to experience. Stop and ponder this question, beloveds: are you ready to move forward through the transforming gift of life, or are you still stuck in the mass belief that you can only move toward the higher realms of expression through the process of death? Yes, we know it seems an impossible feat, and it may be some time in the future before many of you can step through the door of transmutation in your physical vessels. But we can help you begin the process of reclaiming the ability and the wherewithal to accomplish that miracle.

Many of you have begun the process of reversing or staying the aging process. You remain youthful, full of vitality, vigor and eager to experience all that Spirit offers you. You are making a difference, in your loving interactions with others, and in your unselfish devotion to be of service and assist others on the path. Now it is time to tap into that memory, to reclaim your immortality. Many of you will, as the forerunners of the process, become aware of when it is time for you to move onward to the next level, or through the higher dimensional portal where your loved ones can no longer see you. You will not become ill. You will still appear healthy and vital, but your Spirit will tell you it is time to make ready for your departure. Yes, for now, most of you will still experience the death process, but a few will open the door for the future transfiguration and embodied ascension of the masses.

With each and every insurgence of cosmic energy, higher, more refined frequency patterns are made available—indeed, the stuff from which miracles are made. You all are being given the golden opportunity to release all that is not in harmony with these frequencies—it is required in order to accommodate and utilize this gift.

You ponder and ask, how will you appear when you step through the portal into the beauty and wonder of the higher dimensions? Imagine yourself without any imperfections; see yourself in the most beautiful, radiant body imaginable, for it will be your choice, your Creation. Will your loved ones recognize you? Indeed, not by your appearance, perhaps, but by your radiance and by the intricate vibrational patterns you project which are composed of light, sound and color. Have we not stressed this fact time and time again: Light, sound and colors are the modalities of Creation and you are very proficient at utilizing these gifts—you have just forgotten?

It is time to make a decision, my precious ones, and even though we have told you many times what the process entails, I will endeavor to clarify further. **THOUGHT FORMS**—please engrave those words in your conscious and subconscious minds. As you become more proficient at manifesting through the Universal Laws and the gift of primal life substance, it is critical that you become aware of how powerful your thought forms are each and every moment of the day and night. If you fall asleep in fear, anger, doubt or feelings of guilt or unworthiness, these will be magnified as they spin out into the astral plane and connect with like energies. The more powerful the thought, or the more emotional energy that is put into a thought, the more powerful it becomes and the more it affects or "colors" your reality. First the energies of the thoughts affect your auric field, either clouding and distorting it, or enhancing and enlightening it. These energies then move through and into your emotional and mental bodies. Each rush of feeling produces an effect: a positive, loving thought adds sparkling colors of vibrancy to your auric field, while negative emotion distorts and adds shadows or faded colors and patterns.

Each of you lives and functions in time and space, enclosed in a field of energy of your own making. You are surrounded by masses of thought forms created by you, through your conscious and unconscious thought patterns. You perceive reality through the filter of vibrational frequency patterns made up of your own thought forms. If your thought patterns are clouded and distorted, then you truly are "looking through a glass, darkly."

The vibrational resonance of your thoughts determines the colors of energy you will project, while the nature of the thought determines form. If a person sends out thoughts of selfish greed or envy, a brownish, green color will radiate forth (thus the saying, green with envy). Anger or rage projects dark clouds of muddy red energy which can almost look like daggers or sharp shafts of projectile-shaped energy. However, if you send forth feelings of pure, unselfish love to a particular person, it is immediately transported to them and enfolds them in an aura of protection. Feelings of worship, devotion and adoration radiate outward and upward in a wondrous pattern of light and color, containing all the colors of the Rays with all the qualities of godliness. We of the higher realms see, feel and absorb these blessed gifts from you, dear ones. Know this and remember: no loving thought or prayer ever goes unnoticed or is ever wasted.

Allow me to give you an exercise to assist you to become more aware of the energies you are projecting. Not only is it important to monitor your thoughts, but to observe from where in your body, beside your brain, that these energies are emanating. Through observation and intent, you have an opportunity to monitor your thought patterns and with determination and the assistance of your Higher Self, you will soon be projecting only vibrant, clear colors of peace, love, compassion, abundance and joy. As most of you know, the chakras are spinning cone-shaped vortexes of energy located in strategic areas of the human body. Each of these energy centers resonates to a particular color (colors which gradually change as you raise your frequencies). However, for this exercise, since these are still the colors in which most of humanity is resonating, we will use the basic colors which are attuned to the seven Rays of expression for your solar system.

Focus your consciousness on your root chakra: here are stored energies of survival and scarcity, or when in balance, this provides a sense of abundance and plenty, security and a connectedness to the Earth. This chakra is located in the sexual area of the body, therefore called the root chakra. Its color is red—see this as a brilliant, pure red of power and strength as you tone or chant the words **I LIVE.** Hold the sound as long as comfortable and then take a deep breath as you move your hand and consciousness to the second chakra, the navel, or the lower abdomen. This is the seat of desire, pleasure, sexual/passionate love tolerance—your goal is to bring your desires into harmony with Spirit, for your highest good and the good of all. Strive to blend your passion and love for another with compassion and a soul union, as well as a physical union. Tolerance and compassion for all will help you make great strides in balancing this chakra so that it resonates purely and harmoniously. See this energy as orange and as you focus on this area, take a deep breath and tone the words **I FEEL.**

Move to the solar plexus, the area of personal power, self-control, and emotions. In the past, this was the area where you allowed others to tap into your energy source with what looked like dark cords, or you tapped into the energy field of others. As you become more empowered, this is no longer possible. The solar plexus along with the heart area has become the power center whereby you project the gift of Christ Light which you have accessed and drawn down from the higher realms. Sharing this gift with the Earth and humanity should be one of your major missions in life. See this energy field resonating to the color of yellow as you take a deep breath and tone **I WILL.**

Move your hand and consciousness to the heart chakra. Here is your life force, your solar power center, the seat of your Higher Self, your Essence and Divine Love. If you filter all the feelings of the three lower chakras and their energies through this power source, beloveds, miracles will begin to happen. See a vibrant, radiant green flowing from your heart center as you tone **I LOVE.**

The next chakra center is the throat, and this is a most important area at this time. Many of you are experiencing stress or symptoms of discomfort in the throat area. That is because it is the power center of the spoken word, communication, discernment, discretion and self-expression. Too long have you allowed others to decide what would be your truth, and have feared to speak your truth. It is time, beloveds, to take back your power, and to speak with honor and integrity, with compassion and wisdom. Take a deep breath as you visualize a brilliant blue color and tone the words **I SPEAK.**

The third eye, or the area of the forehead between the brows, is the next chakra. As the veil of forgetfulness is lifted and you reclaim your gifts of Spirit, you will regain your clear inner vision, intuition guided by Spirit, clairvoyance and perception beyond the limitations of duality. See this area resonating with a lovely violet color as you tone the words **I SEE.** Finally, move your consciousness to the top of your head, or the crown chakra.. Here the beautiful lotus of Spirit is unfolding to allow the radiance of the Creator to once more flow to and through you. Here resides Divine Wisdom, Spiritual Will—where you may tap into the wisdom of your Higher Self and Divine I AM Presence and where you are, once again, moving into Oneness with all Creation and the Infinite. See this area radiating an iridescent white as you tone the words **I AM** three times.

As you begin to move more into your mastery, dear hearts, you will begin to see through eyes filtered with love and hear with ears tempered by compassion. You will project an energy field which will enfold you and radiate out further and further, thereby creating peace, love, joy and abundance. By your example others will learn, and within this force field you will build the vortex by which you will eventually transcend and leave forever the trials and tests of the Earth plane. It is time for you to remember that there is no death, only a transcendence of Spirit. Matter, or the stuff your physical body is composed of, may change and decay, but Spirit—the Essence of you—only becomes brighter and stronger as it reunites with more fragments of itself on the upward spiral to Oneness with our Father/Mother God.

Beloved, brave warriors, we have put out this clarion call before, but we ask you to listen and heed, for time is of the essence as we move into this critical phase of the dance of evolution for your earth, solar system and galaxy. **We ask you to unite, beloved ones. It is time once again to gather our forces, to make ready for the mighty march across the heavens, reestablishing the dominion and power of all the legions of light, the forces of God!**

We see you in your beauty and perfection; we encourage you to envision that perfection as well as reclaim your birthright, "made in the image of God," which is the pure radiance of Spirit made manifest. I surround and enfold you in an auric field of love and protection. I am with you always. I AM Archangel Michael.

47. OVER THE RAINBOW BRIDGE OF LIGHT

*B*eloved masters, the radiating effect of your endeavors
to tap into the higher realms is beginning to bear fruit.
You are making a difference on the Earth, in the Earth and
amongst all the inhabitants of the Earth. As you integrate
and become the bearers of Divine Light, you become guide-
posts, focal points and beacons of love, radiating harmonized
frequencies for others to follow and emulate. There is now
enough power and impetus for these refined energies, which
now are encoded with the heartbeat and memory of humanity and the Earth, to resonate out into the solar system, the
galaxy and even this universe. Indeed, it is a time of great
change for all forms and expressions of life.

Allow me to give you another overview of what is happening as you reclaim those vaster parts of yourself that you
had to leave behind in the higher planes as you descended
into the consciousness of duality and physical expression.
We have told you time and again, but it is still hard for many
of you to accept the fact that you are a master and a soul
fragment of a great and magnificent Being. As you made the
journey down through the different dimensions, you had to
leave parts of yourself behind, or to look at it another way,
you had to refract or separate into smaller and smaller portions of yourself. You have experienced many levels of your
"Beingness" down through the ages, one of which is your
wondrous Christ Self. Another is what we call your Higher
Self, when you still had the remembrance of your origins
and the purpose of your journey. You have also functioned
and expressed your uniqueness on the mental plane of
awareness, and in the higher astral planes (the emotional
facet of your multidimensional self), as your soul-self was
working its way down and compressing your magnificence

into a form which would fit into your physical vessel.

The good news and the miracles are evident; you are now reversing that process, the INBREATH of Creation, or the journey home, has begun. As more and more of you radiate your love, and balanced and harmonious energies out into the ethers, it opens up and builds what has been called the rainbow bridge. This bridge is the pathway of Light, radiating the energies of the Twelve Rays of this galaxy which are infused with the virtues, aspects and attributes of the Creator. It is an arc of Light and a covenant between you, us and our Father/Mother God. The rainbows you see in the sky are changing; more Light beams and colors are being added as you access and draw down the energies from on High. It is the promise made manifest, **"We will leave you with a visible path to guide you back to your home among the stars."**

All that you are experiencing now—the discomfort within your bodily forms; the releasing of many of the aspects of your life that you thought were important, stable and necessary; the crumbling of old belief systems and the feeling that you are no longer in control of your destiny—is all part of the accelerated transformation process now in progress. You are shedding the layers of etheric matter from your auric fields which no longer serve you, which cannot exist where you are going. When you integrated your soul-self, you diminished the power and control that your ego-self had over you. As you integrate your Higher Self and it takes over the guardianship of your energy and destiny, the soul-self moves into the background or, to put it more clearly, it becomes integrated into the energy force field of your Higher Self.

Many of you are now in the process of integrating your Christ Self. This is the Second Coming, beloveds. As you are able to tap into the higher frequencies, you will tap into and integrate more and more of the wonder of who you really are. Not only do you have the potential for your Christ Self to take dominion and guardianship of your physical vessel, but you will also open the way for the masters and blessed Beings of Light to OVERLIGHT you and infuse you with even greater radiance which carries the gifts and wisdom of Spirit that you had to leave behind.

When you allow your Christ Self to emerge and that refined energy becomes the dominant force in your life, the path is cleared for you to begin the process of accessing the rarified frequency patterns of your Divine Self. These are the gifts of the myriad parts of yourself, those fragments who also made the journey into density, who are ready to share their wisdom and adventures with you. Therefore, you do not have to have all the answers, just as it was not necessary for you to experience every single facet of earthly life. Your Divine Soul Mates have done that for you, just as you have your unique experiences and wisdom to share with them. That is as far as we will take you on this reintegration process, but know this, beloveds, it is only the beginning of the miracle of returning to the ONENESS of SPIRIT.

Many beautiful souls have agreed to play out the dramas in which all Earth residents are involved, at one level or another. They agreed at a soul level to bring to the attention of all humanity the imbalances and inequities that need to be corrected and addressed. There is no need to name these negative traits again; you all know what they are. Many are so quick to pass judgment and express their self-righteous indignation. We tell you that none of you is blameless. You all have played the same game or role to some degree, or been involved in a similar scenario at one time or another, whether you remember it or not. So you see, you are only judging yourselves.

Indeed, it is a time of accountability, a time when nothing can stay hidden, a time when all are seeking to return to balance and harmony. A time when the energies of cause and effect return to each of you very quickly, so that you must face the consequences of your thoughts, deeds and actions. But we ask you to be the observer, beloveds, and radiate love to those who seem the least deserving, the victimizers, as well as the victims. Radiate love to their inner Essence, not condoning their actions, but seeing the highest outcome for all; this will avoid adding more negative energy to the situation. Move to a level whereby you are observing all that transpires from the objective viewpoint of a master, knowing that out of every adversity there is the potential for a greater good to emerge. Become aware that everything that is being destroyed or torn down is making way for something more appropriate, refined, and en-LIGHT-ened to take its place.

On your journey toward reunification, as we endeavor to bring into your consciousness the many facets of your true self, we would also like to address the subject of the masculine and feminine aspects of the Creator. There was a time in your ancient past when the aspects of the Mother Creator were the dominant energy and focal point of worship. For many thousands of years it has been a patriarchal world and the Creator has been envisioned and acknowledged in only the male aspect of its greatness. Just as you are bringing together all the parts of your vaster Being, it is time to reunite and acknowledge the wholeness, as well as the many expressions, of the Creator. The Goddess aspect, the Mother God, or the feminine energy of the Creator, is radiating more of her attributes and energy throughout the universe at this time—the attributes of Divine Love, Compassion, Illumination, Nurturance, Gratitude, Faith, Creativity and the Inner Focus and Awareness of Spirit. These blessed energies will enhance, refine and complement the masculine aspects of the Creator, Divine Will to Create, Wisdom, Truth, Valor, Decisiveness and Power.

Before many of you came into this lifetime, you agreed to be the bearers of the gentle, sweet energy of the Goddess. Yes, many in the male body, as well as those in the female body, agreed to allow the energy of the Goddess to Overlight them so that they would become the examples for others to see, and hopefully, to emulate. As a result, it is no longer so radical for the male in a family to be the one who is the nurturer and caretaker of the young ones. Many brave men are allowing their gentle side to emerge as they begin to express their feelings and acknowledge their emotional nature. The difference between the male psyche and the female psyche is narrowing as each begins to integrate the masculine or feminine aspects of Self. On the opposite side, many born in the female body agreed at a soul level to integrate and allow their male side to take dominance, thereby becoming more active out in the world of business and government. While playing their feminine role, they are also assertively making their mark in other areas of endeavor which were, heretofore, the exclusive domain of the male population. It is one more aspect of the integration that is taking place on many levels.

You have learned about the Rays and the energies they radiate, and you are becoming familiar with the Beings of Light, or the archangels who represent and carry the solar aspects of the Creator via the Rays. It is time for you to become reacquainted with the beautiful feminine aspects of the Archangels, or Archaii as they are sometimes called, who are the Divine Counterparts of these magnificent solar Beings of Light. Also, please begin to call on the many lady masters, who have served so unselfishly throughout the ages. Seek out their names and the qualities they offer to assist you on the path of illumination. Those in the feminine body are leading the way in this awakening process, thereby breaking the tight control that has been in force for so long by the masculine population. It is not about right or wrong, or judgment, it is about bringing all into balance and harmony, once again.

My beloved **Lady Faith** is ever ready and anxious to answer your call, and help you to bring forth and integrate the energies of the First Ray of Divine Will. She will help you to strengthen your faith in yourself and assist you to access and integrate your higher truth, while enhancing your courage, as you go forth in your endeavor to bring forth the New Age of Creation.

The beautiful **Lady Constance,** who at times has been called Christine, is the Divine Counterpart of **Archangel Jophiel,** the **Angel of Illumination** and the Second Ray. She can assist you to manifest and integrate the Divine Qualities of Wisdom, Perception and Comprehension. How wondrous it would be if those of you who are educators and caretakers of the young would call on this wise, benevolent one. She will help you understand the Universal Laws of cause and effect, or Karma, and to bring forth the enlightenment needed to turn knowledge into Wisdom.

The beloved **Charity** is the Divine Complement of **Chamuel,** or known by some as Kamiel. Please know that at different times and with different races the names may

change slightly, but the blessed Beings of Light are t.
There is oft times confusion in this regard, just as th.
been some confusion in the colors and energies of the ∪
We have explained this in great detail in the past and so ⌐c
will not address that issue at this time, but we will give you
this bit of advice: accept only that information that rings
true within your heart center, whether it is a name or a radical new concept. Chamuel radiates the energies of the Third
Ray: Divine Love, Adoration, the Spoken Word and the
Abstract Intellect. Beloved Charity can strengthen your
Tolerance, Tact and Forbearance.

Archangel Gabriel, the **Angel of Resurrection,** and the
bearer of the Fourth Ray, was the predominant force during
the 2000 years of the Age of Pisces, bringing forth the
Immaculate Concept—Hope (what an appropriate name for
Gabriel's Divine Counterpart). **Lady Hope** inspires and gives
Hope to those who seek to bring forth their creative visions
and emphasizes Purity, Clarity of Action and Humility.

The Fifth Ray is under the influence and direction of two
of the better-known figures in your history. **Archangel
Raphael** radiates the scientific attributes of the Laws of
Creation, Concentration, and the Listening Vocations. **Lady
Mary,** the beloved **Angel of Consecration,** who sent down a
facet of her Being to become the blessed mother of Lord Jesus,
is the overseer of those in the field of Healing. This lovely
lady will guide you in the process of surrendering to your
Highest Good, the rewards of Selfless Service and in matters of the Heart.

The Sixth Ray of Devotion, Forgiveness and Idealism is
under the radiance of **Archangel Uriel** and his beloved
Donna Grace, or Aurora as she is sometimes known. This

lovely lady will help you attain Peace and Tranquility, and to bring your emotional nature into harmony with Spirit.

Finally, we come to the most important Ray of this coming era, the Seventh Ray of Freedom, Redemption and Transformation. **Archangel Zadkiel** and his beautiful **Lady Amethyst,** bearers of the Violet Flame, will enhance your Invocations, and magnify the Flame of Purification and Forgiveness as you seek to release all that is not in harmony with Spirit and for your highest good.

Beloveds, seek to know and integrate all the facets of Creation that are yours for the asking. Do not deny any part of yourself, for when you do, you are denying a facet of God that is waiting to assist you to come into your wholeness, or **Holiness.** As you become more comfortable with the workings of the universe and the perfection of God's Creation, you will know, without doubt, that you are in control of your destiny. All the tools, magic and miracles are within reach. So turn inward and claim your Divine Birthright. We are there waiting for you, in the stillness **WITHIN.** I AM Archangel Michael, and I bring you these truths.

48. WHAT IS YOUR ENERGETIC SIGNATURE?

*B*eloved masters, you are approaching the end of your year, and preparing for an even more important era on planet Earth. It is a time when many celebrate, give thanks for the harvest and observe sacred events of the past. We of the higher realms also observe a harvest and come together in celebration. Also, under the direction of our Father/Mother Creator from the Great Central Sun, we lay out our overall plan for the coming year.

The great Beings of Light and the entire spiritual hierarchy, as well as the angelic forces, from the archangels and the great devic angels, to the multitude of precious elementals, all come together in celebration in the shining, etheric city of Shamballa during your earthly months of November and December. We bring a list of your accomplishments and we bring the radiance of the love you have projected to us and the Creator. All is recorded and entered into the great cosmic record, and the magnificence and magnitude of your inspired deeds and thoughts are added as fuel to the supply of primal life substance that we will have available to us for the next year. Each of you comes before the high council in your etheric body, and we take measure of your individual radiance and your energetic signature. From this, we decide who will be nudged and encouraged to come to the fore, who will be offered more responsibility, and who will have an opportunity to work more closely with the spiritual hierarchy. We decide which of you are ready to receive higher wisdom, and the greater gifts of Spirit, knowing from your past performance that you will use these for the highest good of all.

I ask you to take an objective analysis of yourself, your persona, or what I would like for you to begin to see as your

Energetic Signature. Please begin to see and observe your-self in a different light—as a radiating energy force, instead of just a physical Being with emotions. What are you radiat-ing, dear ones: a sense of guilt, fear, discontent, self-hate, shame, a sense of helplessness or hopelessness, or being dis-connected from your Spirit Self? Even if you have moments of hope, inspiration and radiate positive emotions or beliefs, is it enough to overcome the negative energy you have pro-jected out into your world? You have created your picture of reality with your energetic signature and your world reflects it back to you. It isn't possible to radiate love, hope, com-passion, faith in the future and joy in expression and not have it change your life for the better. Each of you, no matter at what stage of enlightenment, is experiencing many trials and tests as you move through the levels of initiation, and are balancing and harmonizing your energetic signature.

The secret, my brave ones, is to move through the **"Fire by Friction"** with ease and grace, as an observer of the pro-cess, seeing your tests and challenges as opportunities to gain new wisdom, and for manifesting your spiritual garment of Light. **Creating your coat of many colors means incorpo-rating all the Divine aspects of the Creator—building a cloak that surrounds you in the glorious colors of the Twelve Rays of this galaxy.**

Please stamp on your mind and in your memory the words: **MAGNETIZATION** and **RADIATION.** You will be hearing them often, and hopefully we can instill in your con-sciousness how important are these words and the concepts they carry. When you first came to Earth in all your glory as a shining Spirit Being on a mission for the Creator, you ra-diated pure Light, and you drew to you or magnetized all that you needed to create the paradise in which you were to live, The Garden of E-Don. You know what has transpired during those long ages of darkness, but what I wish to bring forth into your consciousness once more is this: as you reclaim your mastery and move into harmlessness, you once again have begun to radiate Love/Light, or the positive aspects of divinity. As a result, the path to the rainbow bridge that connects you to your I AM Presence is opened so that you can begin to magnetize all that you desire to recreate your paradise on Earth.

Beloveds, we have given you the Universal Laws of manifestation and the rules you must abide by; now we will add another component. After you have gone through the process of formulating what it is you desire to create and have asked that it be brought into harmony with your Divine Blueprint for the highest good of all, see the radiance of your energetic signature beaming out from you around the Earth. See it flowing out into the higher realms, thereby magnetizing to you the primal life substance needed to bring your vision to fruition in the physical realm. As you radiate all the aspects of love, you build a powerful force field which allows you to magnetize and manifest more and more of the gifts of Spirit, from which all Creation stems.

I would like you to experience a different kind of visualization. **I would like you to imagine that you have only six months remaining in your life in this incarnation. You are in good health and full of energy and vitality, so you are not restricted physically in what you can do or accomplish. Before you start, remember that what we are focusing on is the energy signature which you will take with you: how much negative energy you have balanced and how much positive radiance you have added to your Golden Etheric Web—or the real you. Are there relationships that need to be healed, things that need to be said, or wrongs that need** to be righted that you have avoided? Have you been putting off or are you waiting for the "right time" to start a creative endeavor that keeps surfacing and pulling at the edge of your consciousness? Have you had a yearning, but never seem to get around to spending more time with your loved ones or enjoying the beauty of the nature kingdom? Have you promised yourself that you would begin to meditate, that you would take a class or join a group that would increase your wisdom or help you understand yourself or others better or that you would heed the nudgings of Spirit that seem to grow stronger and stronger, but you just never make the time?

What have you occupied your days and nights with, beloveds? We know you must take care of your families and support them financially, but what has been your energetic signature while you spend your "allotted time" performing these tasks? Please take stock and view your life from the perspective that each day is a beautiful gift, wrapped in love and containing all energy you will need to make all your dreams come true. If you will only add your inspiration, your dedication and faith in the outcome, along with your gratitude for the gift, and then mold it through your actions into your own special Creation, oh, what miracles you could create!

Please allow all the little, inconsequential events of your day that usually bring frustration and keep you from focusing on what is important to flow around you and not impact you. Do not accept others' negative viewpoints and energy as your reality. See yourself as a shining, crystal rock in the middle of a fast-flowing stream, and whether the water is flowing gently over you, soothing and refreshing you, or it is raging and roaring past you, it matters not. You will stand firm and radiant in your solar power center and nothing

can move you from the certainty that you are in control of your world—and that your world is loving and perfect.

During the new year that is almost upon you, many prophecies, both positive and negative, will come forth and it is important how you perceive and accept what is being said. Yes, each and every thought, expression and action has an energetic signature and adds to or detracts from the overall radiance of the Earth. The Earth is being monitored carefully as well, beloveds, to see when your planet will be ready to move forward to the next level of illumination. As you all are aware, there has been much devastation and cleansing on the Earth this past year, and yes, it will continue as a necessary part of the overall plan for the highest good of all. We know it is difficult for you to not focus on the negativity and destruction occurring in the world. But we ask you to also be aware that all of those who have experienced these cataclysmic events agreed at a soul level to make the supreme sacrifice so that you and the Earth can move forward. Those who have made their transition from the Earth via the cataclysms are watching with great joy from the higher realms, knowing that they have made an important contribution to the whole and that their evolutionary journey will be made easier because of the role they agreed to play.

Your test is to be the loving, compassionate observer, helping those you can, knowing that there is a grand plan being played out on Earth, while projecting your contribution of radiant energy out from your heart center into and around the Earth and to the whole of humanity. The Earth is not being destroyed, nor are you being punished, but the emotional and mental bodies of the Earth must be brought into balance and harmony so she can move into her proper place within the solar system and galaxy. All of you, and that means each and every one on Earth, agreed at a soul level to the roles you have been asked to play in the drama now unfolding. Most are fulfilling their promises unconsciously, many have abdicated and fallen by the wayside, but many more of you are endeavoring to fulfill your contracts in their highest form with full awareness of what they entail. We know who you are and we commend you, our radiant Warriors of Light.

It is crucial that you understand how essential you are and that time is of the essence. Know that this is the most important lifetime you will ever experience on planet Earth and that your active participation is vital to the successful outcome of the plan. That is why we ask you to change your perception as to why you are here, what life on Earth is about and what is truly important. We ask you to turn your focus to the temple of your heart and begin to build your paradise within, filling it with love, beauty and harmony, and then projecting that perfection outward so that it begins to un-fold around you. Your refined, energetic signature will gradu-ally radiate out into the world, affecting and changing everything it touches. See each moment as precious and per-fect, as a gift from our Father/Mother God allotted to you, its caretakers, to use as you so desire. Know that if you will integrate these concepts into your reality and if you will see yourselves as a radiating force capable of magnetizing all the wonders of Creation to you, that you can transform your world and create the world of peace, abundance and harmony you desire within six months of your time.

You, my brave warriors, have the formula to recreate Paradise on Earth. We are here to assist you with all the forces of Heaven at your beck and call. Reach inward and upward; we will respond. In love and gratitude, I salute you, beloved ones. I AM Archangel Michael.

49. MESSAGE FROM RONNA

Beloved Friends,

This has been quite a month of miracles. Several things happened that reinforce how wondrous are the workings of Spirit, and I would like to share them with you.

First of all, I have for some years driven a 1982 Buick Riviera, which my husband, Kent, has kept in wonderful condition. I always bless a car when I get it and ask the name of the elemental who watches over it. Felicia was the angel of my Buick and lately she has been letting me know that she was getting tired and that it was time to let her go—little things with the electrical system, etc. Kent began looking for a new car for me. My contribution amounted to telling him if I liked the color and the style. We went to a couple of dealerships and finally made an offer on one I really liked. My husband is a great negotiator, which I am not, so I just sat and listened (with butterflies in my stomach). The dealer and Kent were miles apart on the first one, and he didn't like the games they played, so we walked out. I said to myself, "It is okay, my perfect car is out there; let it be." The next day Kent took me to see a car he thought was a good buy, a 1998 Nissan Maxima with only 12,000 miles(we never buy new cars). I fell in love with her—she was an iridescent, deep blue/green with dove-grey upholstery and drove like a dream. I REALLY wanted her. After over an hour of negotiations, Kent and the salesman were still $500 apart (I would have given in an hour before), but this is his area of expertise and I did not interfere. We finally walked out. I was disappointed, but said again, "My perfect car is there waiting, and will manifest when the time is right."

I had taken a booth at a psychic/art/crafts fair for the

weekend and had to get up very early the next morning. Just as I was about to drop off to sleep, Lord Michael whispered to me, "Do not fret, beloved one, you will have your sweet chariot." I smiled and dropped off to sleep.

The next evening, after telling Kent about my day at the fair, I asked what he had done that day. He mentioned several places he had gone, and then he said, "Oh, and by the way, I bought your car."

So, I am now the proud owner of Sweet Chariot, "Cherry" for short—and Lord Michael came through again.

Another miracle I would like to share with you happened the next weekend. My husband and I went to the University of Nevada, Reno, homecoming game with our son and daughter. It was a glorious day and our team played a terrific game. I was observing the people as much as the game—feeling all the energy that they were radiating when Archangel Michael nudged me and said, "Use it."

So, I began to visualize all the energy going up into a big spiral and then coming down through my crown chakra and radiating down into the Earth and then back out into the higher realms. My body began to vibrate until I could hardly sit still. Kent looked over and said, "What's the matter?" and I replied, "Oh, nothing, I'm just excited." I looked up into the clear blue sky, and there from the northeast to the southwest as far as I could see, were two perfect angel wings. They were telling me that the energy had been received and would be used for the highest purpose.

The next day, I had scheduled a mini-event here in Reno on 11-1-1998 (an 11-11) with a dear friend of mine, Dorothy. It was rather impromptu, but we ended up with 38 paid

participants (also an 11) and we had a glorious afternoon—
special people, awesome energy and a wonderful, special
message for them from Archangel Michael. The next day, I
received a call from a lady saying she had seen me on the
public-access station here in Reno on Sunday. After quizzing
her, I realized that they had shown my one-hour TV show
from last year on Bridging Heaven and Earth where I talked
about and channeled Archangel Michael. I don't know the
particulars, but dear Lord Michael managed to get us on the
air here in Reno at the same time I was holding the seminar.

It is indeed a wondrous time to be alive. Claim your
miracles, they're waiting.

I love you all so very much, Ronna

50. Celebrating a Spiritual Reunion

*B*eloved masters, let us join together during this sacred time and share our hopes, dreams and aspirations for the coming year. Yes, we also have great hopes and visions of what miracles will be wrought by you and for you, the Starseed of planet Earth. **Close your eyes for a moment and breathe deeply as you settle your awareness into your heart center. Now envision, if you will, that in this timeless moment we are all coming together to rejoice, remember and reestablish our Divine Relationship, one with another. See in your mind's eye and feel with your soul's heart as your vast spiritual family, past, present and future, come forth to greet you. Watch as all the shining, radiant beings from the Great Central Sun and throughout the universe from our Father/Mother God, down to the tiniest elemental Beings, present themselves in all their magnificent splendor and walk amongst you. There are no limitations here, no one is excluded, for in this great gathering in the higher dimensions there is room for all—every soul who has ever incarnated on Earth is present, as well as all the precious Beings from throughout your solar system and galaxy. You see, it is a grand reunion reminiscent of the time when you all gathered in celebration before beginning your long sojourns in the physical on planet Earth.**

Have no doubt, beloveds, that you are welcome and belong at this gathering. We see you in all your glorious radiance—your unique, auric color pattern shines forth for all to see, and the sweet tones of your special vibratory harmonics add to the celestial music of the spheres, blending and merging in Oneness. You naturally migrate to those who radiate the same colors and patterns as you, and whose tones blend perfectly with yours, for these are your dearest

and closest soul companions from whom you were separated so long ago. Let your mind wander a while, what new insights come to mind, what words of wisdom surge forth, what do you remember that is of great importance to you? Allow the possibility to enter your consciousness that, henceforth, you will have access to new information, thought patterns, creative ideas and wisdom which have been stored in Light packets in your brain structure waiting to be ignited during these important and momentous times.

As you blend and flow, merging with group after group, you will gain the benefit of their experiences and particular insights, as well as offering your own to them. See yourselves sitting with the beloved masters dearest to your heart, as they surround you in love and compassion, and suffuse your auric field with their radiance. Each in turn offers their special attributes: truth, faith and protection; perception and illumination; gratitude and forbearance; clarity and humility; concentration and dedication; peace and tranquility; and transmutation and purification, to mention only a few. These are just some of the attributes of the seven Rays of your solar system that we have spoken of so often. Which of these attributes do you lack? What is your "weakness in Spirit?" Again, sit quietly with yourself, turn inward and honestly take an inventory of your strengths and weaknesses—no judgment, dear hearts—just observe. We are offering you a grand opportunity to tap into the Divine Stream of Light, the Source from which all blessings flow. Take all you need, but then we ask you to please use what you take to assist others to awaken and reclaim their birthrights.

It is our greatest desire that all on Earth awaken and remember the Spark of the Divine that each of you carry within, that you remove the barriers, boundaries and restrictions which separate you, one from another. We envision you, each and every one, healing your body, mind and soul and returning to the sanctity and harmony of Spirit. We see your Earth returning to its pristine beauty once again with sparkling, clear waters, fresh, pure air, and rich, fertile soil. We will encourage and assist any and every one who is willing to nurture and care for the animal and nature kingdom, as you remember that you were given stewardship of these great gifts of Creation. We offer guidance, direction and assistance to you each time you move to a higher level of awareness and step out into the unknown. We give comfort and nurture you as you release many things in your lives that you hold dear. We assist you to the maximum that Sacred Universal Law permits in your endeavors to overcome your shortcomings and imbalances. We see not your imperfections, beloveds, only your radiance and its intensity.

We watch as you timidly, and then sometimes boldly, reach inward and upward toward the higher-dimensional frequencies, as you glimpse and feel, possibly only for a moment, the wondrous joy of the Oneness. As those of you who have experienced this miracle know, you are never the same and you will ever yearn to return to that state of bliss. You are being pushed to the limits of your physical endurance as you release old energy encodings which are not for your highest good, as you, through conscious or unconscious agreement, accelerate the mutation process. You are leaving your animalistic instincts behind; you are refining and releasing your human impulses, addictions and limitations as you integrate all aspects of your Beingness into a fully aware master of the physical plane. Once again, you are becoming Spirit Beings of Light in garments of human flesh.

Before you began your great adventure so many aeons ago, you left your garments of Light in the safekeeping of your I AM Presence, just as you allowed us to remove from your memory banks much of your true identity. You agreed to take only a portion of your talents and wisdom with you into each incarnation, storing the remainder in the heart of your I AM Presence. You eagerly and joyfully participated as a cocreator in the great drama that unfolded on planet Earth over the many aeons of time, as you experimented and experienced all the rich diversity that the material world had to offer. But as the Earth and humanity sank into the denser frequency patterns of the lower fourth and the third dimensions, your lives became so painful and stressful that you moved into resentment, fear, anger and a sense of separation. And thus you have remained for these many thousands of years. But that time is now drawing to a close as the shackles of fear and limitation fall away, and each of you boldly moves through the fog of illusion into the shining Light of truth. Remember, beloveds, as we heal and weave the past anew.

No matter the appearance, or the circumstances, whether the lowest or the highest, each of you is a beautiful, unique Spark of God, a blessed Creation. You are a refracted Ray of Light sent forth from one of the great Rays of expression which radiated from the God mind in order for God to experience and express more of ITS ever-unfolding uniqueness. This is the magic and wonder of your long earthly sojourn— the Prime Creator expressing and experiencing through you, a blessed Spark of ITSELF. Now do you remember?

All aspects of Creation on your Earth are awakening, the Mineral and Animal Kingdoms, as well as the Devic and Elemental Kingdoms, who are assuming their proper roles again as the guardians and caretakers of the Nature Kingdom.

The whales and dolphins, who are the record keepers for the history of planet Earth, and the cosmic telepathic communicators between Earth and the galaxy are desirous of reestablishing their relationship with humanity. You have forgotten, but they have not. They have willingly and lovingly served humanity down through the ages, only to be killed and maimed. Please help to stop this abomination, beloveds. The dolphins and whales resonate to the element of water and therefore are very conscious of your emotional frequency patterns and have suffered along with you down through the ages. Many blessed souls have blended their energies with these beautiful ones and are making you aware of how precious and important they are in the scheme of evolution.

The call has gone forth for those of you who remember, those of you who were there in the beginning, to reunite in the physical in order to awaken to your own magnificence and heritage, and to reconnect with your brothers and sisters, the whales and dolphins. There is a reunion in the higher realms, but just as important, there are many grand reunions taking place on your planet. You are being reunited with many precious members of your soul family, some of your intimate soul mates, and groups with whom you have journeyed from the beginning of time, and with whom you have had many wondrous experiences. Know that these reunions are gifts that you have earned, an opportunity to share, support and enjoy the harmony and beauty of compatible soul companions.

Will you, from this day forward, endeavor to sense our presence more fully in your everyday life? As you do so and give us permission, we can take a more active role in assisting you over the times of uncertainty, sadness and stress. As you strive for harmony, we can project more loving energy toward you and place a buffer of protection around you. Will you stop for a moment before berating yourselves or another and think, **How would a filter of loving energy change this situation? What is the good in this event and how can I realize the highest outcome?** Give the gift of love and compassion, beloveds—not more material gifts. Make gratitude and thanks-giving an integral part of your everyday thought habits. Look for the Spark of Spirit in the eyes of those you meet and acknowledge that Spark with a smile or kind word. Move out of isolation and separatism into an ever-expanding sense of unity and Oneness with others. You will not be so quick to judge or criticize when you realize they came from the same Source, another precious facet of the Divine.

Let us now address the issue of New Age philosophies versus religious philosophies, so that you may come to a better understanding of what spirituality is and is not. There is much fear, resentment and criticism among those who are followers of a particular established religious philosophy and those who embrace the so-called New Age concepts. Unfortunately, religious beliefs have led to isolation and separatism instead of unity, and there have been conflicts and war down through the ages in the name of God or a certain religious belief. The Creator does not embrace, support or condemn any one religion. All Beings are sacred and blessed in the sight of our Father/Mother God, and there are many paths that lead back to the Oneness.

A person attuned to their Higher Self knows that there are beauty and truth in all religions, but they also are aware that spirituality is not about dogma, ethical codes, or a certain rigid morality. Spirituality transcends all religions and connects each soul to their own Divine Truth. Spirituality loves and embraces life, and does not condemn or reject anyone. Spirit functions within the framework of sacred Universal Laws and these are unchanging. And the core of this law is love—love of self and love for all God's Creations. Spirituality is not about being psychic, such as inner seeing, clairvoyance, and inner hearing (clairaudience) or telepathic abilities. These abilities are your natural birthright, you have just forgotten and these abilities have atrophied from non-use. Your extra sensory perception will return naturally as you clear the static and negative energy patterns from your auric field and reconnect to your Spirit Self. You can be a religious human being and not be spiritual, but you cannot truly be spiritual if you are not willing to embrace the good in every religion and every person, honoring and allowing each one to express their spirituality in their own unique way. You will see the Spark of the Divine in everyone and everything, and you will incorporate and manifest within yourself all the wondrous attributes of the Creator as you become a living example for others to emulate.

When you attune to your I AM Presence which is your connection to the God Source, you will integrate the Love/Light of the Divine and spirituality in all its glory will radiate forth. It is happening now, beloveds. You see and sense it in yourself and in many of those around you, as your numbers grow by leaps and bounds. Spirit walks the Earth and it is **YOU.** Know that you are loved beyond measure. I AM Archangel Michael.

51. SEVEN STEPS TO MASTERY

*B*eloved masters, many of you are feeling that you are regressing instead of making progress as you endeavor to move forward on the path of en-LIGHT-enment. I assure you that this is not the case. Higher and more refined frequencies are constantly bombarding you and the Earth, and as a result, you are in the midst of the emotional intensity and distortions of the astral plane, or the fourth dimension, which you must traverse on your way to the fifth dimension of balance, peace and harmony. For many of you, it is a clearing of the residual, core energy patterns that you must release so that you can accommodate the higher vibrations. Even so, it can be a very intense and even painful process as, once again, you are faced with situations and reactions which trigger overwhelming emotional responses. Know this, beloveds, it is a golden opportunity for you to, once and for all, release those impacted energies that you have carried with you as excess baggage for many thousands of years. Face them, process them and see them be transmuted into pure-Light Substance, and in the process you will feel LIGHTER and BRIGHTER, for it will be so.

More and more precious souls are just stepping onto the path of awareness as they begin to heed the nudgings of their soul-self. Often this is brought about by an intense "dark night of the soul" process as they face the distortions of consciousness that they have created and the full measure of the law of Karma, or cause and effect, is brought to bear. It is not punishment, even though it may seem so in the beginning, but an opportunity to turn and bravely face yourself and what you have created. All the forces of the universe are at your disposal to help you reclaim your perfection and once more align with the multiple aspects of yourself. Thanks to the brave souls who are called the Wayshowers, or the vanguard of Light workers, the golden path is clearly defined and all the information you will need to quickly move through the process is available. The time is fast approaching when each of you will be asked to bring forth and share your own particular wisdom garnered from your vast experiences on Earth, as well as the jewels of wisdom stored within your brain structure which you brought with you from the far reaches of the universe.

There is a plethora of information available to you on every facet of spiritual awareness and advancement, as the brave ones ahead of you are able to access the higher and more refined levels of the higher causal mind and the great Beings of Light. Much of this information is helpful and love-filled, but some of it confusing and distorted, and therefore, we ask you to use your discernment as to what you accept as your truth. Some of the information stretches the imagination and you wonder how you will ever attain the multiple levels which are described. It seems an almost insurmountable task, and so once more, let us return to the basics. After being shut off from your Source for so long, you are eager and desirous of knowing all there is to know and to attain the heights of illumination as quickly as possible. But, my precious friends, you must make the journey one step at a time, fully learning each lesson as you release what no longer serves you so that you can step through the next door of incandescence, attunement and integration.

Do you remember the Universal Laws of manifestation that were previously outlined to assist you? You must have a clearly defined picture of what you want in your world of the future. You must have clarity of thought and vision by defining your purpose and bringing it into alignment with your Divine Blueprint for the highest good of all. In great detail you must write out and script your thoughts as you formulate your plans and the steps you must take so that you have a clear road map to follow. Be prepared to take action as Spirit nudges you in the right direction, often catapulting you out of your comfort zone into the unknown. Always keep your focus on the moment and see it as perfect and appropriate. Maintain an attitude of joy and gratitude, thereby opening the way for greater and more wondrous gifts to be showered upon you.

Let us emphasize again, these next few years of your Earth time are the bridge to a bright, new future for you and the Earth, as well as your solar system and galaxy. It is up to each of you as to how easy or difficult the journey will be; however, please keep this in mind, beloveds: your success is assured. Also, remember, it is your choice as to how long it takes you.

I ask you to study and meditate on the following steps to mastery until they are firmly engraved in your mind. As you familiarize yourself with the process, you will realize which areas you are presently focused on—no judgment, please, just observe. You are probably further along than you imagine and you may be working within several different steps or processes at once. As with the dimensions, there is no firm demarcation, so you may experience several levels at one time.

FIRST STEP ON THE PATH · You begin to feel a desire to turn inward in order to seek out the origins of your emotional responses and pain. There is a willingness to look at all aspects of the ego-self or your subconscious personalities, thereby giving you an opportunity to closely examine your emotional beliefs and to better understand how your emotions control and direct you through your ego desires and needs. You begin to be comfortable in surrendering to the wisdom of your Higher Self as you move further into the process of healing your emotional wounds and aligning your emotional desires with your soul print and Divine Mission.

SECOND STEP ON THE PATH · You begin the process of reprogramming your subconscious emotional beliefs as you release old, self-sabotaging emotions and replace them with self-empowering emotions. As you establish a personal connection/relationship with your guides, teachers and angelic helpers, you start to realize that you have a Spark of God within your physical Being and strive to bring even more of that radiant feeling of love into your life. You become aware that your emotions affect your actions, just as your actions affect the balance or imbalances in your physical world or everyday experiences.

THIRD STEP ON THE PATH · You make a conscious effort to align your will with the WILL of your Higher Self. The emotional body begins to vibrate within a more balanced and harmonious frequency pattern. The ego desires are gradually replaced by the desires of Spirit/Higher Self. You turn inward for nurturance or a sense of love, self-worth and validation, instead of seeking it from a source outside yourself. You begin the process of becoming emotionally detached from outward events and occurrences as you allow Spirit to guide you toward the highest and best outcome for all, and you become an observer instead of an instigator or reactor. You know that there is a higher purpose within everything that happens; that everyone is exactly where they should be for their greatest growth; and that you are not being judged or punished, but being given an opportunity to attain balance and harmony via the situations that arise in your everyday life. You move from an I, or separateness focus, to a WE, or UNITY consciousness.

FOURTH STEP ON THE PATH · You turn your awareness to your mental body and your linear, analytical thought processes, or your conscious, conditioned mind. With the help of your Mental Higher Self you start to examine old beliefs, superstitions, and dogma which are limiting, inflexible or controlling. As you re-evaluate what you have accepted as your truth, which has formed your attitudes and judgments, you become willing to objectively investigate or study new, expanded, self-empowering concepts. You develop a faith and belief in a POWER greater than yourself, and therefore, are willing to release control and allow Spirit to guide you via your intuition or inner knowing. You claim your spiritual power by expanding your vision, speaking your truth and living your integrity, while allowing others to do the same.

FIFTH STEP ON THE PATH · You begin to understand and use the UNIVERSAL LAWS OF MANIFESTATION. You meticulously and in great detail formulate how you envision your future world to be, and then relinquish control of the outcome to your Higher Self, knowing that your Creations will come to fruition at the proper time and in the best way for all concerned. As you learn to live in the moment, in peace, joy and harmony within yourself and those around you, you become aware that you are building your future reality each and every moment with your thoughts, words and deeds. You stop trying to be the director of your destiny, as you move from intellectual to spiritual awareness and step into the flow of your Divine Destiny. You stop trying to change or control other people's lives and begin to focus on their positive traits instead of their faults, as you recognize the Spark of the Divine within each person.

SIXTH STEP ON THE PATH · You come to the realization that you are more than just a physical body with a soul. You understand that you are a soul fragment of a great and magnificent Being experiencing physical embodiment, a radiant aspect of our Father/Mother God. You also know, without a doubt, that Earth is not your home, you are only a visitor here on an important mission at the request of the Creator Gods of our universe. You move out of the illusion of the mass-consciousness and live in a higher-dimensional reality of your own making while still being grounded on Earth and efficiently functioning in the everyday world—BEING IN THE WORLD, BUT NOT OF IT.

SEVENTH STEP ON THE PATH · You are now moving quickly along the path of ascension, as your ego becomes the servant of the soul and your soul is incorporated within your Higher Self. You have cleared the pathway to your I AM Presence so that now you may receive Light and wisdom directly from your Source. If it is your desire and a part of your Divine Mission, you will gradually be over-Lighted by the ascended master or angelic presence whom you are to represent, or from whose lineage you came. You radiate the pure Love/Light of the Creator through your heart center and your auric field blazes with the iridescent spectrum of the Twelve Rays. You cease trying to "become" anything and move into a state of BEINGNESS.

Beloved friends, until we come together again, I would ask you to concentrate on your root chakra · red energy (the exoteric color of the First Ray on the material plane). Which of the negative attributes of red energy are you experiencing?

A lack of vitality · A sense of depression or helplessness · Hate, judgment or resentment for anyone or anything in your life · Lacking a sense of security · Survival or scarcity issues · In need of grounding to Mother Earth?

Then transmute these using the positive attributes of red energy to: Create strength · Develop power in thought, action and deeds · Claim and manifest abundance · Develop courage · Use your "will power" to speak your truth and stand in your integrity · To stimulate you into action in order to manifest all you desire and to live your highest potential.

I suggest that you wear red often for the next month and use a red pen or colored pencil to write down your thoughts and to chart your progress. Review each day and become familiar how you used red energy—how it felt and where it affected you. We will progress through the color spectrum of the chakras and Rays until you have a good understanding of the energies involved and you can quickly determine which energies you are drawing on and how they are affecting your picture of reality. As you develop a closer working relationship with your bodily form and with your spiritual counterparts, you will be able to define and rectify any discordant energies that arise, thereby moving you into the flow of balance and harmony.

This information is given to you in hopes that it will assist you to move quickly through the multiple levels of initiation and into the state of mastery that is your natural state of Being. Be brave and courageous, my warriors of Light; youhave nothing to lose but your imperfections. I surround and enfold you in an aura of love and protection. I AM Archangel Michael.

52. YOU ARE BECOMING BOLD MASTERS WITH BRAVE HEARTS

We will add a new name to describe who you are, beloved ones—Brave Hearts. The solar flame of the Creator burns more brightly in each of you who have given your Higher Self permission to assist you, and it has fully ignited within the bosom of the Mother Earth as well. Soon you will be able to accommodate the full measure of your Higher Self and I AM Presence, but at the present time it may seem as though your body cannot contain the power and intensity of this wondrous energy. Many are experiencing surges of Kundalini energy (the Spirit/life force welling up from the root chakra and moving along the path of the spine, igniting each of the seven major bodily chakra vortexes along the way). Many are also experiencing activation of other major and minor chakras in the body, especially in the head, neck and shoulders, hands and feet (the refined chakras of your Light body) which are causing symptoms of distress or temporary pain. All a part of the process, dear ones: do not be alarmed.

We are asking you to focus on the energies of your body's seven major chakras at this time for the purpose of assisting you in integrating and accessing the influx of Divine Energy with ease and grace. If you know what to expect, and are familiar with the positive and negative attributes of each chakra, it will help you tremendously to move forward to the next level of awareness.

Before you can reach for the stars and lift your consciousness into the higher-dimensional realities, you must have a firm foundation to keep you anchored and connected to your Mother Earth. You must not forget that you are a spiritual

Being experiencing the material realm of duality/polarity for the Creator. So, dear ones, do not yearn to abdicate your missions even though the desire to return to your true states of Being burns brightly in your heart and mind. You, the Starseeds, are needed to integrate and transmit the ever-increasing infusion of cosmic life substance from the Great Central Sun as it radiates from the heart of our Father/Mother God. You are the examples of the new Spiritual/human Beings that are emerging: the precursors of the forthcoming refined, root race of the New Golden Age.

In our previous message we gave you the Seven Steps to Mastery and touched briefly on the root chakra and red energy, the color of the root chakra and the exoteric (material plane) color of the First Ray of Divine Will and Power. We asked you to spend some time examining your actions and reactions to root chakra/red energy.

If you did so, did you take notice of what makes you angry? Were you able to handle your negative emotions differently? Did you experience red energy in its positive form as a stimulus, using it for strength, will power and courage; or as a negative force causing you to be fearful, angry, hateful or resentful? Did you observe how moving the red energy from your mind as a thought form affected your auric field and how the energy was mirrored back to you by others? Or, did you recognize and transmute it before it resulted in a cause/effect situation? Where in your body did you experience the most red energy?

The soul fragments you have created down through the ages resonate to a particular frequency and feed on the energy you create, both positive and negative. If allowed to increase and continue in the negative form, it will cause you to be irritable, unforgiving, bitter and frustrated. But if anger, resentment or hate is recognized for what it truly is—distorted energy—you can process and transmute it back into pure universal Light Substance. It will assist you in learning the wisdom of a particular thought pattern, event or encounter without having it mirrored back to you by others in its negative form. It will give you insight as to what you need to address and where you are out of balance. It shows you where you have impacted energy that needs to be transmuted and healed. In its positive mode, red energy helps you strengthen your resolve and heal the soul fragments you have created so that you can lovingly incorporate them back into your auric field as you gradually regain your mastery and assume control of your destiny in the highest way.

We will now focus on the second chakra and orange energy, which is located in the lower abdomen and affects the adrenal glands. It focuses on the energies of sexual/passionate love, the emotions and is the seat of the instinctual nature. Using the energies of the second chakra negatively creates self-doubt, envy, addiction, ego/desire body/sexual issues, overindulgence, compulsive behavior, guilt, judgment, criticism, sense of superiority or inferiority, embarrassment, meddling, control and manipulation, defensiveness, stubbornness, and causes self to follow only the instinctual nature.

Positive attributes: use orange energy tinged with pink (love energy) to help you overcome ego and allow your soul-self to become the director of your life. It will help you gain self-confidence, and it is also revitalizing and healing. It will help you to surrender to or come into alignment with your highest good and purpose. It helps your concentration and to attune the ego desires with the desires of Spirit, which are always in harmony with your Divine Blueprint or Mission. It brings your giving and receiving nature into balance. (It is blessed to give, but you must also feel worthy of receiving.)

The seat of the ego is the first, second and third chakra (the solar plexus). The ego has been in control of the emotional and mental bodies ever since the fall into the third-dimensional experience. Ego is an important facet of the personality; however, it is not meant to be the director, but under the guidance of the soul-self. Ego feeds on red and orange energy, creating over-self-confidence, self-importance, or self-doubt. When ego is in control, you are always looking to someone, something or some event to mirror back to you a sense of worthiness. The ego is never satisfied and so you are usually disappointed, for you are judging yourselves by others' standards and looking externally for validation.

When the ego is under the guidance of the soul, you turn inward for validation and know that you are a Spark of Divine Energy, unique and precious, and you allow yourself to BE where you are, as you constantly strive toward greater balance and harmony. It can be revitalizing, inspiring and motivating when you stop caring what others "think" of you and you begin to monitor your actions and feelings by your internal awareness as it is transmitted to you by Spirit.

How strong are the soul fragments that you have created that feed on GUILT—guilt regarding others; guilt regarding responsibility; guilt regarding past actions, performance or having to be perfect? How strong are your soul fragments that feed on JUDGMENT OR CRITICISM—about yourself or others; about not accepting and loving yourself the way you are at the moment; comparing yourself to others;

criticizing others who do not think as you do, or criticizing yourself for not measuring up to someone else's standards or expectations?

After you identify the areas that need to be balanced, see yourself radiating the imbalanced energy up through your Higher Self to your Divine I AM Presence, and then see your Divine Self sending it back to you tinged with beautiful, iridescent-pink love energy. See this refined energy moving into the second chakra and all the places where you have stored imbalanced red or orange energy. See it revitalizing and healing your four lower-bodily systems as it brings you into alignment with the highest vibrations of the first and second chakras. Henceforth, monitor how you project red or orange energy of ego as you strive to reprogram old habit patterns and thought forms. You must be consistent, dear ones, until you have formed new habit patterns of mastery.

When functioning in a third-dimensional reality, the three lower chakras connect you to the Earth and the pain and illusion of mass-consciousness. You are ruled by the ego until you begin to balance and harmonize your vibrations through the process of healing core energy patterns, eliminating old negative unconscious attitudes and responses and replacing them with the empowering thought forms and attributes of your Higher Self and I AM Presence.

Again, I assign you a task, if you are willing. For the next month, meditate on the energies of orange, wear or carry something orange, and do your writing and scripting with an orange pen or pencil. Be aware of this color and how it affects you. Orange is not a favorite or well-liked color for most people. Discern how you feel about orange and why. Experience and become comfortable with orange/second chakra energy until you are using it in its most positive form.

Let us now focus on the wondrous gathering that recently took place on the sacred island called Maui (February 1999). It was a grand reunion of blessed souls who came together long ago to experience the beauty and perfection of planet Earth during the Golden Age of Lemuria, and who also experienced the sense of devastation, despair and failure when that beautiful continent sank beneath the waves and settled onto the ocean floor. It was a time of recognition, a time of celebration, and a time of releasing old pain and core memories as each one, in turn, remembered, reclaimed soul fragments and healed old wounds. Day by day, beautiful souls from around the world, of diverse cultures, experience and beliefs, opened their hearts and reclaimed the gift of love and oneness they had known in ancient times past. There was a sense of coming home, a glimpse of paradise, unique to each one, but precious beyond measure to all.

Each person who attended took home their own personal miracles, life altering and often mind boggling, knowing without a doubt that they had communed with masters, Divine and angelic Beings, both in physical and etheric bodies. Remember, beloveds, when you come together in harmony with an open heart and mind, there is nothing you cannot accomplish. It is only the beginning, my brave ones; you are moving rapidly to the next level of enlightenment and it will be with your beloved ones by your side, hand-in-hand. No longer do you have to tread the path alone, you have earned the right to be reunited with your soul mates, your soul family and with your loving guardians, teachers and us of the spiritual realms. Congratulations, Brave Hearts, victory is in sight. I AM Archangel Michael and I bring you these truths.

53. MESSAGE FROM RONNA

Dearest Friends,

The WHALE QUEST event held at Maui, Hawaii, was incredible and beyond any of our expectations (I heard this over and over from those who attended). The way the group blended and soared together as we sang, toned, danced and listened to the words of wisdom offered by an impressive group of presenters is an experience we will all remember. It was rainy and blustery the first two days we were there (but still pleasant compared to the northern climes). The reported temperature at Mt. Haleakala (over 10,000' elevation) was around 10 degrees with a wind-chill factor well below zero. That morning we left at three a.m. to make the journey to the crater for our sacred ceremony—the further activation of the crystalline energy beneath the crater and an initiation and infusion of the First Ray of Divine Will and Power from Archangel Michael. The sky was clear and ablaze with stars. The wind was blowing strongly when we arrived, but as we came together at the summit and started our ceremony, it died down to a gentle breeze. The same thing happened when we were there in 1997, and if you have ever experienced the energy and elements atop the crater, you know that this is most unusual.

One day, the group went out on a large boat to commune and connect with the whales and we were fortunate to see a number of these beautiful creatures in the distance as they breached the water and sounded. It was suggested that we sing our soul notes to call the whales to us (sounding and toning, which we had experienced and practiced often during the week). As we lifted our voices in harmony, suddenly there was a pod of whales with beautiful, recently born babies among them. *These angel beings cavorted and played around their mothers, flipping and jumping out of the water, while we watched in delight.*

During our time together, many of us connected with our star families and quite often the recognition was instantaneous and the tears of joy were continually flowing as we laughed, cried and embraced. Archangel Michael helped many to remember their origins and their missions as he gently opened their minds and hearts to their own magnificence.

There is one special, magical story I wish to share with you. Remember, Archangel Michael told us he would join his Essence with the whales and it was certainly evident that, indeed, this took place. There is a lovely lady we will call "D" (a newly found, old friend of mine), who lost her beloved husband last summer. D has had a difficult time adjusting to life without her mate and has not ventured far from her home since his transition. She owns a condo on Maui (coincidentally, right next door to the Embassy Suites where the seminar was held). Another dear friend suggested that she go to Maui and attend at least part of the Whale Quest conference (she was hesitant because she had so many wonderful memories of the times she and her husband spent there and she was afraid it would be painful and lonely). My name came up several times from different people, until she became convinced that she was supposed to be there.

We met and spent several hours together the day before the conference began and the reconnection was instantaneous, "old friends being reunited." D thoroughly enjoyed the seminar and the whale watch and was glad she came, although there were still some painful memories and doubts regarding her loss of her beloved mate (who without a doubt was a master of Light). The evening before the final day of the conference, she asked me if I would like to take a drive the next afternoon after the closing ceremonies. We could explore another part of the island, enjoy some of the beautiful scenery, have lunch and maybe even do a little shopping. I gladly agreed and D said she would call me the next morning to firm up our plans.

Now I must set the stage for what took place the next morning: D's condo faces the ocean, and she stated that in the many times she had visited there, she had never seen a whale from her front window. I had already gone down to the conference hall and so my roommate and friend, Helen Huber, answered the phone when D called. D was looking out her front window as they spoke, when she commented about a lovely half rainbow radiating down through the clouds over Molokai, and then she gasped and could hardly talk, for there in slow motion, a beautiful great whale breached in the ocean right in front of her. She could clearly see his right eye and a beam of Light seemed to radiate from it. In her mind, the immediate thought came, "NO, it can't be true—I didn't really see what I thought I saw," and so again, in slow motion, the whale breached and this time turned its eye to look at her as the beam of Light radiated forth. D started crying and could not talk any longer. After trying to collect her thoughts and calm her emotions, she went into the bathroom to wash her face and as she looked into the mirror, she smelled the fragrance of her husband's favorite shaving lotion all around her. Archangel Michael had told her (in a message channeled in her book) that she would see a miracle and when she looked into the mirror she would reclaim some of her Essence (paraphrased).

After D returned home, she told several of her friends about her miracle, and each one was so touched that it brought tears to their eyes. She told the friend who had encouraged her to attend the conference and it touched him deeply, as well. He then called one of his "angel friends," and as he told her the story he turned toward the TV. There before his eyes was a great whale, breaching the ocean with his eye clearly visible— an advertisement for an upcoming whale event. Now what are the odds that, at the particular moment he was telling the story of the miracle of the whale, he would see a whale breaching the ocean with its great, compassionate eye turned toward him on TV? Pretty astronomical, I would say.

And so, precious friends, Archangel Michael the Whale is giving us wondrous miracles and signs as to his presence among us. He is alive and well and his Essence is within us all.

I will share one more beautiful miracle with you. The day I was to channel Archangel Michael, Helen Huber, another dear friend, was awakened in the wee hours of the morning with the music and lyrics of a lovely, angel song pouring through her head. She has a magnificent, high, clear voice, and after she sang it for me, I said, "You must sing it for the group." And so we called Charley Thweatt, a wonderful musician who played his guitar and entertained us with many special songs throughout the conference. They practiced for only a short time and then sang and played "You Are An Angel," as the people filed into the room and then we all sang the beautiful words together.

It was a special moment and also another indication as to what can happen when we are visited by angels.

Love and Blessings, Ronna

54. IF YOU WERE GOD

*B*eloved masters, it is a time of remembering, a time of integrating all the multiple facets of yourself, both the beauty and wonder of who you are, as well as the imperfections. It is time for the game of illusion and separation to come to a close. We watch as you struggle to accommodate the influx of higher vibratory energy which often results in symptoms of discomfort and confusion. But we assure you, dear ones, that the outcome will be well worth the experience. You will look back over the last few decades and smile as you wonder why you were so fearful and hesitant. Your passage out of the darkness into the Light was a promise given when you answered the clarion call and agreed to be a part of this great adventure. You are reversing the process by ascending into "Lightness" once more, after compressing your incredible vastness into the density and limitations of physical form.

Let us play a game which we will call "Let's Pretend." Imagine that you are a god and you decided it was time to visit the planet Earth. You wanted to experience first-hand this unique and wondrous physical world which you had birthed within your mind's eye. You projected out from your heart center the perfect thought form and primordial cosmic substance that the great Elohim, builders of form, archangels and the mighty force of angelic Beings would use to bring this dream form into manifestation. You wanted to walk amongst your children and enjoy the great diversity of god-expression that had been created so many aeons ago.

Would you see the imperfections, the suffering, the pain and negative emotions that are rampant in the third-dimensional illusion? I think not. You would see the beauty and wonder of the many diverse Creations that adorn this extraordinary planet, where all the magnificence of the Creator's dreamscape from the far reaches of this universe is represented. That is why the Earth is so important and unique. That is why all of the forces of Creation are here to see that you do not fail.

Would you judge your children and admonish them for their failures? No, you would not. You would see the beauty of their Essence as it aspires to burst forth from the confines of its physical prison. You would look upon them with compassion and understanding, knowing that the task you have given them is a monumental one—an undertaking that had never been attempted before; therefore, there were no manuals or guidelines to follow. Free will and a complex composite of memory patterns, experiences, attributes and desires set the stage for this grand experiment on planet Earth. After our Father/Mother God birthed the creative thought form, they relinquished control to you, their precious children. Why would they judge you for trying to fulfill your mission in your own unique way?

You would see your children through eyes filtered with love so that their imperfections were diminished to shades and patterns of lesser or greater light. You would hear their words with compassionate ears, knowing that the illusion of separation and suffering are very real to them. You would extend a gentle hand to support, soothe and comfort, while knowing that you do not have the right to remove the lessons that must be learned by each individual soul. Each of you agreed to experience a special facet of Creation and then learn to manifest it in its physical expression. When your Creation was perfected you would then present this as a gift to the Whole.

If you were a god, you would walk boldly upon the terra firma, relishing each sensation and experience of your physical embodiment, knowing that only in this form of material expression could you learn to truly appreciate the freedom and magnificence of Spirit in its pure form. You would use all your mental capabilities to impart wisdom, but within the confines of non-infringement. You would be fully aware that each soul must find their own true path and abide by that truth as they perceive it.

You would cherish your physical form and be fascinated by its intricate design. You would honor it, knowing that it is a precious gift, but not a true representation of who you are—only a disguise. You would know that you have played many roles with various parts, and in a multitude of situations—some great and important roles, and some small and insignificant, some where you were the hero or heroine, and some where you were the villain or portrayed the shadow side of duality. Would you judge those whom you asked to play the game of polarity and duality—taking first one side and then the other? No, I think not.

The game of let's pretend is coming to a close. It is time for you to know that it is you who decided to visit Earth and participate in this grandest of experiments—you, who are gods-becoming. You, just as we, are precious Creations of our Father/Mother God, and you are on a mission that others were not brave enough to undertake. Reclaim your virtuous God nature, beloveds. That is what we are offering you as we endeavor to lighten your path and smooth the way for your return to your magnificence as a master of cocreation.

Let us now turn our focus to the continuation of your

lessons in mastery. Have you done your "soul-work" over the past month, concentrating on the second chakra? Do you have a better understanding of the dynamics of this center and orange energy?

Do you feel different about guilt? Were you able to acknowledge the energy of guilt and alleviate or transmute it? Did you feel the self-empowerment or freedom of that action? Do you now recognize the energy of judgment or criticism when it arises? Is it directed more toward others or yourself? Are you better able to take a stand of neutrality, or of not having to have an opinion on every issue? Are you more aware and tolerant of your bodily form? Have any sexual issues or awareness arisen that you have not addressed before? Have you acknowledged and begun the process of embracing your addictions and behavior so they can be healed and transmuted into a more positive form? Have you gained any insight as to what core needs your addictions and compulsive behavior stem from? Have you experienced any embarrassing situations, and were you better able to handle them? Have you begun to honor and please yourself first, and then express more compassion and love toward others as a result?

The solar plexus chakra—yellow energy is the focus of our next lesson. This chakra affects the liver and spleen and governs the attributes of self-control and mastery of desire which results in the ability to project love from your solar power center. Use of this energy in its negative or imbalanced form results in emotional trauma, anger, fear, stress and impacted psychic energy. Be aware that when you experience a lack of self-control, fear-based emotions, a lack of personal power or an intolerance for others, you are using the yellow energy of the solar plexus in its negative form.

When you are allowing the third-dimensional frequency patterns of the solar plexus chakra to prevail, your feeling nature becomes shut down due to emotional trauma of the past. You respond and react to other people's emotional needs and energy rather than your own (allowing psychic energy intrusion by others). Many of you have forgotten that all the life-force energy you will ever need is available from your soul/Higher Self and I AM Presence—drawn vertically down through your crown chakra. Instead, the practice of horizontally attaching energy cords to each other's emotional body via the solar plexus to syphon off energy has become the norm. This resulted in allowing others to control you, disempower you and drain you emotionally. This practice has kept you off balance in a push/pull struggle to get or keep your share of emotional energy. When you are ruled by your ego emotional body rather than your Higher Self emotions, be assured you are experiencing the negative polarity attributes of the solar plexus chakra—yellow energy.

Intuitively examine your relationships and determine who has tapped into or is syphoning off your emotional energy. Also, whose energy are you tapped into or dependant upon? Do you try to control or manipulate your spouse, your children, friends or family? Who in your circle of relationships is trying to control or manipulate you? This is called emotional blackmail. Ask yourself: if I reclaim my personal power, how will I use it? Will I control it or allow it to control me? How will it affect my relationships? After attempting to inspire those with whom I am closely connected to move forward, am I ready to allow relationships with those I have "outgrown" to come to an end, without judgment? Can I love and bless them while allowing them to find their own path as I follow my path to a new level of awareness? Am I ready for "personal empowerment" to change my life, and quite possibly move me out of my "comfort zone," resulting in greater responsibility and an opportunity to be of service— no matter in what form or capacity?

As you tap into the positive traits of yellow energy (which gradually incorporates the higher frequencies of golden energy from your I AM Self), you begin the process of reclaiming your personal power and self-control of your emotional/desire body. You become more tolerant and patient with others and learn to use tact and diplomacy in your interactions. This radiant energy brings clarity of thought and the knowledge that you are a self-powered or empowered Being. A sense of sovereignty will return, even as you reclaim your ability to radiate the love energy of your I AM Presence to others through the solar plexus center (front and back), thereby becoming a receptor and transducer of the higher-frequency patterns of Light.

Beloved warriors, as you begin the process of aligning your "ego will" with the will of your Higher Self, the emotional body begins to vibrate within a more balanced and harmonious frequency pattern. You turn inward for nurturance or a sense of love, self-worth and validation instead of seeking it from a source outside yourself. You begin the process of becoming emotionally detached from outward events as you allow Spirit to guide you toward the most beneficial outcome for all. As you reclaim your mastery, the ability to create your version of paradise on Earth will accelerate at a tremendous rate.

It is time for the Earth and humanity to burst forth into a new level of expansion, expression and awareness. The magnitude of cosmic life force that is now being radiated down upon you and your planet has not been experienced for many thousands of years. The clarion call to step forward into the next level of mastery is now being sent forth. Acceptance carries great responsibilities, beloveds, but also great gifts and rewards.

Are you ready to don your cloak of many colors, your garments of Light? We await your answer, my faithful friends. Know that whatever your decision may be, you are loved eternally and will forever be a precious Creation of God. I AM Archangel Michael.

55. MESSAGE FROM RONNA

Dearest Friends,

I held a one-day intensive on March 14, 1999, in Sierra Madre, California. The setting was Dr. Helen Huber's lovely home, which looks something like a miniature Spanish mission, and is situated in the foothills of the San Gabriel Mountains. It was a wonderful, magical experience. The energy of the angel devas and elementals was much in evidence in the lovely, unique setting of trees, flowers and shrubbery, set off by fountains, statuary and winding walkways. The two days before the event were sunny and warm, and we felt it was important to hold the event outdoors on a large patio while the fountains supplied sweet, rippling sounds in the background (we felt sure that the Devas and Archangel Michael would give us the gift of a perfect day on Sunday). Our wish was granted and it was glorious; a clear, beautiful day with wispy angel wings dancing and floating in the sky behind me almost all day. The energy was so high, I thought at times I would not be able to stay in my body, and when our beloved Lord Michael radiated his energy through my body, the vibrations were such as I have only experienced a few times before. His message was wondrous—part of which he shares with you in this month's message. It had a joy and "Lightness" that was incredibly touching, and the sense of union with him and the other beautiful Beings of Light was overwhelming. Everyone who attended felt it and went away with their own miracles. He told us that in the golden times of Lemuria, a Temple of the Flame was located in the area where we were, and the surrounding territory was graced with beautiful gardens, fountains and statuary in that time, too. He gave us a beautiful vision of why the California Coast is so special.

Sunday night, around midnight, a strong front moved in dropping copious amounts of rain, even some hail, and a sprinkling of snow on the mountain tops. It was a cold, blustery winter day, but we had received our miracle and so we didn't mind at all. Lord Michael is helping us to remember how it was in those times of glory so that we may recapture them in our hearts and minds' eyes and manifest them in the physical once more. Walk in the beauty of wherever you live, and ask to know how it was and what it represented in those times of perfection. Then ask what you must do to assist in creating paradise on Earth, once again.

Love, blessings and joy, Ronna

56. I AM THAT, I AM

*B*eloved masters, as the promise of spring is fulfilled and new life bursts forth on the northern hemisphere of your world, the southern hemisphere is preparing for the sleep and rest of the winter season. These cycles you may depend upon, but there are other cycles which are changing and evolving rapidly in your world and solar system. As you know, time is accelerating on your planet, but what you may not be aware of is that your mutation/initiation process is also accelerating so that there is very little time spent at one level before you step into the next higher-vibrational plane.

There is much unrest and turmoil on your planet and that, too, is accelerating so that it seems no country or race is immune. We sense your concern, and rightly so, for it is a critical time for all humanity. Therefore, once again, allow me to familiarize you with the Universal Laws as to what is, and what is not, appropriate for you as a master of cocreation. We know it is your heart's desire to assist those who are suffering and in distress, and this is as it should be. There are those whose mission it is to be directly involved, whether it is defending, nurturing, healing or helping to relieve the misery of those displaced or in need. There are those who will be called into the thick of turmoil, and those who must make critical decisions as to what is the best course of action to take in various situations and dramas that are being played out. Others will give support by sharing their wealth and that too is appropriate. However, the majority of you, especially those of you who have claimed the frequencies of the higher dimensions as your reality, are somewhat removed from these stressful dramas. And even though you are very aware of what is transpiring and have a heartfelt desire to be of service, it is imperative that you function within the universal laws of non-intervention.

More frequently, calls are going out for group, even world, meditations, and this is a wondrously effective project and offering. Please remember the guidelines that we have asked you to follow if you wish to be of the greatest service: you must send loving energy to ALL THOSE INVOLVED, the victimizers as well as the victims, those playing out their shadow side as well as the innocent ones who are caught up in the trauma of these life and death situations. You cannot know the greater dramas that are being staged around the world, or what these blessed ones have agreed to experience for the higher good of all. Remember, we speak often of unconditional love, and if you are sending "conditional love" to stop something or eliminate someone, you are playing God and that is not appropriate. We ask you to draw forth the maximum Christ Light that you are capable of incorporating and see it radiating down through you and into the core of the Earth. We tell you that it does not stop there, but will radiate out to the other side of the world as well. Also, breathe this energy back up through your feet and into your solar-powered spinal column (which is becoming a spiral column of Light), and then out your solar-plexus power center as you envision it moving through the honeycombed grid of crystalline Light that now surrounds the Earth. It is important that you affirm before you begin this blessed process, **"I ask for the highest and greatest good for all humanity and the Earth."**

You may call on our beloved Saint Germain to send forth the radiance of the Seventh Ray, the Violet Flame of Transmutation, to whomever you wish without infringing on anyone's free will. This is the Flame of Freedom, Purification and Redemption. You may activate this radiant Flame through invocation or visualization, with the intent of calling this powerful energy forth so that change, forgiveness and transformation into a more perfected state may take place. In order to facilitate and utilize this gift, there must be a magnetic force which draws it forth. This is done through you, either in groups or individually. You must ask for, claim and then radiate this energy to you and through you, and then see it flowing out into the ethers to the area of your intent or where it is most needed. In this way, you are performing a great service and doing God's work in harmony with the Divine Plan.

There is another way you may be of assistance, utilizing your energies to the fullest with the greatest effectiveness and for the highest purpose: as you have been taught, draw forth the maximum primal-life substance that you are capable of, by envisioning a column of crystalline golden/white Light radiating down from the God Source through your I AM Presence. See this rarified energy radiate through your body, thereby blessing and purifying you more each time, as you send it down into the core of the Earth, anchoring it there and then breathing it back up through your precious physical vessel. Now, instead of sending it out from your solar plexus, see it streaming back up and out from your crown chakra and up the column of Light to where we reside as you affirm, "I offer this gift to be used for the highest good of all."

This is a very effective process, beloveds, for you will be supplying us with refined energy that has been attuned to Earth's higher frequencies. Through your free-will offering, we then are allowed to send forth this gift of higher-vibrational frequencies to those places which are in dire need and to those who are incapable of accessing it themselves. We have told you that the frequencies which are being radiated down from the Great Central Sun can no longer be sent forth in a blanket effect upon Earth and humanity without creating even more chaos than is presently taking place. We have often called you the transformers, the transducers and the lightening rods who are capable of magnetizing, integrating and then radiating this refined energy down into the Earth and around the Earth. You might say it defuses the impact of the Light hitting the darkness, so that the higher frequency vibrations may gradually be incorporated by those ready to accept this gift of transforming Christ Light. In this way, my brave warriors, you are truly functioning as emissaries of Light and cocreators with God.

And now, with our remaining time together, let us again focus on your lessons in mastery. During our last time together, we asked you to turn your attention to the third or solar plexus chakra and yellow energy. Are you more aware of the times when those around you tried to tap into your energy source (solar plexus)? Are you better able to discern when you are being bombarded by emotional energy that is not your own, but which is being projected into your auric field by someone else? Are you learning to set boundaries, or to state your wishes in a firm but compassionate way, or practice personal empowerment? Are you becoming more adept at handling problem situations or power struggles by not reacting in an ego-motivated way? Take time to contemplate what kind of situations and people "push your buttons" the most and why.

The energy center we will investigate and experience next is the fourth, or the heart chakra center, which resonates to the color green. TRUST, LOVE, COMPASSION, KINDNESS,

AND CONTENTMENT are all signs of a "HAPPY HEART." However, even these energies must be used in a balanced way and in their highest form. TRUST is a wonderful attribute, but blind trust allows others to take advantage of you. You must temper your faith and trust with wisdom and discernment. You can be duped by those who are less than trustworthy when you have blind trust or faith. How can you LOVE too much, you might ask? When you love the wrong things, it is called addiction: love of power, wealth, food, drugs, alcohol, or an obsessive love for someone. Temper your emotions/love with mental logic and allow your soul-self to help you monitor your "love interests."

KINDNESS sometimes becomes a means of controlling others, or of keeping a person from learning their lessons by doing everything for them, or shielding them too much. Too much kindness, which usually also involves self-sacrifice or a sense of superiority, can destroy relationships, for it is out of balance. You cannot buy love by continually doing too much for someone. You must also allow others to return the kindnesses you give, which creates a balance of giving and receiving.

CONTENTMENT—Being too content leads to lethargy and dullness, a lack of a sense of purpose. Nothing stays static; you must always strive to move forward to the next level of awareness, and to maintain a sense of excitement and challenge while also being content in the moment. Those who are content with who they are without, at times, seeking new avenues of self-expression, are setting themselves up for stagnation and degeneration.

The heart chakra is the doorway to the higher states of consciousness. The energy of the Earth and the material plane flow up from the Earth to the heart and the energies of your Divine Higher Self flow down through the crown chakra and merge in the heart and solar plexus, whereby you may then radiate unconditional love to others and back down to the Earth, as well.

Beloved ones, it is time to transcend the ego-focused energies of love. Release your need to be loved as validation of your worthiness. As you acknowledge and accept the unconditional love of your Divine Self—that precious gift that resides in the Essence of your heart—you will no longer yearn to have others project or mirror back to you that you are lovable, desirable, or right. The true test is love of Self and with that assurance comes the ability to love others. You will know without a doubt that you are loved by your Father/ Mother God. You are a child of Light, and the more you radiate love, the more love is magnetized toward you.

As you begin to draw on the positive attributes of the heart and green energy, your heart center will open and be receptive to the life force from your Higher Self and I AM Presence, which feeds the Threefold Flame of Divine Will, Wisdom and Love. It also heals the impacted energy in the heart, which brings balance, peace and harmonious feelings into your awareness, which in turn creates a sense of well-being and promotes good health and vitality. Your world takes on a rosy hue as you look through eyes filtered with love. You focus on the positive traits of those around you, and your patience and compassion grows as you transcend the physical limitations of love, whereby you join the Beings of Light in the radiant harmony of Divine Love for all God's Creations.

Now, if you will, ponder this concept until we meet again.

You have all heard the expression "I AM THAT I AM," and many have questioned the true meaning of these words. Envision, if you will, the Great All-That-Is projecting a thought form that manifests instantly—an expression of Self—outside of its Divine Self. This Omnipotent Being looks upon its Creation and admires this extension of its consciousness, affirming, "I AM THAT." This process continues as universes, galaxies, solar systems and planets are formed and brought into manifestation. And with each new Creation, the Creator states, "I AM THAT." When the Creator looked upon your shining Essence as you were externalized and given God-consciousness, the Creator also stated, "I AM THAT, I AM." Remember and know that you are a fragment of God-consciousness—are you ready for the Creator to gaze upon you and say, "I AM THAT?" Possibly, not quite yet, but you are well on your way, precious ones. And remember when you gaze around at the world you have created, you must claim, "I AM THAT, I AM."

We shine the radiance of Divine Love down upon you. In you, we are well pleased. I AM Archangel Michael and I bring you these truths.

57. A CALL TO ARMS

*B*eloved masters, we have spoken of the clarion call that was sent forth so many aeons ago in which each of you eagerly responded, "Yes, I wish to be a part of this new experiment." Boldly and bravely you have endured a multitude of trials and tests throughout many lifetimes, as you repeatedly agreed to return to Earth to experience a rich variety of physical embodiments and expression. Many of you feel you have failed, and many of you feel you are not worthy of being a part of the "miracle of ascension" you have heard so much about. Did we not tell you that your success was assured? Even though you descended into the depths of the third-dimensional illusion and forgot your heritage and Divine Birthright, we have not forgotten our promise to you.

As we tap into the etheric record of your individual life stream, somewhat like viewing one of your movie dramas, we can review all that has transpired during your journey into the material world. In moments of your linear time, we have the ability to see and sense what you have felt: your dreams and aspirations, fears, feelings of guilt, rejection and failure, your ever-changing visions of the future, and your courage as you bravely tackled each challenge placed before you. But mostly, we have felt the Spark of love burning within your heart, your constant yearning to be loved, and your deep-seated desire to return to the harmony of Oneness.

Another call is now resounding throughout the universe, **"A CALL TO ARMS."** Many have expressed the opinion that the terms, "Spiritual Warrior" or "Warriors of Light" sounds militant. Let us dispel the confusion and clarify what these terms really mean. The Champions of Light have always wielded the sword of the First Ray of Divine Will under my direction, with Valor, Truth and Integrity as their motto. We have been the guardian overseers of humanity from the first moment the grand plan for the experiment on planet Earth was initiated. We have held the vision and brought forth the thought form of the Divine Creator's desire to create and express his power and will in a solid, physically manifested way. **The power and radiance of the Creator have been our armor; love and integrity have been our shield, and we have wielded the blazing sword of truth and valor as we strove to protect, support and guide you.** This has been my mission, just as each of my brother and sister archangels, with their unique virtues and attributes, have their assignments to fulfill.

The CALL TO ARMS that is reverberating throughout the universe is the call to return to the blessed arms of the Creator, to the enfoldment within the heart center of the All That Is. Yes, you are being called to take up your spiritual armor, to make yourself receptive to the dynamic frequencies of the First Ray of Divine Will and Power by clearing the old, negative energy patterns in your auric field. The Earth and humanity are crying out for peace, understanding, compassion and justice for all. Spiritual warriors radiate love, not hate; they extend kindness and a helping hand to those who project fear and aggression; they teach by example, living their truth as they know it; they practice spiritual empowerment by being actively assertive in setting and obeying rules. A warrior of Light strives for balance and harmony in body, mind and emotions in order to be a pure conductor for the radiance of Spirit, thereby receiving and relaying the higher and higher frequency patterns that are being showered down upon Earth.

The CALL TO ARMS is also a call for the reuniting of star families and soul companions—those from whom you were separated when you were asked to follow your own special path, seemingly alone, in order to fulfill your unique mission. It is becoming the norm to see a person you have not met before in this lifetime and feel a deep, resounding recognition within your soul. "I know you," your heart whispers. You instantly feel at ease and are able to speak and express your thoughts as if you have been friends for many years and you feel a deep sense of loss when you are separated. At the same time, many of the friends you have had for years are like strangers to you. You no longer have anything in common, or to share, and it becomes harder to express who you truly are when you are with them.

The shadow side of life on Earth is roiling and bubbling to the surface as each of you, individually and collectively, are given the opportunity to look into the mirror of life and face the fears and imperfections you have created—an opportunity to heal core-pattern distortions with love and understanding. Many blessed souls have agreed to play the aggressors in this drama, and many others to be the oppressed or the victims. Make no mistake; you carry the energy patterns of each role within you in varying degrees. None is totally innocent and none is totally to blame. Know that when you judge others, you are also judging yourselves. You must each turn within and face your shadow-side and as you do so without fear or judgment, with love and compassion, miracles begin to happen. As a bold Light Warrior, you must face **your worst enemy: your own shadow-self.** As a spiritual Warrior you accept the gift of the Divine Sword of Truth and anchor it within your physical Being once more. The **THREEFOLD FLAME** of Divine Wisdom, Power and Will, Love and

Compassion begins to blaze forth from your heart/soul center and it radiates out from you, creating a powerful aura—a force field of Light.

You, the advanced guard, are radiating the love of Spirit, wielding the sword of truth, as you clear the path and smooth the way for those who are following behind you. You are horizontally radiating the frequencies of balance and harmony from your heart center around the Earth, and to those who are ready to accept this gift of transformation. You are lifting the frequency patterns of the mass-consciousness as you vertically open the gateways to the higher dimensions, thereby creating the bridge of Light which will allow all the beautiful Creations awaiting in the higher etheric realms to begin to manifest on the Earth plane once more: great Light centers, beautiful Light communities, etheric cities and the blessed retreats of the masters that graced your planet in those bygone golden times of perfection. And so, we ask you, are you ready to answer the **CALL TO ARMS,** to don your spiritual armor and carry the sword of power, truth and valor? Do not hesitate, beloveds, this is the call you have been waiting for since you first took on your cloaks of flesh.

And now, to assist you to increase your awareness of the energies, both the positive and negative forces at work within you, let us continue our lessons in mastery of the physical vessel. Our last lesson addressed the heart chakra and green energy. Have you become more aware of the "heart-centered" emotions you feel? Can you truthfully say that you are beginning to listen to your "angel-heart" which only radiates love and acceptance to you and, therefore, to those around you, as well? Do you feel less tightness or pressure in the heart? What negative attributes have you experienced that were focused on the heart or green energy? Were you able to move through these negative emotions more quickly, which allowed you to return to a sense of balance and well-being? Are you better able to move out of a "victim mode" and into the awareness that each and every event or person who makes an impact on you presents a gift for your learning? If you can process the negative emotions by consciously using the green energy of the heart, you are well on your way to becoming the master of your world/reality.

The next chakra, or energy center, we will address is the fifth, which is the throat chakra · blue energy. The throat and thyroid gland are an important part of your new SOLAR POWER CENTER which incorporates the throat, thymus and heart. Remember, **THOUGHT-FREQUENCY PATTERNS, EMOTIONS AND SOUND YIELD FORM.** Your multi-mind (subconscious, conscious and superconscious minds) and your life experiences are tools for greater awareness. Your subconscious mind is a thought processor that takes literally the ideas, images and words you allow to filter through your consciousness, especially those you accept as your truth or beliefs. A part of the transmutation process is to elevate your subconscious mind into conscious expression and for your conscious mind to merge with your superconscious mind. The ability to speak powerfully, truthfully and eloquently is one of the first steps toward self-mastery.

Etherically, the throat chakra is often bound and constricted by energy cords from past lives so that it is difficult for you to express your thoughts clearly or speak your truth. The self-defense mechanism of the ego lashes out by judging or criticizing others when fear, a sense of unworthiness, or doubt dominate the subconscious or conscious mind. Please be aware that the use of negative language of lower vibrational frequencies creates discord in your auric/energy fields and that the spoken word is an important component in the law of cause and effect.

As you reclaim your spiritual power, the first step is to begin to speak your truth as you know it with discernment, discretion and compassion. **"SOUL TALK"** and empowered, creative language are the fuel and frequencies which allow you to tap into the universal energy of Creation. Thoughts, words, emotions and actions are all forms of energy.

Please blaze within your consciousness the awareness that **"I AM"** are the most empowering words you will ever speak. Affirmations, visualization and changing the language you use is one of the fastest ways to deprogram and reprogram your subconscious mind. Creativity, revelation, channeling, telepathy, imagination—these are all part of your birthright— gifts of Creation—part of the virtues and attributes of our Father/Mother God. When you learn the language of "heart-speak" and "Soul-talk" you will automatically use words of empowerment such as: **I AM, I LOVE, I WILL, I CREATE, I CHOOSE, I ENJOY** and **I HAVE.**

Starting now, dear ones, make it a habit to monitor your thought patterns and replace negative thoughts with brief, concise affirmations. This is the best way to shut out the static of your ego-mind and instill new thought patterns. See Spirit perched on your shoulder as an observer as you go about your work/play week and then be honest with yourself: would a master use the language you are using, say the things you are saying? When you move into criticism or judgment, **STOP!** Think before you continue. A master is someone who transforms knowledge into wisdom. When this wisdom is combined with the power of intent and the spoken word, it creates miracles. We are endeavoring to assist you; to give you the wisdom and tools necessary to make an easy transition back to your natural, Divine State as an emissary of Light and a master of Divine Cocreation. We embrace and enfold you in our strong arms of protection and radiate the love of the Creator through our hearts to yours. I AM Archangel Michael.

58. MESSAGE FROM RONNA

Hello again, Dear Friends.

I have just returned from almost three weeks in Europe. The 1999 Wesak Festival I participated in was held about an hour away from Frankfurt in a village called Michelstadt. Judy Vermeulen, my business partner, translator and dear friend, and I stayed in a quaint, old hotel where we learned that there are some very interesting legends in the area about Archangel Michael. The Wesak Festival was held outdoors in a big field, at a nearby hotel. In case of rain, two large tents had been set up and benches for the participants were placed out in the sun facing a raised, covered stage for the musicians and speakers. Our sales tables were placed under some lovely shade trees nearby.

There were between 250 and 300 people present from several countries: England, France, Denmark, Switzerland, as well as many from Holland, Belgium, and Germany. Friday was a glorious, sunny day and I gave my portion of the day's program just before the Wesak Full Moon Ceremony in the late afternoon. Lord Michael had requested that I take the people through the first phase of the initiation process before the Wesak Meditation. Saturday morning was overcast, but it looked as if the dark rain clouds would bypass us. I was busy both days signing books and channeling messages in them for the beautiful German and European people, and then Judy would translate the messages for them. There were many tears of joy and many touching moments shared with both men and women as they received their gift from Lord Michael. It sprinkled rain a bit, off and on, but no one seemed to mind. However the cloud cover was getting much thicker and the sky had darkened considerably. (The thought, "emotional cleansing," came into my mind.)

In the late afternoon (4 p.m.) just as Judy and I, with the help of some angel friends, walked across the field to go to the stage for our part of the day's program, the clouds overhead parted in a circle and some beautiful beams of Light radiated down on us all. Many people were exclaiming and pointing, and some took pictures. I spoke for a short time and had just started the first meditation when a group of teenage, German boys and girls (maybe a dozen) came racing across the field, shouting and playing their boom boxes very loudly. They came right up to the edge of our group, and several of our people went over to them and asked them to please not disrupt. As they turned to go, a young man held out his hand to one of the young women who was trying to get them to quiet down—in his hand was a red tulip. He offered it to her, saying, "Here, please give this to the lady," (meaning me). They moved a little way off into the distance, but kept up their shouting and playing loud music. Judy and I were almost shouting as well, so that the people could hear us. Suddenly, there were several loud claps of thunder and bright lightning flashes—it was as if a whirlwind of energy swept across the field bringing the elements of wind and rain. The young people rushed for cover and disappeared.

As I brought the energy of Lord Michael through me and began his message, it was the most powerful energy I have ever experienced. The people were enthralled, and although many had moved back into the protection of the tents, many others sat out in the rain with their faces upturned, enraptured in the beauty of the moment. The storm passed as quickly as it came, leaving a freshness and the feeling that we had all just experienced a profound miracle. I knew that these beautiful, young ones had given us a gift by presenting our shadow side to us. Many people were angry and dismayed at the disruption, while others had wanted to ask the young people to join us and were fully aware of the drama that was being played out.

Lord Michael told the people there that they had created a beautiful Fatherland and were Divine Architects, but now it was time to open their hearts and allow the Mother Creator to heal their emotional wounds and the Earth, and to bring them back into unity-consciousness. Those who were there will never be the same. I know I won't, and I feel blessed to have been given the opportunity to share this wonderful experience. As with every place I go, the people were so beautiful and so eager and hungry for truth and the love of Spirit. I always feel as if I am in the midst of a wonderful family reunion—a reunion of my star family, as Archangel Michael tells us. You were there, I felt your loving presence and strength as we joined together in the higher realms and anchored a powerful, new level of Christ-consciousness on Earth.

We held another one-day event in Brussels where there were about forty people from Holland, France, Germany and Belgium. It was a sweet, glorious day, much gentler, but no less profound. The people there were told that they were the center focal point of a radiating energy vortex that would spread across Europe—healing, cleansing and unifying. Before I went, I was told it was of the utmost importance that I make this journey and now I know why.

I send you all my deepest love and gratitude. Your sister in the Light, Ronna

59. WE OFFER YOU THE KEYS TO SELF-MASTERY

*B*eloved masters, I radiate to you the loving blessings of the Creator via a glorious outpouring of Light, refracted into the colors of the seven Rays of your solar system, and infused with the luminescence of Christ Light from the five higher Galactic Rays: twelve Rays in all that contain the attributes, aspects and virtues of our Father/Mother God. See and feel this **ROD** of **LIGHTEN-ING** as it fills and surrounds you—enfolding, permeating and transforming all it touches. This is the gift that is being offered to you as you move deeper into the throes of transformation. Close your eyes for a moment and feel with all your senses as we draw you closer into our auric field of Love/Light.

You now know what it is like to be in the **"Flow of Spirit"** at times, and it is easy to maintain composure and control of your emotions and thought processes when all is going well. You are more aware of the Universal Laws, have a broader knowledge of why you are in the physical body, and that you have a Divine Mission, and an ultimate goal of returning to unity-consciousness. But you are still caught up in the game of polarity, whereby the pendulum swings back and forth as you seek balance, which throws you off kilter in the process. This is disconcerting because you feel you are not succeeding or living up to the guidelines that have been revealed to you. Look up the word "guidelines" in your dictionary— it means instructions, criteria, directions—a standard or principle to follow in order to determine a course of action.

Beloveds, we encourage you to relax and not judge yourselves so harshly. Many of you are accomplishing in one lifetime what would ordinarily take dozens or even hundreds of life experiences. You are learning to think and act through the filter of the heart and with the wisdom of the soul/Higher Self. You are bravely delving into and seeking to transmute thought patterns that were instilled in your mental, emotional and etheric bodies over many hundreds of lifetimes. You are striving to maintain a sense of balance while facing your shadow-self and seeking to integrate all the fragments of imbalanced energy you have created since you first took on physical embodiment. We are aware that this is no easy task.

One of the pitfalls of the process, or "glamours" as they were called in the esoteric teachings, is judgment of self, or comparing yourself to others—an action instigated by the ego-self. Just as we have instructed you to be the observer in your interactions with others, we ask you to be the observer of your own thought-processes—to stay focused on what is occurring at the moment, and not waste energy on reviewing the past or projecting your thoughts into the uncertainty of the future. Within the moment is the key to self-mastery, for this is when you have the opportunity to draw on the harmonious resonance of your Divine Self. You cannot access the wondrous gifts of Spirit if you are engulfed in the mists of self-doubt or the swirling thought patterns of discord. Spirit requires harmony and an environment of tranquility in order to plant the seeds of illumined wisdom.

So you see, it is not what you have accomplished, what you know or how much wisdom you have garnered, nor is it even about the service you have given to others—it is about creating a fertile field within the physical vessel in which Spirit can descend and take dominion. As this is accomplished, all else follows at the right pace, within the right time frame and with ease and grace. This is a simplistic explanation of the ascension process, but it is given so that you will stop judging yourselves and trying so hard to live up to the measurements or guidelines that others have set forth. This is the old way where rules, regulations and restrictions were set down by others who wished to control and dominate the masses. You are becoming sovereign Beings once more, with your own personal, intimate connection to the Creator via your I AM Presence and your own true path to tread, which will lead you back into ONENESS at the proper time.

Remember, each of you is a unique aspect of the Creator; each of you has a specific mission and journey to accomplish; each of you has within you experiences, impulses and memories from many lifetimes. Therefore, your journey back to wholeness will also be unique. Here is where you claim one of the most important keys to mastery: choosing your own path back to enlightenment by claiming your own truth and living that truth to the best of your ability, and allowing everyone else to do the same. Self-respect and self-love are also important components of self-mastery whereby you allow the Essence of Love/Light to flow to you and through you and then radiate out toward others. This helps you to put your trust in Spirit as you let go and **LET GOD WORK THROUGH YOU.**

Down through the ages, the number of souls who aspired to become initiates or sought enlightenment were few. There were the elite esoteric schools of wisdom in ancient times where initiates were subjected to a long and rigorous training process, sometimes for many years. However, few succeeded and even fewer were able to take the abilities they had gained and put what they had learned into action for the good of all. The training techniques of the Eastern world also entailed years of meditation and strict discipline in order to attain a level of self-mastery. But there were few who came out into the world and put to practical use what they had gained. Those times are past, beloveds. The keys to self-mastery are being offered to the masses, but must be accomplished while living and functioning in the world of cause and effect and then, practiced until they are fully integrated and put to practical application in everyday life. This facilitates the healing and harmonizing of the energy patterns with those around you, as each of you becomes an example for others to emulate. This is part of coming back into the awareness of the ONENESS of all things. The times of isolation or separatism are over.

Just as you would not expect a child who is in the first grade of schooling to act or take on the responsibility of a youngster in a much higher grade, so it is on the soul path of initiation. It is a gradual process, and your soul/Higher Self knows what is best for you, if you will only listen to the guidance of Spirit. We do not expect you to be perfect; you are not judged if you make a mistake or take a wrong turn once in a while. Live each moment to the best of your ability, while allowing yourself the latitude of acknowledging all the emotions that arise, but by not permitting them to throw you into discord. Step by step, and experience by experience, old habits and thought patterns will fall away—you will move out of the entrapment of limitation and the ego, into the empowerment of Spirit, whereby you will gradually become the master of your destiny and the director of your reality.

As you move into the new millennium, we ask you to begin to build a vision of how you perceive the future of humanity and the Earth for the next century. The secret is for each of you to create your own vision of perfection, or how you would imagine Heaven on Earth to be. You are becoming much more powerful in tapping into the thought forms or cosmic substance of manifestation as you join together in conscious, loving intent. So it is important that each of you adds your vision to that of the rest of the world. Remember, the miracles of manifestation begin within each heart/soul center, then it radiates outwardly and connects with like energy, thereby magnifying and creating powerful thought forms which are eventually manifested on the physical plane. Allow Spirit to begin "downloading" the wisdom and inspiration you will need to gain clear insight as to what your highest vision is to be, so that you can add your inspired thought and energy to that of the whole. **Remember, beloveds, we are all in the process of ascending back into unity-consciousness together. It is the desire of our Father/Mother God that you experience peace, love and joy—NOW!**

We have stated many times before that part of the initiation process and becoming a cocreative master of peace and harmony is to come to a better understanding of the workings of Spirit and the Universal Laws. When you know the rules and the consequences of not following the rules, it helps in making the proper choices. In our attempt to assist you in this endeavor, we will continue our lessons of integration of the higher attributes of the chakra system by transmuting and healing the imbalanced aspects.

Our focus last month was on the fifth, or throat, chakra which resonates to the frequencies of the color blue. It is important that you understand that colors vibrate to specific energy patterns, as does everything in the material world. Envision the words you speak taking form and radiating forth in specific colors and shapes: sharp red daggers of anger, hate or rage, or the blazing-red sword of empowerment and strength; muddy-green hooks of jealousy or attempts to control and possess, or words which radiate vibrant-green energy of healing and harmony. It is not by coincidence that your Earth is predominately made up of the colors of blue, which carries the energies of peace, serenity and truth, and green, which relays life-force energy, healing and balance. Whatever it takes, it is vital that you accept the universal truth that within every word you speak and every thought and deed you project, there is a quality of energy projected as well, either positive or negative.

If you have observed and focused on the energy of the throat chakra, you should be more aware of the language you are using in everyday conversations and the thought patterns that run through your mind. When you endeavor to integrate the higher aspects of each chakra and color, you invoke the assistance of your Higher Self. This enables you to transcend old habit patterns, to speak your truth with discernment and express your feelings in a positive way. You will also learn discretion and to be brave enough to not always have to express an opinion—to know when to be silent. A master speaks softly and often remains silent, observing and listening, unless he or she is in a teaching situation. It is also important that you begin to eliminate language that carries low-vibrational frequencies and replace this with positive words of empowerment. Practice listening with the inner ear of Spirit to the messages or meanings behind the words others speak. Monitor your speech constantly to see that your words match what you truly feel.

We will now turn to the sixth chakra · the third eye which radiates the frequencies of indigo energy. It is time to clear the static and distortions from your third eye, which is the doorway to the gifts of transcendence and mastery. The pituitary gland is being reactivated and is opening like a beautiful lotus blossom, which allows access to the light packets and encoded wisdom stored within your brain structure.

When the veil of forgetfulness was drawn across your memory, you became disconnected from your Higher Self, and the natural abilities of clairvoyance, clairaudience, creativity and intuitive wisdom began to atrophy. The higher-dimensional levels of the brain shut down, resulting in fear, headaches, negative thought patterns and a sense of isolation or being shut off from your soul/Higher Self and God. Humanity began to focus on the lower-dimensional frequencies, or instinctual patterns of the brain, rather than the higher frequencies of the Superconscious mind.

The human mind is awakening as part of the resurrection/ mutation process and you are coming to the realization that you have all the tools necessary to create any reality you desire. All Creation begins first with a thought—the intensity and consistency of the thought determines how fast it will manifest in the physical plane. Your sensitivities will increase and your needs will change, as you move up the path of refinement. As you develop belief in yourself and your abilities, and learn to live attuned to your Higher Self and in harmony with the Universal Laws, your world will become magical and your desire for love, peace, joy and abundance will naturally unfold as you move into the higher frequencies of balance and harmony with Spirit.

The path for you to follow is clearly marked, and there are signposts and guidelines along the way. All you have to do is go forward, one firm step at a time, with loving intent and firm resolve. We are near to support you when you stumble, to whisper encouragement when you are discouraged, but most of all we are here to radiate the empowering love of God to you so that you will know you are never alone. I surround you in an auric field of love and protection. I AM Archangel Michael.

60. ARE YOU READY TO DON YOUR CLOAK OF LIGHT?

*B*eloved masters, even when you have gained the ability to be a conscious observer and view all that takes place from the vantage point of a master, there are times when it is difficult to understand what the larger picture may be, and the true meaning of what the world sees as a great tragedy. Let us explain, and hopefully, give you comfort as more and more unusual and unprecedented events begin to unfold during these swiftly changing times.

First of all, you are in the midst of a major infusion of Christ energy from the galactic core, which is affecting everyone on Earth at some level. Many of you have diligently worked to clear old energy patterns from your physical/etheric, emotional and mental bodies, along with the impacted energies from within your chakra systems in order to be clear receptacles for this Divine Influx. (Chakras are focused, concentrated energy in specific locations of the body.) The chakras hold all past memories, both positive and negative, and along with your subconscious mind are instrumental in creating your picture of reality. Envision your chakras as they begin to spin faster and faster in perfect harmony until they reach maximum velocity—suddenly there is a burst of Light from the core of each chakra transforming it into a new color and resonance. When this takes place it means you have opened a sacred seal within the body and you are experiencing an infusion of Christ Light and the refined energies of the five higher Galactic Rays. We will explain this more in detail at a later time, but it is important that you understand what is happening presently.

There are openings taking place in the chakra system of

the Earth—seals being broken or opened, and it is the same within your physical body. Many of you have opened the sixth or seventh seals (the third-eye and crown chakras), and some even the eighth or higher. Please, do not get caught up in numbers or the game of "What level am I?" And, do not compare yourself to anyone else. Know that you are at the perfect place for your growth and empowerment—you are on your own, unique journey, as is every soul on Earth.

We have also talked about the Second Coming, and you are in the midst of that process as well. Each of you has available to you the maximum Christ energy that your physical vessel can accommodate. And so, here again, there are small infusions taking place in some and a wondrous merging with the Christ Self by those of you who have diligently worked to balance and harmonize your physical vessels. You are swiftly moving through the multiple levels of initiation and the sub-planes and higher planes of consciousness on your way to the fifth dimension.

There are also momentous astrological configurations taking place—celestial events of momentous proportions. On your calendar date of August 11, 1999, a total eclipse of the sun took place, which of itself is not that unusual. However, at that time there was also a powerful Grand Cross formation in what are called the "gates of power," which are the fixed signs of the zodiac: Taurus, Leo, Aquarius and Scorpio. There have been a number of interpretations, predictions and explanations, but allow us to give you one more. Before you can step into harmony with your new spiritual/human, Light-body reality, you must release all fixed, rigid concepts—all your linear, analytical thought forms that are keeping you stuck in the confines of a third-dimensional reality. Are you ready to shed your rigid armor of limitation, your fixed concept of what life is about and who you are? Yes, it is a portal way, a gateway to higher consciousness— an opportunity for you to give birth to a new consciousness and to help the Earth return to her rightful status as a shining, sacred planet of Light.

During times of great change such as those the Earth and humanity are now experiencing, there is the potential for cataclysmic events to take place—not as punishment, but a natural process as the higher frequencies of Light hit the rigid energies of imbalance or darkness. You have become much more powerful than you know as you join together in greater and greater numbers focusing on "the highest good for all" with loving, unified intent.

Know that the beautiful, wise soul called John Kennedy, Jr. and those with him were not just hapless victims of tragedy. It was a contract fulfilled in the highest order. Envision millions of hearts opening in a great outpouring of love, made even stronger with the emotional sense of the loss of a "shining one." See this aura of unified love as it surrounds the Earth and acts as a filter for the influx of energy now being showered down upon the earth—tempering, softening, blending gently and harmoniously as it transforms the rigid energies of fear, anger, greed and ignorance.

Know that you have chosen lifetimes in which you were destined to live to an advanced age—experiencing the fruits of success or failure, and the infirmities of the flesh. Please remember that you have also chosen to experience life as a blazing, shining star—radiant and bright—affecting the lives of all those you touch, but returning to your spiritual home at the height of your glory. You did not come to stay; you came only for a brief visit to gift the world with your loving radiance and such was the mission of the one called John Kennedy, Jr. Remember him and bless him for his gift.

Beloved ones, know that I will be with you during these times of momentous change and the initiation process you are presently experiencing, as will your personal angelic helpers, the masters who guide and direct you, and the many other great Beings of Light who are participating in this wondrous process of ascension.

This initiation symbolizes an outward acknowledgment and affirmation of an inward transformation process that has been incubating for some time. It symbolizes your personal experience of the **SECOND COMING OF CHRIST**—the absorption or integration of your **CHRIST-CONSCIOUSNESS.** One of the benefits of this Divine Gift is direct interaction with the Beings of Light and to know, without any doubt, that you are under the guidance and protection of these radiant Beings. You are now free to interact in a multitude of ways with the higher-dimensional planes and frequencies

Your petitions and decrees have been heard and duly recorded—just as all sincere petitions are heard. In Spirit, during your sleep time, you have been brought before the Hierarchy's Council of Light and judged worthy to be added to the rolls of the **Disciples of Light,** or bearers of the Christ Flame. That is the reason you have experienced so much turmoil and drama over the past few years. In order for you to attain this status, you had to confront, process and clear much of the residual karmic patterns within your energy field. It is not to say that you will not be faced with challenges and stressful events in the future, for you are still influenced by the third-dimensional environment of duality

and polarity, even though you are resonatı
dimensional frequencies and higher. The differeı
you now have all the tools and resources you need, ɑ
as the vast energy of the higher dimensions to draw on,
that never again will you have to struggle alone.

So that you will know that we are ever near and ready to
assist and guide you, the ascended masters, the archangels,
and the Goddess in her many forms ask that you call upon
them to instill within you their virtues, attributes, power and
blessings. Choose one, or more, which you wish to
OVERLIGHT you, to be your source of inspiration and guidance. Your needs may change and so, do not hesitate to call
on any of us whenever it seems appropriate. We will always
answer. If the Being of Light that you wish to attend you is
not here listed, call on it and an inspired mantra from it
will come to you.

**These petitions are given in the form of a mantra which
will call forth that which you need to fulfill your mission
and will radiate love and protection to you as well.**

**I CALL UPON THE BELOVED LORD JESUS/SANANDA
to be my mentor and guiding Light. I ask that he, who is
the perfect embodiment of Christ-consciousness, fill me
with his compassionate wisdom, steadfast intent and determination. Each and every moment, I will endeavor to
be a shining example of manifested Spirit in action. I go
forth in the assurance that the highest path will always be
made clear to me, and each task that is put before me I
will accomplish with ease and grace.**

**I CALL UPON THE BLESSED LADY/ARCHANGEL
MARY for whom I feel such great affinity, to guide and
sustain me in my quest for truth and creative power. I**

claim all the gifts that have been imprinted on my soul and within my brain structure and I gratefully manifest them in their highest form for the blessing of all. I am continually inspired to give birth to things of great beauty to delight and encourage others to do the same. I draw upon the laws of Creation and dedicate my life in service to humanity.

I CALL UPON SAINT GERMAIN to be my inspiration. I claim the gift of the Violet Transmuting Flame—the Divine Alchemical Energy of transformation and transmutation. I will accept the challenge to be the full embodiment of the perfected masculine and feminine energy, showing all what it means to walk in power and strength while personifying love and compassion. I claim and pronounce my MASTERHOOD NOW!

I CALL UPON KWAN YIN to infuse me with all the healing energy, love and compassion of her wondrous nature. Allow me to be a nurturer and healer of all those who seek comfort, hope and inspiration. Allow me to be the instrument by which they attain wholeness in body, mind and Spirit. May all whom I meet and serve be infused with balance, peace and harmony.

I CALL UPON MASTER KUTHUMI, world teacher and bearer of truth and wisdom, to be my inspiration. May I bring forth hidden truths and the higher wisdom of the masters in such a way that it can be understood by all who seek to know. Be my guiding Light and inspiration; teach me discernment and to give wise counsel to those who are led to me. I seek only to be a clear channel and I know the more I give, the more I will receive.

I CALL UPON ARCHANGEL GABRIEL to send forth

in a blaze of glory the declaration of my triumphant emergence from the restrictions of all physical limitation. I am now ready and willing to assume the full mantle of my dynamic power and authority. I declare myself to be a servant of the Christ energy and I will be a shining example and inspiration to others.

I CALL UPON ARCHANGEL RAPHAEL, who has been my teacher, guardian and protector since time immortal. I claim peace and harmony for myself and convey the beauty of my loving nature to all those I meet. I go forth in the knowledge that I am a Being of great purpose and that each day brings me the opportunity to use and manifest the perfection of my Spirit.

I CALL UPON ARCHANGEL URIEL to use me as a herald of the new truth and wisdom that is being poured forth upon the Earth and humanity. I dedicate myself as a voice of the future and a conduit of the healing energy from the universal Source. All I AM and all I do henceforth will contribute to the manifestation of the new Heaven on Earth. I will be an emissary of the DOVE OF PEACE.

I CALL UPON ARCHANGEL MICHAEL; I ask to be his representative on Earth and a messenger in his Mighty Legions of Light. I will dedicate my life, my energy and all I have to the fulfillment of the promise I made before taking on physical form. My greatest desire is to fulfill my Divine Mission on Planet Earth. I will be a bearer of the sword of truth, honor and valor and will stand fast until the dream of the new Golden Age is brought to fruition.

I CALL UPON ARCHANGEL ZADKIEL, who has been an inspiration and Divine Overseer of many of my incarnations. With his help, I will boldly carry his banner of the Violet Flame of Redemption. I will always strive to be an example of right action and justice. I will not hesitate to step forward, whether it is to serve or to be an example of the perfection I now seek to embody.

I CALL UPON THE BEAUTIFUL LADY/ARCHANGEL FAITH to inspire me and lead me through the many unknown pastures. I will go forth in full faith and knowledge that I am being led by my SPIRIT and I will be a shining example for all to see. I will show others that with courage and faith the impossible becomes possible; that by giving up all that is safe and secure, I attain comfort and am blessed with riches untold. I will show the weak of heart that we can step off the cliff and soar among the stars.

I CALL UPON THE COMPASSIONATE LADY/ARCHANGEL HOPE. I will personify hope and inspiration in my manner, speech and actions. I will give loving assistance where needed. I will gently inspire and encourage where there is despair; I will speak words of hope so all may hear. By my very presence, I will bring comfort and leave in my wake an aura of peace and beauty.

I CALL UPON THE LADY/CONSTANCE, ARCHANGEL OF JUSTICE. I, who have known ignorance, bigotry and injustice will be a shining example of unconditional love and pure intent. I will always endeavor to understand and forgive. I claim the purity of my Divine SELF and it shines radiantly for all to see and share in its warmth. I will personify the qualities of understanding, perception and Divine Wisdom.

I CALL UPON THE GODDESS OF LIBERTY to liberate me from any limitation that is keeping me from fulfilling my highest destiny. I assume the mantel of MASTER-HOOD and go forth in constant assurance of success. I know I am a teacher of the new, emerging wisdom and truth. May I never hesitate to speak my truth and share my wisdom when my SPIRIT leads me to do so? I accept the role of a gentle guide to all those who are led to me.

I CALL UPON THE GODDESS OF TRUTH to fill me with the desire to know and experience the hidden wisdom of the ages. As I gain true knowledge and wisdom, and manifest it in my life, may I become an example and disseminator of higher truth, sharing it with all seekers of the Light. I will give comfort to those who are discouraged and inspire those who feel defeated. I will be a courageous example for the faint of heart and give loving succor to those who do not feel worthy of love. I will honor and listen to the nudgings of my Spirit and walk in the way of truth and love.

I CALL UPON THE SHINING GODDESS OF LIGHT/ THE HOLY SPIRIT to fill me and infuse me with her glorious radiance. Make me a beacon for all to see so that they will know whom I serve as I use the Light of Spirit to heal, comfort and inspire. I will bask in the glow of her radiance and create such a brilliant aura of love that all whom I come in contact with will be blessed, and seeds of transformation will be planted and will come to fruition at the proper time. My Spirit rejoices as I spread wide my influence of Loving Light.

I CALL UPON THE LOVING GODDESSES OF THE DEVIC AND ELEMENTAL KINGDOMS to shower their radiant loving energy down upon the Earth, calming all the elements of nature, and to join us in our efforts to heal our wounded Mother Earth. I petition them to work in unison with us once more to reclaim the beauty and perfection of the Earth. May we remember that we are stewards of the Earth and the animal, vegetable and mineral kingdoms were put in our care—MAY WE WALK IN PEACE AND HARMONY, HONORING ALL GOD'S CREATIONS, FROM THE LOWEST TO THE HIGHEST.

Affirm: I hereby don my shining cloak of spiritual armor and accept the gifts and responsibilities of a Divine Master of Cocreation. I dedicate my life and my all to the glory of God/Goddess/All-That-Is and to the manifestation of Heaven on Earth. And so it is!

May the radiance of God's Light pour down upon you. Know that you are loved beyond measure. I AM Archangel Michael and I joyously bring you these truths.

61. A SPIRIT BRIGHT

When I heard what happened on that sad and tragic day,
With tearful eyes and heavy heart I knelt by my bed to pray.

"Why did you have to take him, Lord? He was so young and gay.
He had so much to live for, so soon to be called away."

Within my heart a stillness came; a soft voice seemed to say,
"A bold and happy heart I need, a spirit strong and true.
I have a universe to run, there is so much to do.

"He'll help me light the stars at night,
And shine the Moon until it's bright,
Sweep away the clouds with a broom so fine,
And tell the Sun when it's time to shine.

"He'll paint the rainbows in the sky,
Teach the angels how to fly,
Design the snowflakes before they fall
And tune the harps in the Celestial Hall.

"Now this promise I will make to those who love him true:
He will never be very far from you.
In your dreams when you sleep,
A date with you he'll always keep.
And when it is your time for the promised land,
He will be there to take you by the hand.

"All his wondrous work he'll want you to see
And you'll be together throughout eternity."

Dedicated to all the beautiful, young angels who came to
Earth to bless us with their radiance for only a little while.
They leave us with memories of their love, joy and what it
means to SHINE BRIGHTLY. They are not gone; they will
remain forever in our hearts. Ronna Herman

62. A Vision for the New Millenium

*Y*ou are at a grand crossroads. Beloved ones, as you move through the process of clearing and cleansing the multiple facets of yourself, you are leaving behind the energies that created all the pain, suffering and distress. Step back for a moment, and view these past months as an observer—are you beginning to "get the picture" of what the grand plan and ascension is all about? Being aware and in control are important facets of mastery, and if you have diligently worked with the lessons we have given you, you should be well on your way to reclaiming the many gifts you brought to Earth so many aeons ago.

We have identified and spent much time on the many negative facets of expression in order to help you identify and correct them. Now it is time to begin to concentrate on the positive attributes you wish to strengthen and perfect. It is time to identify and reinforce what is right with your world instead of what is wrong. As we have told you so many times before—what you focus your attention on is what you give energy to, which magnifies and strengthens whatever it may be, positive or negative. Therefore it is, once again, time to take inventory, for you must have a clear picture of what you want your world of the future to look and feel like. It does not serve you to try to fit yourselves into the dreams of another person or persons—it is a time to envision your dream in its fullest measure and then allow it to come to fruition within the "dreamscape of the future for humanity and the Earth" by affirming, "for the highest good of all."

Have you clearly defined how you would like to be of service in these rapidly changing times? That should be first and foremost in your vision, dear ones. It can be as simple as becoming an anchor for the constantly increasing influx of **Divine Life-Force Energy** or using the Violet Flame of Transformation to surround and assist others. Remember, there is a Universal Law which states that you must use or pass on the gifts of wisdom and enlightenment you receive, so that you make room for more to be given unto you. Are you speaking your truth and sharing the insights you have gained through your own trials, tests and experiences? Are you not only claiming the gifts that Spirit is offering you, but using and exercising those spiritual muscles that have atrophied from non-use, such as acknowledging and writing down the inspired insights or wisdom teachings that pop into your mind? As with most dreams, they drift away like smoke if you do not capture them and write them down. Are you willing to step out of your comfort zone when asked to participate in some event or exercise that makes you nervous or sets your heart pounding? It is ego that makes you hesitate. Do not fear to make a mistake, my sweet friends, or to admit that you do not know the answer when asked a question. This is what makes you human, makes others comfortable, and gives them permission to practice and perfect their spiritual skills around you as well.

Have your relationships with others changed? You can tell how you are doing by the people you are drawing to you—those who mirror back to you your concept of self-worth. It is like a dance—you constantly change partners and tempos—sometimes flowing and merging in perfect harmony; yet with others, it seems as if you are constantly out of step, tripping each other or stepping on toes. It does not make either wrong, better or less than—it just means you are not in harmony with each other. As you all blend more and more into unity-consciousness, it is important that you become aware of those you are not in harmony with (without judgment), and those with whom you are in harmony, complementing and empowering each other. As long as you are in the physical body, you will have relationships which will constantly challenge you to stay centered—dramas that you agreed to play out with partners, friends and family. However, the secret in such situations is to not get caught up in their journey and their picture of reality—to stay centered, to assert your spiritual awareness by setting boundaries and being the example, and from knowing that you are not responsible for anyone's spiritual growth but your own. Do not be diverted from your path, beloved ones. Move gracefully through each test and situation with love and compassion, under the direction of your Higher Self—if you do so, you will not fail.

Also examine your present concepts of abundance, health and your bodily form, your right to all the beauty, bounty and abundance the Earth has to offer—your Divine Birthright. After you define and claim all the facets of SELF—believing and affirming that you are a loving, beloved SPARK of GOD— you are ready to move into the mode of SELFLESSNESS, which means no longer focusing on the little self, but on the whole. You know without a doubt that your needs, desires and aspirations will be fulfilled as you move forward into service as a Master.

You will begin to live transpersonally, viewing life and circumstances from the vantage point of "WE," not "I," and looking at the larger picture of life with expanded Spiritual awareness—not the "small story" of the ego. Place yourself in the center of your vision and new reality (identify who you are in this new reality: characteristics, talents, abilities and attributes which describe the highest expression of who you are). Be bold and outrageous in your vision as you claim yourself to be a loving, sovereign entity, and then formulate in great detail how you will operate and function multi-dimensionally as a cocreator of LOVE, LIGHT, PEACE, JOY AND ABUNDANCE.

Take time to contemplate what kind of relationships you want to have with the people in your life. If you desire new relations in your life, place them in your vision—describe in great detail what kind of relationships you want: mate, play-mate, soul mate, business partner, friends, etc. Put them in your vision without identifying them; only state the types and qualities of relationships you desire and then let your Divine Self create the miracle. Always keep your vision as clear and concise as possible. Seek joyful, delightful love and fulfillment. Say every day: I HAVE THE MATE THAT IS PERFECT FOR ME, NOW! (or perfect friend, partner, etc.). If you are in a relationship at the moment that is not of your highest desire, focus on the positive attributes of that person and still affirm: I HAVE MY PERFECT MATE, NOW! They may surprise you and become that perfect mate. Please know that sometimes it is appropriate for you to be your own perfect mate.

You must have a well-defined concept and a firm foundation for all aspects of your life in the physical world as you begin to soar multi-dimensionally. You need to learn to flow within the natural structure and guidelines of Spirit (or follow your Divine Destiny with ease and grace).

We will give you more guidelines for your vision next month, but let us give you this mantra to use until we come together again:

"I have all the resources I need and desire to be comfortable and to assist me in fulfilling my Divine Mission. I live in the perfect place to nourish my Spirit, and my physical, mental and emotional bodies. Abundance flows to me and through me as I hold it lightly in my hands and allow it to flow out into the world to constantly be replenished. All my desires, needs and wishes are fulfilled even before I am aware of them. My timing is perfect in making decisions and taking action. I always listen to and follow my Spirit in every endeavor; therefore, my decisions and actions are for the highest good of all. I cherish and nurture our Mother Earth and she cherishes and supports me. I radiate love and blessings to all and they are returned tenfold. My world is filled with love, joy, beauty, peace and comfort, always."

Now allow us to continue our instructions about the chakra system within your body, the attributes of the seven Rays of your solar system and eventually, the total integration of the five higher Galactic Ray energies. We last discussed the sixth chakra · the third eye and the frequencies of indigo Energy. Hopefully, you have spent some quiet time focusing on this area and delving into your personal perceptions of how it affects you, how you have been using the gifts of the sixth chakra and what distortions you need to release or reprogram. Many of you desire the gifts of clairvoyance and clairaudience, but you have deep-seated memories of times when you misused these gifts or of being punished or persecuted when you used your gifts to help others. These are the memories or impacted energies that we want to help you heal and transmute.

It is important that you have an intimate relationship with each chakra and become familiar with the vibrational resonance you are radiating into your auric field. The third eye is the doorway to clairvoyance or INNER SIGHT—or to put it another way, your Higher Self via your intuition uses the pituitary gland to send pulsations or Light packets of information to you, or to assist you to tap into the creativity or wisdom stored within your brain structure. As you become an observer of your thought processes with the help of your Superconscious mind, you become more conscious of your habitual thought patterns and how they distort or enhance your reality. It is easier to function in a state of light meditation with Spirit perched on your shoulder as the observer, giving guidance and clarity.

You are becoming more sensitive to the feeling sensations of what is "right or wrong" for you. Lucid dreaming becomes the norm and your creative "input" is enhanced as you begin to tap into the great reservoir of higher-dimensional reality under the guidance and direction of your Divine Self, your guides and teachers. As you harness the emotions of the ego and learn to trust your intuition and the nudgings of Spirit, miracles happen more frequently and become a natural part of your reality. Your human mind is awakening as part of the resurrection/mutation process and you are coming to the realization that you have the tools and abilities to create any reality you desire. It is time to tap into the wellspring of **JOY,** which is your natural state of **BEING.** Know that you are in an intense transmutation process in which you are moving into higher-dimensional levels and frequency patterns at an ever-accelerating pace and there is very little time in between initiations.

Now we will direct our attention to the crown chakra · the Seventh Ray · and violet energy. As you integrate the seventh step on the path, you move quickly along the path of ascension. Your ego is now functioning under the direction of the soul-self, and your soul-self is gradually being incorporated into your Higher Self. Your subconscious mind is becoming conscious and your conscious mind is being flooded with the wisdom of your Superconscious mind. The energy is now focused on the pineal gland and as your crown chakra is opened and the distortions cleared, you begin the process of rebuilding the rainbow bridge of Light to your I AM Presence. The Christ energy or higher frequency patterns of Light will reactivate the pineal, pituitary and hypothalamus glands which, in turn, permeate and affect every gland, organ and cell in your body (this is called building the Light body). It is also a descension of Spirit or allowing the higher aspects of your vastness to take dominion within the physical vessel once more (which is a very important component of the ascension process). The process of surrendering to Spirit becomes natural and you know, without a doubt, that there is a Divine Plan at work within your life. Light, sound and color takes on a totally new meaning for you as you begin to resonate to the "language of Creation."

The process of integrating the seven chakras of the physical body with the higher Galactic Chakras and Rays is well under way. As you release the imbalanced thought patterns from your seven chakras, they begin to spin faster and faster—in perfect harmony—and the higher Rays pour through your spinal column, turning your energy vortex system into a blazing, iridescent column of Light. The Light that permeates your auric field begins to radiate further and further out into the world, blessing and positively influencing everything it touches. Use an amethyst stone, wear violet, or submerge yourself in this color—it has wondrous, magical properties, for it is the color of the Violet Flame of Transmutation and Transformation.

We are offering you the gifts of enlightenment, wisdom and inspiration, and you are building a bridge between the third, fourth and fifth dimensions by integrating and anchoring new ideas and frequency patterns via purification, transformation and inspiration. Yes, you are at a grand crossroads, my brave warriors, stepping onto the spiral path of en-LIGHT-enment, and leaving behind the rigidity of the third dimension. Allow all that no longer serves you to gently fall away and be dissolved in the blessed Violet Flame of Transmutation—leave behind the burdens you have carried for so long and step into the bright, golden future that is your reward and destiny.

We cherish and love you beyond measure. I AM Archangel Michael.

63. Speaking of Angels

*B*eloved masters, as the world turns and moves upward along the spiral of illumined awareness, it is leaving behind the old distorted views and concepts which have kept its inhabitants cut off from their origins and true identities. A curtain is lifting between the dimensions, giving you a glimpse of where you are from and where you are going. The small voice within is speaking to you more distinctly and more often—you are having lucid dreams, many of which are in vivid colors beyond anything you have seen in the physical world. All of this is part of the reclamation process—the process of reclaiming the gifts and garments of Light on your journey homeward.

The beliefs you are releasing and the new, expanded vision of Creation that is being filtered into humanity's consciousness can be likened to the time when everyone thought the Earth was flat and that ships would drop off the edge of the world if they sailed too far into the unknown waters. Once again, you are charting a new course, beloveds, but it is into the unknown realms of energy and space. Fear of the unknown has always limited those who are cut off from the guidance of their Higher Self, and so they give away their power by relying on the truth and direction as supplied by others—those bold enough to have a vision and the determination to manifest it. Unfortunately, quite often those pioneers did not have the best interest of others in mind, but were serving their own selfish interests—desire for control or wealth. Humanity is being shaken to its very depths, as Spirit tries to jar loose the shackles of the third dimension that have held all of you in bondage for so long.

These are unsettling times of great change, and seemingly,

unending catastrophes around the globe. That is why we wish you to know that we are here to assist you and show you the way. One of the greatest gifts of this "time of awakening" is our reunion with you. It has been told and explained many times before, but allow me to refresh your memory as to how the angelic realm fits in the Creator's grand plan and what our functions are.

There are many levels and departments in the celestial hierarchy of angels, which is still only one facet of the Creator's conscious expression of self. We, the archangels, carry the attributes and virtues of God-consciousness, just as you do. But the difference is that we radiate a specific attribute of the Creator—you might say, the driving force for one aspect of the God Mind. We embody faith, love and absolute obedience to the Creator, always. The angelic realm in its many expressions was created by God to assist, guide, nurture and instruct you, the bold ones, who agreed to diminish yourselves into lesser beings in order to experience God-consciousness in its most fragmented form. Originally, you embodied all the aspects and attributes of the God Mind, but gradually as you journeyed down through the ages and the higher dimensions, you left your higher consciousness in the care of your I AM Presence.

When you first came to Earth in your beautiful shining Light body, you radiated the seven Rays of God-consciousness for this solar system, with the Ray of your I AM Self as an overlay. Gradually, over time, you have enhanced some attributes or "Ray virtues" at the expense of others, or have used them in their negative, limiting form of expression. Some of you are more mental, some more emotional, some are enthralled with creative expression, others with a scientific, devotional, or service-oriented focus. All of these expressions are desirable, but remember, we have spoken often of balance and what is needed at this time is to integrate and use the positive aspects of all the virtues and attributes of God's creativity while mastering and enhancing the specific gifts of your I AM Presence or your major Ray overlay.

The Elohim, the mental radiance of the Creator, the great builders of form, and the wondrous Devic and Elemental Kingdoms, who helped create and now oversee all of the nature kingdom on Earth and in other worlds, are all standing by to assist you in these turbulent times of transition. We hope you have accepted as your truth that you all have guardian angelic Beings who were assigned to you at the time of your birth and who will guard and serve you faithfully within the limits of Universal Law and to the degree you allow. There are other wondrous angelic Beings ready and willing to serve you, but you must ask, for they are not allowed to infringe upon your free will.

Love and joy attract angels like a magnet—whose greatest desire is to be of service to humanity. Begging is not the way to gain their favor, but asking them to assist you in your endeavors will assure their cooperation. They will help you to manifest your dreams if what you desire is for the highest good of all, but know that it will happen in their time and in their way. The concept of money is confusing to them, instead ask them to assist you in manifesting abundance, joy, love and peace—this they understand. But you must also do your part by taking the necessary steps, as well as eliminating any self-sabotaging beliefs that you still harbor in your subconscious mind.

There are loving, angelic Beings to help you with affairs of the heart, and your mental or creative endeavors—they will help you firm your resolve and work with your body elemental to bring about good health and well-being in your physical form. The wonderful, playful cherubic angels are waiting to bring you joy and a sense of lightheartedness. These precious, little Beings of God Light love to be near you and to surprise you with little miracles or coincidences. Ask them to help you find things that are lost, and you can learn to communicate with them as well, but their language is a language of feelings and thoughts rather than words. They will cause "angel bumps" to rise on your skin when a truth has been stated, and they will buzz you with an angel kiss or sometimes surround you in a lovely fragrance. The angelic realm brings the love and radiance of God to humanity and the angels' greatest desire is to be of service.

The Essence of angels comes to Earth in embodiment through people like you and you and you—they come to be the representatives of the great archangels and to walk amongst humanity to share the virtues and attributes of God-consciousness. Yes, they are just like you, and you may be one, my precious friends, making your way through human evolution as you grow from the lower rungs of the evolutionary ladder through study, work and service. There are representatives of every level of God-consciousness on Earth at this time, embodied in the physical expression in order to anchor the most lofty, rarified aspects of the Creator. Have we not told you that you are more magnificent and precious than you could ever imagine?

Dear ones, let us now continue to build the vision for the future of your world. You must realize that first, you begin to build your vision in the higher realms of unlimited possibilities. Your thought forms slowly take form as they draw forth more cosmic Light Substance, and then gradually begin to manifest in the physical expression on Earth. The greater the focus and intent, the more quickly the vision manifests. As you come together in unified, conscious intent with the good of all as your motivating force, you create a synergistic thought form of dynamic proportions. This is why you are now making such inroads in the mass-consciousness mindset. As spiritual Light warriors, even though your numbers are fewer than that of the masses, you are making great progress because of your unified, empowered thoughts of love, peace, abundance and harmony for all.

It is time to be bold and outrageous in your vision. Envision yourself as a loving, masterful sovereign entity, and then formulate in great detail how you will operate and function multi-dimensionally as a cocreator of love, Light, peace and joy.

State daily, *"I am healthy and have a youthful attitude. I am energetic with a zest for life. I sparkle with vitality and treasure each day and opportunity to express my ever-expanding awareness. I inspire others to release their old outworn reality. I dance with joy, going forth bravely into the future, day by day, living life to the fullest. Each day I AM becoming more empowered by my Christ-consciousness as it descends and takes dominion within my body, mind and emotions. I AM ascending in this body, but will stay on Earth until my mission is accomplished and my destiny is realized."*

Begin to look at fear in a new way. State to yourself until you believe it, *"I have a new relationship with fear. Fear is an emotion that serves me and I AM always in control of my emotions, therefore I AM in control of fear."* Transcending fear means you can experience it, observe it, learn from it and then move through it. In this way, fear will serve you as a warning bell as to what you need to be aware of, what is out of balance—what you need to bring into harmony. Emotions are made of negative- or positive-energy thought forms and you must control them instead of allowing them to be your master.

Lay the foundation for the emotional nature of your vision. What makes you joyous and fills you with gratitude? You must allow your Spirit to soar but you must also nurture the inner child as well as the soul. Be willing to express and claim that which touches or nourishes the innocence within: joy, delight, spontaneity, or sadness, anger and fear—feel these emotions, but realize that you are not these emotions. Freedom of expression should be an important facet of your vision. Know that you have a right to be completely spontaneous and follow your own inclinations and desires as long as they are for the highest good of all. Begin to expect the best of people and they will meet your expectations. Claim and envision your life being filled with miracles, beauty and joy and gradually, your grandest affirmations will come true. As you support, love and cherish all things, you will receive support, and you will be loved and cherished in return.

Develop your own philosophy of life and living. Listen to your inner guidance and practice discernment. Begin now to interact with the multiple parts of your Being as if they were all around you, in your presence every moment—for in truth, they are. You are consciously accessing information and wisdom from the fifth dimension and above, and as you accept it as your truth, you will be able to clearly and truly communicate with your guides, teachers, masters, angelic helpers and all the Great Beings of Light. State and affirm,

"I AM a Divine Instrument of Light through which the higher-dimensional frequencies of Creation flow. From this moment forward, I will fully and completely live my perfected vision of Heaven on Earth. Each day, I AM becoming a master of Divine Manifestation in the world of form, and I move beyond the restrictions and limitations of the third- and fourth-dimensional reality. I carry the torch of God Light. I radiate the love of angels. Henceforth, each and every day, I draw to, through and around me more and more of my perfect I AM PRESENCE OF GOD."

Do not allow the barriers on the path to deter you; boldly walk through or over them. Do not allow the discomfort and pain to discourage you; call on your angelic helpers to soothe and support you. Do not allow the doubts and judgment of others to weaken your resolve—show them by your example and be bold in your convictions. Do not take your eyes or your attention from your goal, dear ones; it is nearer than you think.

We relay the loving thoughts of our Father/Mother God to you, "Beloved children of Light, blessed are you in our sight. In you, we are well pleased."

And so, the spiral takes another turn. Are you ready for the next awakening? I AM Archangel Michael.

64. YOU ARE DIVINE COURIERS

*B*eloved masters, are you daring enough to accept the truth that you are in the physical vessel to assist the Creator to become more conscious of **ITSELF?** Each facet of God's expression of Self, however large or small, was sent forth to create, expand and magnify the grandeur and majesty of the **ALL THAT IS.** This is an ever-evolving process, without beginning and without end. Although the experiment on planet Earth is just a minuscule portion of the Creator's grand plan, it is an important, integral part of the evolution of your solar system, galaxy and universe, as well as the Omniverse. You might say that the Earth is the focal or starting point for the reunification of Spirit.

Your Earth was chosen to be the home base for the greatest fragmentation of God-consciousness ever experienced. You, who were brave enough to answer the clarion call, agreed to allow your magnificent I AM Self to be divided into greater and greater numbers of lesser and lesser Sparks of consciousness. This was indeed a bold endeavor. The risks were great, but the potential to expand the consciousness of the Creator was enormous. For this reason, no other planet or solar system has ever had so many angelic helpers or great Beings of Light assigned to it, nor has any planet been observed or monitored so closely as Earth. You know some of the ancient history of Earth and its beginnings, as well as some of the failures and a few of the bright periods in Earth's more recent past, yet you still do not comprehend how important you are in the cosmic scheme of evolution.

Even though, from time to time, you are remembering who you are and have caught a glimpse in your dreams or visions of your true home and of your many wondrous adventures, you are still confused and your heart aches when you see the pain and suffering which is rampant on Earth. You wonder why so many of the good and beautiful ones seem to die young, and why tragedy strikes the sweet and innocent ones as well as those who are seemingly unworthy. Please remember that none of this is the Creator's will and no one is being punished. Please remember that each and every one of you were gifted with totally free will when you agreed to assume a body of flesh on the material plane of polarity and duality. Also, remember that you are living a culmination and composite of all your many lifetime experiences and at times, have agreed to experience a devastating illness, accident or tragedy of some sort as a way to balance all past karmic imbalances—or to be an example to others, showing them that even in adversity you can radiate the love, peace and harmony of Spirit. Every experience, no matter how tragic, can be used to make great strides in awareness, to uplift others and to inspire and show the way. How is this possible?—by allowing your Christ Self to OVERLIGHT you in order to bring peace and comfort to the physical vessel; by surrendering to your highest good and purpose, even if this means giving up your present identity and bodily form; and by believing in miracles and that all things are possible.

Did not the beloved Christ Jesus, who was without blemish, experience the most extreme pain, suffering and degradation for the benefit of humankind? Your pain and suffering are also duly noted and do not go unnoticed if you place yourself in the cradle of Spirit's love and ask that "thy will be done." Death and disease as you are presently experiencing them are unnatural and not a part of God's Divine Plan. Part of the process of reclaiming your Light body is to remove the distortions in your physical, mental, emotional and etheric bodies, so that you will no longer have to experience these abominations. Only in your fragmented state in the third dimension can you experience the pain, suffering, fear, and sense of unworthiness that is the norm for so many on Earth. Regardless of whether you believe it or not, all the imbalances that have created your present reality are changing as the Earth stirs and reclaims her Divine Status and as those like you, the Light Warriors, lift your consciousnesses and bring forth into manifestation a new vision for all humanity.

We are doing everything allowed by Universal Law to assist you: to help you reclaim your Divine Birthright, to help you remember, to smooth the path and ease your burden. We are not only sending down the radiant Rays of God-consciousness to you, but we are reestablishing our intimate connections with you. The connecting link between physical expression and spiritual awareness is the intellect tempered by love. That is why we have endeavored to activate the wisdom stored within your brain structure by helping you to remember that you are a Spark of the Divine as you strive to reconnect and integrate your Higher Self, your Christ Self and your Divine I AM Presence.

We have given lessons on the seven Rays of God-Consciousness for your solar system and an overview of the five higher Rays of Galactic Consciousness. Allow us to capsulize the virtues radiated to you through the seven Rays—virtues that you should strive to reintegrate. Also, know that as you bring your physical being into harmony with Spirit, you have the potential to draw upon, magnify and radiate the dominant Ray of your I AM Presence as a living example to others—to be the personification of that aspect and virtue of the Creator.

THE VIRTUES OF THE FIRST RAY:

THE WILL AND POWER TO CREATE, TRUTH AND FAITH. Under the First Ray you will find the leaders, pioneers, the dynamic types full of Will and Determination. It is important for First-Ray types to balance their dynamic drive for action with the Second and Third Ray energies of Love and Wisdom. The First Ray will enhance your courage and determination as you boldly go forth to manifest your version of the New Golden Age.

THE VIRTUES OF THE SECOND RAY:

ILLUMINATION, PERCEPTION AND WISDOM. Those with a Second Ray Monad, or Divine I AM Self, are seekers of Truth and Knowledge and ultimately illumination. The major focus of this Ray is to turn knowledge into Wisdom, and temper Wisdom with Love and Compassion. The ideal second-Ray person is calm, intuitive, with sharp, clear intelligence; a seeker of Truth and Spiritual Wisdom.

THE VIRTUES OF THE THIRD RAY:

TOLERANCE, ADORATION, FORBEARANCE AND TACT. The Third Ray is the Ray of the Refined Mind, the Spoken Word and Abstract Intellect—the plane of Spirit and the higher causal mind. Here you will find the sages, philosophers, dreamers and visionaries. The Third Ray strengthens Tolerance, Tact and Patience, and tempers the desire for perfection and intellectual pursuit with Common Sense and Sincerity.

THE VIRTUES OF THE FOURTH RAY:

PURITY, ACTION, CLARITY, HUMILITY, COMMUNICATION AND HARMONY. The Fourth Ray is the Ray of Beauty, Harmony and Artistic Endeavor. It is the plane of Intuition. It is often called the Ray of Harmony Through Conflict or the Ray of Struggle. In order to tap into your higher intuitive mind you must tame the ego and the emotional body, which most often results in years of struggle and frustration. A Fourth-Ray person needs to heal and harmonize the emotional body and strengthen the mental body in order to allow the illumined qualities of the intuition to manifest, thus creating a balance between the spiritual and physical worlds of reality.

THE VIRTUES OF THE FIFTH RAY:

HEALING, SURRENDER, SELFLESSNESS, CONCENTRATION, LISTENING AND DEDICATION. The Fifth Ray is the Ray of Concrete Knowledge and the Mental Plane. Here you will find those with scientific minds, researchers, the great intellectuals or those who are more linear thinking, analytical types. If you are overly emotional, bringing in the energies of the Fifth Ray will help you to strengthen your mental focus and create balance. The Fifth Ray focuses on the scientific attributes of the laws of Creation, and will enhance your desire for Truth and Justice.

THE VIRTUES OF THE SIXTH RAY:

DEVOTION, FORGIVENESS, HEALING, MERCY AND GRACE, HARMONY, PEACE AND TRANQUILITY. The Sixth Ray is an emotionally-based Ray and since one of its purposes is to help dissolve the energies of the lower astral planes, it is focused within the subconscious mind—endeavoring to return it to consciousness and into Harmony with the conscious and Superconscious minds. Use the energies of this Ray to move out of religious dogma and a sense of separation into spiritual awareness and unity-consciousness;

use it to enhance your Devotion, Tenderness, Peace and Tranquility. Take the emotional intensity of the Sixth Ray, strengthen it with the mental focus of the Fifth Ray, and then blend it with the transformative energy of the Seventh Ray and you will be well on your way to mastery.

THE VIRTUES OF THE SEVENTH RAY:

FREEDOM, PURIFICATION, REDEMPTION, SERVICE, INVOCATION, MANIFESTATION, DIPLOMACY AND REFINEMENT. The Seventh Ray is the Ray of the New Age. It brings forth the Violet Transmuting Flame. It is the Ray of Invocation, manifesting in the highest form of Service. It is the Ray of Conscious Transmutation and the Violet Flame is also the Flame of Forgiveness. Use this Ray to enhance your abilities of Invocation and Visualization. **Call on the beautiful Angels of the Violet Flame to assist you in transforming misqualified energy back into neutral Light Substance and to help you move through the transmutation process with ease and grace.**

Remember, beloved ones, the most important of all the virtues is LOVE, and this blessing from the Creator permeates and OVERLIGHTS all the other virtues.

Your goal is to integrate, use and radiate all the virtues of God-consciousness, with the Ray of your Divine Self as your overlay or guiding influence. As you gradually balance the seven major chakras and the many minor chakras of the physical vessel which are the magnets for the energies/attributes of the corresponding Rays, you will begin to attract and integrate the incandescence of the five higher/more refined Galactic Rays as well. When this happens, your spiritual growth and awareness is greatly accelerated, for you are tapping into the radiance of your Christ Self and your I AM Presence.

Know that you are **DIVINE COURIERS** bearing the Spark of God into the world of form. You are creating and experiencing the expanded consciousness of God in **ITS** most delightful, wondrous form as a result of your brave journey into the unformed, unmanifested realms of the cosmos.

Now, if you are willing, let us take a journey together. I wish to help you remember and recapture how it feels in the rarified worlds of the higher dimensions. You may wish to transfer this meditation onto a tape, or have a soul mate read it to you so that you may derive the maximum benefit.

Close your eyes, and move in to the golden temple of your heart—there stands a beautiful, shining Being, your Higher Self. You move forward to meet this loving, radiant one, and you embrace. The love that flows from him/her is so exquisite it brings tears to your eyes. Together you move toward a spiraling crystal staircase and begin your descent down through the Earth until you reach the crystalline core. Here stands a lovely lady dressed in a gossamer, green gown. She has flowers entwined in her hair and there are birds and small animals all around her, as well as representatives of the mighty Devic and blessed Elemental Kingdoms. This is the Essence of Mother Earth, she who has been your loving host, and who has borne the trials, tribulations and abuse of humanity for many long ages. She steps forward and you embrace one another and the love you exchange is rich, powerful and profound. She asks if you are willing to assist her in her transformation/mutation process. She promises you that she will do everything earthly possible to keep the cataclysms of the elements at a minimum: the raging fires, the turbulent winds, the torrential rains and the shaking and quaking of her body, but she needs your help, your

love, your radiating Light and positive thought forms to do so.

Together, you step onto the crystal spiral and quickly move up and out of the Earth's atmosphere—out into the galaxy and beyond, into the higher dimensions. You step onto another spiral which takes you to the worlds of the Seven Spheres of God-consciousness. This is the place where you integrated the attributes and virtues of the Creator, which were then infused into the seven chakras of your physical vessel and which are the dominant energies of your solar system. Suddenly, you are in a place filled with RED ENERGY, the energy of the root chakra—look around, what must you release in order to return to harmony with this world which focuses on strength, power, abundance, will and courage? Are you carrying residual energies of anger and scarcity? Are you still functioning in a survival mode? Are you afraid to use your WILL to claim your POWER? See the luminescence of this world change your root chakra into a sparkling magenta or red, tinged with blue/violet. Let go of all the negative energies that are keeping you from claiming your birthright of abundance, love and joy.

Now you move to the ORANGE ENERGY world, the focus of the second chakra. This is the world where your spiritual-desire body was aligned with the mental, emotional and physical aspects of your Being. It is where the energies of desire, sexual/passionate love, emotions and your instinctual nature are stored in the physical body— the area in which the ego-desire body has ruled for so long. See all the stored energies of the ego-desire body (which is never satisfied)—jealousy, envy, overindulgence and addictions—being transmuted as this world floods your second chakra with a sparkling orange, tinged with pink or a beautiful peach color as Spirit reigns once more.

The next world is made of YELLOW ENERGY, which you carry in the third chakra, or the solar plexus. This is your emotional/personal power center, self-control, sense of authority and where, in unison with the heart, you project love/Light. See this yellow world radiate a brilliant-gold color to this chakra as you release all negative attachments and clear the emotional trauma—all the psychic energy you have absorbed from others down through the ages, as well as all the hurt, anger and fear. How does it feel to take back your authority, self-control and to project only love and Light out into the world?

The spiral now lifts you to a GREEN ENERGY world which is anchored in the heart or life-force center. Ask your Higher Self to quickly take an inventory of the Heart Chakra—are there energies of jealousy, envy, selfishness, guilt, or unworthiness lurking here? Invite your Higher Self and your I AM Presence to take up permanent residence in your heart/soul center and watch as you are flooded with the pale pink/violet radiance of this sphere. Feel your heart expand with love for yourself, all humanity and all Creation.

It is difficult to leave this world of love, but it is time to move on to the next level. You find yourself in a place filled with BLUE ENERGY, corresponding to the fifth chakra, or throat center. All the impacted energies and restrictions which have kept you from speaking your truth, the dark energies of ignorance, words of judgment and criticism, reside in the throat-center chakra. Feel your throat being bathed in a beautiful deep blue/violet from this wondrous sphere as the bonds of restriction are removed from your throat and you take back your power of the spoken word. Affirm that, henceforth, you will speak your spiritual truth with discernment, discretion and compassion. Remember how it was in this world where you learned to make the sounds of Creation; how you held a perfect vision and then made the wondrous sounds that brought your vision into manifestation. Breathe deeply of the prana of life as you reclaim the power of the spoken word. As you purify your thoughts and heal your throat, the eloquence of your words will be secondary, for the resonance of your voice will sound like beautiful celestial music to the ears and heartstrings of those around you.

The sixth chakra is the area of the third eye, a world of INDIGO ENERGY. Here is where you integrated your intuition, clairvoyance, telepathic skills and wisdom—the gifts of Spirit you would need to function in the physical world. Here the light packets of higher wisdom and your Divine Blueprint were prepared to be encoded at a later time into your brain structure. See all the impacted energies stored in this chakra—fear, tension, inability to concentrate and bad dreams—dissolve and turn into brilliant golden-white as you tap into your higher wisdom, intuition and telepathic skills, thereby strengthening the bridge to your Divine I AM Presence.

The seventh chakra is located at the crown of the head, and this world is a blending of the blue color of the Father Creator's will and power with the pink of the Mother Creator's love and compassion, resulting in a lovely violet color, or the VIOLET ENERGY of the Seventh Ray—the Ray of the New Age. See all the impacted energies of confusion, depression, hesitation and lack of inspiration, and

the static or distortion in your column of Light that connects you to your Higher Self and Divine I AM Presence
being transmuted in a blazing Violet Flame—the sacred
fire of freedom. It will transmute ALL the discordant energies of the past. All you have to do is invoke it and it
will blaze up from your feet and surround you and fill you
to overflowing with a never-ending supply of its transforming, magical energy.

Affirm that you will bring back into the world of the
physical all the radiance, balance, harmony and gifts of
the Seven Spheres as you tap into the Universal Oneness—
the Christ energy of our Father/Mother God.

State, if you are willing: In the name of our Father/
Mother God, I hereby reclaim my birthright. I AM a radi-
ant emissary of God. I AM a blazing spark of the divine. I
AM the Light. The Light I AM.

Beloved ones, our mission is to set you free from your
self-imposed bonds. My pledge is to stay with you—to guide
and protect you until every angelic being, every human on
Earth and in the astral planes, and every sweet elemental is
freed and all are redeemed and returned to the state of perfection from whence you all descended. You cannot even
imagine how much I love you. I AM Archangel Michael and
I reaffirm my pledge to each of you.

65. A Creed for the New Age

*B*lessed warriors of Light, let us set the stage for your "coming out party," for you truly are at the state of your evolutionary process where you are ready to don your cloaks of Light and claim your cosmic identity—if you are bold enough to take the next step. We might compare you to the pupa of a butterfly, wrapped in a cocoon at a fragile stage in your development, and in a semi-dream state in which you have to be protected. But now you are ready to emerge as you shed the shifting, dissolving distortions of energy that bind you—as you fully integrate the attributes and virtues of God-consciousness that are being filtered down to you via your Higher Self and I AM Presence. Precious friends, once more, you are ready to unfold your radiant wings of Light and reunite with your spiritual family (at many multiple levels) as you step onto the next rung of the ladder of ascension on your way back into the higher realms.

Do you find that you are more in synchronicity with Spirit—living in joy and expectation even amidst the chaos around you? There is an excitement building and expanding around the Earth, even in places where oppression and deprivation rule. As more of you awaken to the nudgings of Spirit and address the inner discontent that is growing stronger and stronger, fear gives way to love and hope, and anger gives way to serenity and compassion. The flood gates of cosmic truth are now open and flooding your planet and everything in and on it with seeds of awareness and remembrance. The intellect of the physical mind is merging with virtuous pure love via your Spirit Self, thereby making way for the new teachings and higher vibrational patterns to infiltrate into the consciousness of the masses.

Allow us to give you a NEW AGE CREED to integrate,

practice and live by. It transcends any religious doctrine and can be practiced by anyone no matter what their spiritual beliefs are. It is time to dissolve the boundaries of rigid dogma, superstition, separation and fear. Make this the year when you begin to practice unity-consciousness, brotherly/sisterly love and respect for all humanity.

1. Love your Father/Mother God with all your beingness. Love yourself unconditionally as a Divine Spark of the Creator. Love everyone else as you love your self.

2. Know that you are caretakers of the earth and all life forms that reside on her—the nature, animal, elemental and human kingdoms. Protect, preserve and honor all expressions of life.

3. Live your life with joy and the spontaneity and delight of a child. Endeavor to leave a legacy of love and hope. Enjoy the journey of life and strive to fulfill your earthly mission to the best of your ability.

4. Maintain a constant attitude of gratitude and live every day as though spirit were perched on your shoulder as an observer. Practice nonjudgment and look for the good in everyone.

5. Your goal is to return to balance in body, mind and spirit. Polarity and duality will no longer affect you when you walk the middle path.

6. Seek and claim your truth and then live your truth with integrity. Allow all others the same right.

7. Learn and use the universal laws of manifestation— the God-given tools that will assist you in creating your version of paradise on earth.

8. Share the wisdom you have integrated with others—first by example, then through your actions and finally through words.

9. Claim your Divine Birthright: the love, joy, peace, health and abundance that are yours as a gift from our Father/Mother God.

10. Each day, call on your mighty I AM Presence to overlight, guide and direct you and then listen to its inner nudgings. Call upon the mighty Angel of Forgiveness and the Violet Flame at the end of each day to balance, harmonize and transmute any discordant energy you have projected that day, thereby becoming harmless and moving beyond the laws of cause and effect and into a state of grace.

I have offered to answer some of your questions each month to help allay your fears and clarify some issues. Many of you are concerned about the countries you live in such as China, Japan, Turkey, Greece, Russia, Yugoslavia, Africa, South America, Mexico and the Mideast, which are experiencing so much strife and suffering. You ask, **"What can we do to help?"** First, learn and live by the above creed—be an example and radiate your Light for all to see and bask in. Join the group meditations that now abound around the world, adding your unique energies and prayers. Draw the maximum cosmic Light Substance to you, as you become an anchor of Light in the area where you live. Envision great crystal pyramids of Light being formed in the fifth dimension, where you all join together in your meditations, with the intent of building the greatest cosmic Light waves possible. These waves, designed for the highest good of all, will sweep across each country as time goes by, awakening the masses—cleansing and clearing the negative energies that have a stranglehold on each country and its people. Know that each country and race is unique, for they were created with distinct attributes, desires, opportunities and challenges. Each of you has been strategically placed in the area where you can be of the greatest service and do the most good. You have vibrational seeds within your brain/soul structure which will assist your country and countrymen/ women, and the Earth has seeds of remembrance to return to you via the great crystalline energies deep within her body which are now revving up to full power.

Be an example by accepting your spiritual power, as you lovingly establish new boundaries while extending love, nurturance and support wherever possible. Set new goals while clearly stating your purpose, and then boldly go forth to create the beauty and perfection for which your country was once known. Seek your spiritual family and reunite in a common purpose, thereby expanding your power and effectiveness exponentially. As you state and affirm your new vision and begin to take the necessary steps to make it a reality, we will join you with all the force and power of creation to assist you in manifesting your dream—in the best and shortest way possible. We are now allowed to intercede and help you within certain parameters, but you must ask our assistance and we must consider the overall plan for the evolution of humanity.

Many of you wonder and are concerned about the conflicting information received via various channels and teachers. Know that some are still caught in the old paradigms of hell and punishment, and doom and gloom. These teachings were created to instill fear and guilt by those who wished to control others. None of the great masters, including the beloved Jesus, taught this philosophy—their words and mission statements have been distorted and changed and are not true interpretations of their teachings. Be aware, beloveds, that to a varying degree, all channels filter the information given them from a higher source through their own belief systems. Some channels are able to move their conscious minds to the side and allow almost pure information to come forth, while many others have not learned this discipline. Also, know that a channel can only bring forth information from the level of vibrational frequencies they are able to tap into with the assistance of their soul, Higher Self or Divine I AM Presence. In other words, the purer the pathway to your Vaster Self, the more rarified vibrational patterns you can access. For example, my messenger whom you know in this lifetime as Ronna Herman—envision her lifting her consciousness up the column of Light to her I AM Presence where we connect with her vibrational patterns and send light packets of information into her brain structure, which are then filtered through her brain/knowledge/wisdom and deciphered into the English language. The more aligned a channel is with Creator Truth, the more accurate are the messages brought forth. (Our messenger is not comfortable with us focusing on her as an example, but truth is truth.)

Many are only tapping into the vibrational patterns of the mid-fourth dimension and therefore are bringing forth thought patterns and probable realities from whatever level they are attuned to and which fit their picture of reality. As we have stated so often before, **DO NOT** accept any information as your truth, no matter the source, until you validate it through your heart/soul monitor. If it is loving, empowering and rings true, then you may accept it as your truth. If you feel fear, tightness or dread in your heart or solar plexus, discard the information. If you are not sure—it may be information that is vastly different from what you thought was your truth. Set it aside, and ask your Higher Self to validate it for you if it is to be your truth. And if it is, it will be validated beyond a doubt—by someone, in a book or article you read, or in an occurrence that is unmistakable.

Now allow me to take you on a journey—a meditation to assist you in merging with the vastness of who you are.

A TRINITY OF SPIRIT— A TRINITY OF CONSCIOUSNESS

Focus your consciousness in your heart center. Breathe deeply as you imagine with your inner senses a beautiful temple. See yourself step through a golden door which sends forth a blazing iridescent light. In the center of this room is a magnificent Being seated on a throne. There is so much love radiating from this beautiful one that it almost overwhelms you.

You slowly walk forward and stand before this wondrous Being and as you gaze into his/her shining eyes, you realize that this is your soul-self. You move into the embrace of your soul and you feel a great surge of warmth and love that penetrates to your very depths as you and your soul merge into a unified Divine Aspect of the Creator. Your heart center bursts open with love as it expands to contain this wondrous gift.

You turn and see another glorious Light Being enter the room and come toward you, a Being of even greater Light. You recognize this beautiful one as your Superconscious mind or Higher Self as it moves forward and gently merges with you and your soul. See your subconscious mind as a

beautiful child, and see your conscious mind as an androgy-
nous form of blazing golden-green energy.

You reach out your hands and form a trinity of consciousness as you merge in perfect harmony with these
aspects of yourself. See all the cells of your body—each with
a consciousness of their own—burst forth in blazing Light
as they join you in the temple of your heart center. Feel
the powerful energy and joy as you expand into greater
unity-consciousness, and as you move deeper into the microcosm of your DNA structure.

You now see a great and majestic twelve-strand helix
spiraling before you and as you step into this awesome
structure, you begin to drift down into the center of the
Earth. There in a beautiful crystal pyramid stands a lovely,
shining lady, the essence of Mother Earth.

You put out your hand and as she takes it, a sense of
gratitude, oneness and love pours through you. Together,
you swiftly move up the spiraling helix formation out into
the higher realms, leaving behind the confines of your
physical vessel—expanding, moving, swirling in glorious
Rays of Light and color—out into the galaxy and into the
heart of the Great Central Sun.

You see a glorious, bright Light that is radiating an aurora
borealis of colors beyond your wildest imagining as rippling
sounds and lovely music surround you. You look around this
new realm with joyous recognition as you reach out your
hands to your Father/Mother God, the Creators of this universe. Every part of your Being expands and swells with love
so sweet and overwhelming it brings tears of joy to your eyes.

Again, you have formed a trinity and together these

splendid, wondrous Beings join you in the temple of your heart, leaving there your heritage: the gift of love, joy, abundance and harmony. You know you will never be the same. You have reconnected with your Source and anchored it deep within the core of the Earth, creating an arching rainbow bridge that will eventually take you back to your home among the stars.

As you slowly begin your journey back down through the dimensions, you see a great outpouring of golden, iridescent Light filled with millions of tiny, diamond crystals surrounding you—another gift from the Creator. See this golden liquid Light surround your auric field, and slowly begin to permeate through all your bodily systems into the very core of your Being. Sense yourself moving back into your physical consciousness, knowing that you have made profound connections with all parts of your Divine Self.

Whether you travel inward or outward, you will find love, support, wisdom and nurturance. From this moment forward, you are the embodiment of all sacred energies with the consciousness and wisdom of a master. All gifts of creation are yours throughout eternity. All you have to do is claim them. By the grace and love of God, so be it and so it is!

Once again, slowly focus your attention on your conscious mind, breathe deeply and feel yourself totally back in your body as you feel the energy surge through you, bringing a sense of wonder, vitality and aliveness into your awareness. Say and know without a doubt, "IT IS DONE."

Come join us, brave and beloved ones, in the realms of all possibilities—you are only beginning to get an inkling of the glory and love that awaits you. I am with you always. I AM Archangel Michael.

66. MESSAGE FROM RONNA

My Dear and Precious Friends:

How truly blessed and privileged we are to be, what I call, major players in this time of awakening. I feel your love and presence radiate across the miles to me, and your sweet notes and letters mean more than I can ever tell you (although I do not always have time to answer each one). These past few years have been times of great challenge (which get easier), and a busy, hectic schedule (which I love).

Daily, I ask our beloved Lord Michael to give me good health and the strength to continue the pace as long as I am needed. The time is now, my friends, for us to become more visible and more vocal. It is amazing how the general populace is beginning to awaken and ask questions—everywhere I go, I find it so. So, step out there, I dare you, and I believe you will be amazed at how much you have to share—how open and receptive most people are. Take the simple truths that Lord Michael has give us over the years and pass them on in whatever way is appropriate. It is as simple as that. My heart is filled with love and gratitude. Give yourself a big hug from me.

I wish you love, Rays and rainbows of Light, joy, laughter and God's blessings, always.

Ronna

ABOUT THE AUTHOR

Ronna Herman is internationally known as a channel for Archangel Michael. His messages of hope and inspiration through Ronna have been featured in more than a dozen New Age and spiritual publications around the world, and translated into most major languages.

A retired business executive and real estate broker, Ronna provides a common sense approach to metaphysics. Her spiritual search began in 1970, and after much intense study and training, she began a second career as a spiritual teacher and counselor. In 1994 she founded StarQuest (www.ronnastar.com).

Ronna has appeared on numerous radio and TV shows, and has spoken twice at the United Nations' S.E.A.T. (The Society for Enlightenment and Transformation). She presents seminars throughout the United States and the world, touching peoples' hearts and connecting them with their soul self. Those who attend her powerful seminars receive valuable tools to move them to the next level of their spiritual growth.

In her first book, *On Wings of Light,* Ronna shares inspirational messages from Archangel Michael. The book, published in five languages, is a best seller in The Netherlands. Following on this success, Ronna has written a trilogy of six stories that she calls "metafiction." Offered now in manuscript form, the stories in *Once Upon a New World* are based in part on glimpses and remembrances of some of Ronna's past lives and some of her current incarnation experiences.

Ronna lives with her husband, Kent, a retired airline executive, in the high desert country outside Reno, Nevada. When not traveling, Ronna and Kent enjoy gardening and spending time with their combined families consisting of 7 children, 19 grandchildren and 4 great-grandchildren.

BOOKS AND TAPES BY RONNA HERMAN

On Wings of Light

Ronna's first book of channelled messages from Archangel Michael is about hope and love: love of self, love of life and how to enjoy the experience of being an empowered spiritual human being. Archangel Michael is made real on the book's pages so that readers feel a tangible connection with his energy, his wisdom and his love.

The messages in this book are positive and life changing. They help us understand who we REALLY are and how to create our perfect realities. Archangel Michael explains why we are here on planet earth and how to be the masters we are in these physical forms.

The Golden Promise

Further messages from Archangel Michael, providing many exercises, meditations, and affirmations to help us release old, self-sabotaging beliefs, and to replace them with empowering, life-changing thought patterns.

If you are ready for the next steps in your spiritual growth, this is the book for you. Many of the principles in the book are also incorporated in the series of I AM Mastery classes Ronna now offers in person and by mail.

Once Upon a New World — A Trilogy

Ronna calls this series of stories "metafiction," since although they are fiction, they are intertwined with a higher truth. They are based on glimpses and remembrances of some of Ronna's past lives, and partially, too, on some of her experiences during the present incarnation. The trilogy is about the journey (incarnations) of one SPARK of the God Force, and Its evolution through time and space. It is an adventure story of love, hope and inspiration.

These stories give new meaning to why we are here on planet earth and where we are going. They teach, in simple language, the Universal Laws and higher truths that are so important to understand and apply masterfully during these times of great change. There are two stories per book.

The Maui Tapes

Contain all the exercises, lectures, meditations and messages from Archangel Michael given at the two-day Harmonic Convergence Anniversary Seminar.

TAPE 1: Brain Waves; Kinesiology; Sacred Breath Toning, Gift of Angelic Helpers; Side B: Meditation: Balancing Chakras; Harmonizing & Balancing Physical, Mental & Emotional Bodies; Connecting with Higher Self · **TAPE 2:** Encode Finger Responses from Higher Self; Break Agreements; Galactic Center Info; Side B: Chakra Center Chants; Language of Light; Universal Laws of Manifestation · **TAPE 3:** Transformational Sacred Breath; Meditation: Clearing Past Lives & Experiencing Reintegration with Divine Self; Side B: Toning with Mudras to Balance the Chakra System & Integrate Higher Frequencies of Light **TAPE 4:** Meditation: Activate & Integrate Five Higher Ray Energies; Build Sanctuary; Commune with Masters & Angelic Helpers; Dropping Into the Alpha State; Side B: Message from Archangel Michael **TAPE 5:** First Ray of Divine Power & Will; Humanity's Descent to Earth; Angelic Origins; Side B: Archangel Michael's Message; Initiation

I AM Mastery Course Tapes

The I AM MASTERY TAPES are support material for the I AM MASTERY PRINTED COURSE—they give an overview and meditation for each chakra, but do not give the full course information.

Tape 99-2: I AM Mastery Course Overview
Side B: Meditation; Class 1: Root Chakra, Red Energy
Tape 99-3: Class 2: 2nd Chakra, Orange Energy, with Meditation
Side B: Class 3: 3rd Chakra, Yellow Energy with Meditation
Tape 99-4: Class 4: 4th Chakra, Green Energy
Side B: Meditation and Message from Archangel Michael
Tape 99-5/6: Class 5: 5th Chakra, Blue Energy with Meditation
Side B: Class 6: 6th Chakra, Indigo Energy, with Meditation
Tape 99-7: Class 7: 7th Chakra, Violet Energy, with Meditation
Tape 99-8: Class 8: Initiation, Overview of 5 Higher Galactic Chakras, Vision for the New Millennium, Message from Archangel Michael

I AM Mastery Meditations (2K-6)

Michael's Messages at Lake Tahoe and Pyramid Lake (2K-5)

Building your Column/Pyramid of Light creating a Sacred Power Vortex where you live.

ORDER FORM

StarQuest, 6005 Clear Creek Dr., Reno, NV 89502 USA
Phone/Fax: 775.856.3654   Email: ronnastar@earthlink.net
Order online: www.ronnastar.com

	Price	Qty	Totals
On Wings of Light	20.00	___	_____
The Golden Promise	23.00	___	_____
Once Upon a New World — Books 1,2 & 3			
Manuscripts available prior to publication	CALL	___	_____
The Maui Tapes			
Tape 1	11.00	___	_____
Tape 2	11.00	___	_____
Tape 3	11.00	___	_____
Tape 4	11.00	___	_____
Tape 5	11.00	___	_____
Complete set of five tapes	50.00	___	_____
I AM Mastery Course — 8 Lessons			
Printed materials	55.00	___	_____
Tape 99-2	12.00	___	_____
Tape 99-3	12.00	___	_____
Tape 99-4	12.00	___	_____
Tape 99-5/6	12.00	___	_____
Tape 99-7	12.00	___	_____
Tape 99-8	12.00	___	_____
Complete set of six tapes	65.00	___	_____
I AM Mastery Meditations — Tape 2K-6	12.00	___	_____
Archangel Michael's Messages at Lake Tahoe			
and Pyramid Lake — Tape 2K-5	12.00	___	_____

SUBTOTAL BOOKS & TAPES _____
Sales Tax of 7.25% for NV shipments ___
Shipping Charges (see table below) _____
TOTAL _____

	Tapes	Books
U.S.	$2 + $.50 each add'l	$4 + $2 each add'l
Canada	$2 + $1 each add'l	$5 + $3 each add'l
Overseas	$2 + $1 each add'l	$10 + $5 each add'l

Send check or money order payable in U.S. Funds, or charge to (check one): VISA__ MasterCard__ AMEX__ Discover__

Card Number_____ Exp._____
Name:_____
Address:_____
City:_____ St:____ Zip:_____
Phone:_____ Email:_____